# GENDER IN REAL TIME

B

# GENDER IN REAL TIME

*Power and Transience in a Visual Age*

## Kath Weston

Routledge
Taylor & Francis Group

NEW YORK AND LONDON

Published in 2002 by
Routledge
29 West 35th Street
New York, NY 10001
www.routledge-ny.com

Published in Great Britain by
Routledge
11 New Fetter Lane
London EC4P 4EE
www.routledge.co.uk

Routledge is an imprint of the Taylor & Francis Group.

Printed on acid-free, 250-year-life paper.
Manufactured in the United States of America.

10 9 8 7 6 5 4 3 2 1

Library of Congress Cataloging-in-Publication Data

Weston, Kath, 1958–
    Gender in real time : power and transcience in a visual age / Kath Weston
        p. cm.
    Includes bibliographical references and index.
    ISBN 0–415–93452–4 — ISBN 0–415–93453–2 (pbk.)
        1. Sex role. 2. Time—Sociological aspects. 3. Gender identity. 4. Feminist theory. 5. Feminist
    economics. I. Title.

HQ1075 .W47 2002
305.3—dc21                                                                           2002068182

FOR ELSIE, ERNA, AND IRENE,
WHO FED ME STORIES

# CONTENTS

# ACKNOWLEDGMENTS

Time waits for no scholar, but even in this hurried era of academic restructuring, friends and colleagues have been good enough to pause. Sabine Gölz and Geeta Patel sparked my initial curiosity about relating gender theory to writing on science and mathematics, including the work of Brian Rotman. Conversations and correspondence with Tressa Berman, Shih-Hui Chen, Akhil Gupta, George Marcus, Julie Murphy, Neni Panourgiá, Lisa Rofel, and Anindyo Roy had the paradoxical effect of sending me off in new directions and sharpening my focus. To Julie I offer special thanks for leading me past hesitation, from the library back to the desk. To other writers I wish a friend and colleague like Tim Diamond, ever the coconspirator in prose.

I owe a debt to Elena Tajima Creef for helping me keep my goals for the book in reach, if not always in sight. Many thanks go, too, to Lindon Barrett, Lauren Berlant, Catherine Lord, Saba Mahmood, Liisa Malkki, and an anonymous reviewer, each of whom made thoughtful comments that led me to rework sections of the text. Kiran Nagarkar appeared in my life at precisely the right moment to spur the book to some semblance of conclusion, if not completion. For that I will always be grateful.

My sister, Judi Weston, creatively illustrated the inseparability of vision, gender, and time through her photographs from the mid-1990s Venice Carnival, which introduce the chapters titled "What the Cat Dragged In" and "Do Clothes Make the Woman?" Nancy Banks generously lent her design talents to the task of preparing the photographs for publication.

Susan Cahn, Tim Diamond, Alice Echols, Smadar Lavie, Paul Luken, Thaïs Morgan, Esther Newton, Roger Rouse, Janet Spector, Suzanne Vaughan, and Jacquelyn Zita all offered suggestions that influenced the final version of the critique of performativity. My editor, Ilene Kalish, deserves my gratitude for many things, not least of them her sagacious advice in the face of less judicious authorial attachments.

Books about political economy must take shape in a political economy. If obstacles are to be acknowledged as well as debts, it must be said that it is not always easy to find the means to pursue research on topics (gender!) that have shifted with intellectual fashions from the cutting edge of tomorrow to yesterday's au courant. All the more reason to thank the institutions that supplied critical funding for the research that informs this book. Grants from the American Association of University Women, the American Philosophical Society, Arizona State University West, the National Science Foundation, the Rockefeller Foundation, and Wellesley College funded the field research and portions of the analysis that are realized here as ethnography. The Bunting Institute at Radcliffe College provided office space and camaraderie during a critical year in the project's development. The Committee on Degrees in Women's Studies at Harvard University and the Department of Sociology at Brandeis University both served as sources of moral as well as material support.

To Geeta Patel I am endlessly grateful, for reasons she knows best. The rest is infinity.

# NOW BOARDING: THE STARSHIP GENDER

Turn the page and step into a time machine. Destination: Gender. Gender not as a *thing* to be understood, or a conceptual *space* to be visited, but as a product of social relations imbued with *time*. Grab your gear and prepare for a trip to another intellectual galaxy.

Since its inception, gender studies has tended to emphasize the visual over the temporal, whether the topic be advertising or performativity or international women's movements.[1] Readers "watch" the gendered surfaces of bodies as those bodies work, love, struggle, and strut. Authors use thick description to make resistance visible to the mind's eye. Analysts consider how the spatial organization of a workplace contributes to gendered inequality, how the visual imagery employed in films helps reproduce gendered hierarchies, what the lavish displays associated with drag can tell about masculinity, femininity, and race. Although each and every one of these instances incorporates very specific conceptions of time, temporality usually remains implicit in the analysis. History may enter by way of background, but seeing remains the privileged metaphor for what the analyst of gender knows, or hopes to know.

After decades of innovative scholarship that galvanized a field and shattered a world of preconceptions, the study of gender now appears to languish. It has been a long while since the publication of a provocative and influential text along the lines of Judith Butler's *Gender Trouble*. These days many scholars looking for cutting-edge research gravitate toward other topics.

*Gender in Real Time* contends that the overwhelmingly visual orientation of gender studies, with its associated neglect of time, has contributed mightily to this malaise. If there is to be any hope of developing a critical perspective on gender and power in the contemporary world, time must figure much more prominently in the analysis. The shifts collectively dubbed globalization have to do with much more than an accelerated drive to buy and sell in ever-expanding markets (although acceleration, too, incorporates a very particular notion of time). Today's globalizing world is a world given over to economic growth and exploitation ("development," "modernization"), discourses of "fast" capitalism and speed, forms of production with distinctive temporalities (just-in-time inventories, repetition), politicized histories that claim an innocence of memory, and insistent attempts to commodify gender along with other aspects of identity.

Commodification, in turn, mystifies temporal processes by treating them as things removed from power plays and all manner of historical context. Globalization becomes a phenomenon, a juggernaut, its relentless progression a matter of inevitability if not of fact. Soon women everywhere will have the "freedom" to choose from a variety of prepackaged ethnic cuisines, the "freedom" to buy seeds that their grandmothers would have saved from the last harvest, the "freedom" to long for the fashions broadcast from satellites, carefully tailored by transnational corporations to (shape) local tastes. Or so the most widely circulated accounts would have it. In order to reflect critically upon these developments, much less to change them, time is of the essence.

It is well known that books, like fossils, are time machines of a sort that can transport readers to another era.[2] Words become the equivalent of a starship that slithers through a rent in spacetime to convey readers to various yesterdays, tomorrows, and occasionally even a parallel universe in which events unfold rather differently than expected. Science fiction conjures up a future, historical narratives evoke a past, origin stories dispute the sequence of chronological time altogether. Less recognized is a second way in which books can provide a vehicle for time travel. By supplying the analytic machinery required to understand time, they serve as devices for examining the workings of temporality. In the case at hand, presumptions about time embedded in theory and practice turn out to affect, intimately, the making of gender.

This book traverses time, then, in both ways. In the first sense, *Gender in Real Time* emphasizes the importance of historical legacies and the historical moment for understanding gender relations. The first chapter, "Unsexed," takes readers to the late twentieth-century United States, where a preoccupation with ambiguity arose that had its academic counterpart in a preoccupation with multiple genders and a terrifying if prosaic correlate in street violence directed at bodies that seemed to resist classification. To understand these linked developments, readers will journey to a much earlier period of globalization characterized by the expansion of medieval trade routes and the golden age of Arabic/Islamic science. The concept of zero circulated during this period has valuable implications for anyone interested in following the rhythms of gender's creation, disappearance, and reemergence in the "real time" of life under the latest in capitalism.

The next chapter, "Do Clothes Make the Woman?" brings readers back to 1980s North America to explore the limitations of the visual emphasis incorporated into performativity theories of gender. The ensuing discussion focuses on how temporal movements associated with repetition helped make these theories attractive in the aftermath of historic shifts in industrial production that relocated manufacturing plants overseas. "The Ghosts of Gender Past" explores the part played by historical memory in the production of gender, especially under conditions when ideologies of modernity have prevailed. "The Global Economy Next Time" underscores the importance of pursing time-sensitive versions of gender studies in order to engage with the new forms of power that globalization brings.

Many of the key concepts developed in the book, such as time claims and a zero concept of gender, address taken-for-granted aspects of consumer capitalism to which gender studies has become unwittingly indebted. What's at issue? The prospects for equality, the work to which we give our days, passion, rage, friendship, survival, resource distribution, memory's wagers. What's at stake? Our theories, our relationships, and sometimes our very lives.

At the same time, so to speak, the book invites readers to embark upon a second sort of voyage that involves close scrutiny of the notions of time entailed in different approaches to understanding gender. The theory of relativity in physics teaches that wherever there is space and vision there is also an implicit reckoning of time. (The two are not really separate phenomena: thus the term "spacetime.") Accordingly, even the most visually oriented approaches to gender studies have temporality embedded within them. This is the case, for example, with the concept of repetition that recurs in performativity theories of gender, as well as social Darwinian notions of evolution embedded in historical memories of the Modern Woman. Even the narrative device of travel and exploration adopted for this preface draws uneasily upon textual conventions of an earlier, colonial epoch of globalization. A book-qua-time machine not only furnishes an apparatus for identifying and analyzing these temporal contours; it also begins to theorize temporality in its own right.

When it comes time to reinvigorate gender studies, not just any approach to time will do. *Gender in Real Time* uses the tools of political economy, the history of mathematics, Darwinian evolution, and a bit of physics to propel gender studies toward a future. Like any spaceship, this one needs provisions. First stop will be an introduction, where readers can take stock of the paradoxically troubled state of gender studies while concepts such as spacetime are loaded aboard, the better to think history and space, movement and vision, performance and globalization, together. (Readers already well-supplied with theory or impatient to cut to the chase can skip the introduction and go directly to the essays themselves. The chapters gain something when served in sequence, although each can also be savored alone.) Then it's on to aspects of time which, left unexamined, make gender studies complicit with marketing and commodification. Step aboard the *Starship Gender*, departing soon for latest capitalism. Just turn the page.

© Judi Weston, reprinted by permission

# CHAPTER ONE

# WHAT THE CAT DRAGGED IN: GENDER STUDIES TODAY—AN ELEGY AND INTRODUCTION

Do the time, don't let it do you.
—*Prisoner at Black Mountain Correctional Center
for Women, North Carolina*

What an impossibly beautiful dream: to live in a genderless world, or if that's not your cup of tea, to live in a world untrammeled by the inequalities historically associated with gender. This was the apparently timeless vision conjured up by women's movements in the United States during the 1970s and 1980s. Somewhere in the course of the changes leading up to the present century the dream died, and with it went a certain critical edge for gender studies.

To study gender relations today is to work in the shadow of paradox. On the one hand, publications on gender are flourishing. Never before has so much been written about masculinities and femininities, variously construed; raced and gendered bodies; international feminisms; honor killings; anorexia; women, sovereignty, and citizenship; the disproportionate numbers of female refugees; transgender movements; reservation of electoral seats for women; the gendering of music; the gendering of architecture; the gendered consequences of inheritance and divorce law. And that is just a start. On the other hand, a certain lassitude now seems to afflict the study of gender, a sense that feminist scholarship, in the North American academy at least, has passed its glory days, no longer offering quite as much in terms of activism or insight.[1] For people working hard to change conditions that bear down harder on women, a women's studies department in a university and the gender studies section in a bookstore may no longer be the first stops, or even the last, when they need to research their subjects.

The unnamed paradoxes that shadow contemporary discussions of gender contribute mightily to this sense of intellectual exhaustion. Yet these paradoxes are hardly recognized, much less debated, as such. They say that bad luck comes in threes, but paradoxes? Perhaps only when untenable. Call the first the paradox of liberation simultaneously achieved and denied. Call the second the paradox of spacetime, in which gender theory exalts the visual at the expense of the temporal. Call the third the paradox that pits survival against representation in an economy with an increasingly global reach.[2] All three paradoxes intertwine. Each incorporates problematic assumptions about time.

The purpose of this introduction is to dissolve or displace these paradoxes in order to prepare the ground for an inquiry into some of the ways that time travels through the study of gender. Nothing of the sort can be accomplished in an era of globalization without locating political economy at the heart of the analysis. It is my premise throughout that a closer examination of the temporalities embedded in the making and marketing of gender (and its theories) will help get gender studies moving again. As the field has been all along. Paradoxically enough.

## LIBERATION WHEN?: THE FIRST PARADOX

An unexpected thing happened on the way to women's liberation: Great hopes for improving women's lives gave way to a strange mix of complacency and despair. Scarcely a decade had passed since the 1970s hunt for ancient matriarchies (on the part of cultural feminists) and heroic women workers (on the part of socialist feminists) before a new generation of scholars began to criticize such quests for their naïveté. As it turned out, women could hunt, join armies, operate bulldozers, and lead groups to political consensus without gender equity necessarily following. The celebrated egalitarianism of certain precapitalist societies looked more and more like a romanticized figment of an overheated twentieth-century imagination.[3] In the guise of history, early feminist researchers had described their yearning for what they found lacking in the now.

Their successors concluded that while contemporary measures of inequality might show some "improvement" for women, the gap that separated women from men would not be closing any time soon. Gender and its attendant inequalities had proved impressively malleable, adapting to new circumstances rather than withering away in response to demands for change. In a rare instance of agreement, feminist and antifeminist critics concurred that gender was probably here to stay. Equality between men and women never had and perhaps never would prevail.[4] Activist groups modified their political goals accordingly. This political volte-face marked the passing of another of what literary critic Susan Buck-Morss has called "mass dreamworlds," utopian hopes for a future, in this case shored up with fantasies of what had once been possible in the past.[5]

Yet this newfound skepticism coincided historically with a growing popular belief that gender oppression, at least in North America, had already been laid to rest.[6] Using the language of progress, many people across the political spectrum argued (and continue to argue) that the lives of women today are better than ever. Women were said to operate on a virtually equal footing with men, their lives positioned at the end of a long timeline called modernization. One look at the gender and color composition of most corporate boardrooms, not to mention the first-class cabin of any plane, should have given these commentators pause. Preposterous claims about women's unlimited opportunities issued not only from the pens of critics such as Camille Paglia, but also from the mouths of coworkers, mothers, and religious advisers. Polemics by writers such as Shelby Steele and Thomas Sowell made similarly inflated (and related) claims about the end of racism. All this, despite ample indications that the rhetoric of inequality's passing has represented nothing so much as a premature burial.

How can such apparently contradictory beliefs coexist? What does it mean for inequality to proclaim itself vanquished even as it demands to be sustained? It is worth taking a moment to consider these narratives of self-congratulation and dashed expectations in relation to one another. The paradox of liberation simultaneously achieved and denied is not a case of some people believing one thing, and some another, when the topic turns to gender. Indeed, it is not uncommon in the United States for a single individual to voice sentiments derived from each of these logically opposed narratives of change. In politics, logic can offer poor refuge.

The narrative of disillusionment begins with a vision—I use the word advisedly—of a world without gender. Many feminists of the 1970s endorsed the humanist position that gender (like war, the state, racism, and poverty) could, perhaps would, but certainly should go away. With a new body of gender theory at their disposal, they appealed to sophisticated (if contentious) explanations for the mechanisms that produce and reproduce gendered differences.[7] Organizers formulated their goals with reference not only to theory but also to an idealized future. In practice the static vision of a world without gender enlisted a thoroughly temporal orientation.

Lisa Rofel, an anthropologist who has done extensive research in China, recounts how European and North American feminists created Chinese women in the image of their politics and their dreams by casting them as living, breathing exemplars of liberation.[8] The Chinese state, for its part, bound gender equity ideologically ever closer to nationalism, holding up women's liberation as a definitive proof of successful modernization. Discrepancies in the official story eventually provided ammunition to opponents of socialism and fostered despondency among minority world (that is, "Western") feminists.[9] Rofel chronicles her own attempts, as a North American scholar, to take seriously the assertions of factory women in China that they were liberated. Women in this sector of the economy worked longer hours than men, yet men complained about getting stuck with "dirty work" such as washing bicycles. What feels like inequality, and to whom? What calibrates oppression? Discussions of equity quickly lead to matters of measurement and interpretation.[10]

It is one thing to understand the conceptual problems with the evolutionary and utopian threads woven into concepts such as "improvement," "advancement," or "liberation." It is something else again to understand how a political goal such as liberation begs for application of disciplines associated with measurement to determine what will count as better, if not best. To take gender studies in this direction is to ask whether colonial histories and national ideologies do not ride gender theory still, carried belowdecks in the hold of very specific assumptions about time and space, counting and accounting.

Over time the rough-hewn notion that "women's status" lends itself to measurement, much less serves as a barometer of progress, became patently insupportable. Subaltern studies scholars pointed out that attempts to use "women's condition" as a marker of "civilization" had a long and undistinguished history in the annals of colonization, where it often served as an excuse for incursions by colonial powers.[11] National liberation movements, which often fought colonial rule with a promise to bring about a lasting improvement in gender relations, fared no better under feminist scrutiny. Legal scholars developed sophisticated critiques of the ways in which postcolonial law codes saddled women with demands to represent the newly liberated nation.[12] Women, more than men, experienced pressure to embody historically constructed but ideologically timeless national/cultural/communal "traditions." Middle-class Indian men were expected to abandon their lungis to close business deals in Western suits while women were supposed to cling to their salvar kameez and saris, regardless. Gender remained in the aftermath of more than one sort of revolution, and multiple were the wellsprings of disillusionment.

Gender had reasserted itself not only in practice, but in theory as well. Disputes ensued about whether a world without gender would be ideal in any case, even if it were possible to achieve. If gender is here to stay, some reasoned, why not treat it as a resource for play and for pleasure, rather than fighting it as a deadly opponent? Why not value some of the ways that gender can come together with race, class, religion, nation, and other aspects of latter-day identity to give texture to everyday encounters? What is a world without color, dalliance, difference? Debate over such questions intensified within late-twentieth-century women's movements against a backdrop of renewed globalization.[13]

Might there be a way to retain gender without perpetuating inequality? Why not reconfigure gender relations so that they need not entail hierarchy and oppression? Why not reconceive power as a positive capacity instead of a resource to be seized or a weapon used to strike somebody down? Shouldn't it be possible to have your gender and eat well, too? Easier said than done, perhaps. Memories of what "separate but equal" meant in pre–Civil Rights America were still fresh. But as women's groups began to claim gender and scholars began to investigate masculinities and femininities, rather than rush to discard them, the genderless world became a lost world, navigable only by the light of nostalgia, betrayal, and good riddance.[14]

Organizing never stopped, despite widely circulated claims about the demise of "the" women's movement. As the twenty-first century beckoned, both local feminisms and transnational women's movements continued to thrive, albeit in different forms and venues than in previous years. In place of a utopian politics, activists in the 1980s United States painstakingly built coalitions and alliances to accommodate multiple, crosscutting, sometimes conflicting identities. North American feminists more consistently specified which women they were discussing, rather than basing assessments of women's needs on middle-class white women or generalizing too broadly about women versus men. By the 1990s Hawai'ian women had assumed key leadership positions in the Hawai'ian sovereignty movement. Sicangu Lakota and Ihanktonwan Dakota on the Yankton Sioux reservation revived a coming-of-age ritual for girls with the goal of fostering a living tradition that could offer young women advice on how to resist the pressures to join gangs as well as knowledge of medicinal plants. Groups such as the Portland, Maine–based Sisters in Action for Power introduced a new generation to direct action campaigns that demanded affordable public transportation and gender violence prevention programs in the schools.[15]

Organizing initiatives abroad during the last two decades of the century were, if anything, more pervasive. Brazilian women banded together to get running water in *favelas* (shantytowns). Urban Afghani women went underground during the years of Taliban rule to teach the next generation of girls how to read and write. With support from UNICEF, a coalition of eastern and southern African artists and researchers launched *Sara*, a comic-book series for young women that addressed problems such as getting an education, sexual assault, running a household with limited resources, and HIV prevention. Women across the globe worked hard to establish nongovernmental organizations (NGOs), then went on in the new century to reevaluate the dominance of NGOs in transnational feminism.[16] Through it all, gendered divisions of labor did not go away, incarceration of poor women did not go away, domestic violence did not go away, restricted access to wealth and land did not go away. Women continued to starve.

How is it, then, that this narrative of great expectations giving way to great efforts but far from utopian results led, not just to disillusionment, not to renewed calls for activism or irrevocable gloom, but (in the United States) to an emergent narrative of triumph and self-congratulation? If you have happened to discuss gender with a group of twenty-year-old Americans lately, you may have learned, to your surprise, that women and men now receive the same pay. Not only that: A woman can do anything she wants as long as she tries, women can legally marry women in some state somewhere, and new technologies inevitably makes women's lives easier. (Needless to say, evidence bears out none of these assertions.) You may not find everyone in accord on each point, but similar statements about women's de facto state of liberation are bound to come up. The term "postfeminism," which implies an equality long since achieved, gained currency to describe precisely these sorts of presumptions.[17]

What matters for an understanding of the first paradox—liberation simultaneously achieved and denied—is not whether various "improvements" to (some) women's lot can be established. What matters is that many women and men alike credit as true *changes that have not happened* in gender relations. Their response to questions about gender differs markedly from the split dramatized in polls that ask about inequalities associated with race or wealth. When race is the headliner, for example, respondents who identify as white are much more likely to perceive a historical shift toward racial equality than respondents from less racially privileged groups.[18]

If logic lay at the heart of the matter, postfeminist claims would be easy enough to dispel. Counter-examples abound. In the United States, women working full-time year-round made seventy-three cents to the male dollar in 1998. Better than 1904, no doubt, but far from on par. In South Africa, rape had become sufficiently routine to make it profitable for companies to invent rape insurance, offering policies that guarantee medical assistance in the event of assault. In Thailand and Vietnam, women who could have been ordained as members of the Buddhist Sangha millennia ago still had no officially recognized standing as nuns; the Bhikkhuni (order of Buddhist nuns) in Sri Lanka was restored in 1998 after a thousand-year hiatus, in response to work by women's groups. Literacy rates for women from Mongolia to Burkina Faso were going down, not up. And these examples hardly begin to examine class- and color-specific renditions of gender as they take shape through other vectors of inequality.[19]

Single women in the United States have a harder time securing home mortgages than single men across the board, but if the woman filing an application is Native American, her chances of securing a loan decrease dramatically. To understand why requires more than an analysis of gender per se. In this case, gender relations unfold in the context of a history of genocide, bureaucratic procedures for state certification of Indian identity, state-sponsored assimilation policies, struggles to preserve a land base, sovereignty claims, and land grabs that have continued from the colonial era up to the present day. Clearing title to Indian land has become a procedure so uncertain and complex that many banks wouldn't touch it even if reservation incomes did not already rank among the lowest in North America. Property law and lending regulations scarcely recognize "alternative" histories of proprietorship or land use. Unless the applicant happens to work with one of a handful of lenders attempting to remedy this situation, she cannot secure money to build or repair. Not because she is *a* woman, but because she is *this* woman.[20]

So what of women's vaunted freedoms in the face of this sort of critique? There is more going on here than a remarkable ability to perceive a level playing field while the majority of one's compatriots are slipping and sliding down the hill. The fantasy of liberation achieved, heralded by steady "gains" that are rife with symbolism but nowhere to be found, allows people to bask in the satisfaction that women now benefit from developments that have not developed. Statistical evidence to the contrary often fails to persuade. A curious lapse in a society where numbers not only carry great authority but also become integral to technologies of power at the disposal of modern states and corporations.[21]

To maintain a belief in uniform social progress, especially when confronted by unevenness and contradictory evidence, requires some doing. Like many evolutionary stories, the narrative of liberation achieved often takes this form: Things were bad once upon a time, but those days are now behind us. "Us" in this context implies a Euro-American subject, by ancestry and/or geographical location. In a classic essay from 1990, Chandra Mohanty called attention to the sleight of hand that allowed "Western" feminists to slough off awareness of their own oppression by assigning victim status to "Third World" women, then targeting them for pity and support from a distance.[22] And what is distance in this case but a metaphor for going back in time, to the extent that majority world women were made to represent an oppressive past, a "backwardness" that Euro-Americans allegedly had already overcome?

The corollary of pity, which denies agency and accomplishment to people "over there," assigns blessings to the supposedly lucky ones right here. Acknowledging the unconscionable conditions in which a woman somewhere else may have to live can help maintain the pretty fiction that none of one's neighbors has to do likewise. In an attempt to clarify some of the obstacles to building alliances across borders, Inderpal Grewal and Caren Kaplan took up the related problem of how to link feminisms around the world "without requiring either equivalence or a master theory" such as progress.[23]

Every self-congratulatory gesture toward all that is thankfully now "behind us" betrays a debt to this time-ridden variant of change called progress. The bad old back-in-the-day gives way not just to today, but to a more enlightened now. Ally evolutionism to the Euro-American center of gravity implicit in "us" and you get a classic colonialist displacement of time onto space. Travel to Egypt or Turkey or India in search of a simpler past; hold up North America or Britain or France to discover Everywoman's far more civilized future. Locations in the South still tend to receive narration in "Western feminist" literature as sites of beatings, burnings, sex tourism, and more mundane horrors, with little notice taken of the opportunities for creativity, earnings, and friendship that open up in places that are differently articulated to what passes for a global economy. In contrast, countries that have the greatest hand in running the global economy continue to be portrayed as sites that give free play to desire. (The European Union as consumer paradise; the United States as the birthplace of gay rights.) No matter that the many cash-poor people in North America make poor consumers, or that legal rights represent an area in which queer movements have had relatively little success. So it is that utopian dreams, supposedly given over to skepticism (liberation impossible) or complacency (liberation accomplished), live on in transnational imagination, each side of liberation's paradox entailed in the other.

In a sense, of course, liberation's paradox poses no paradox because liberation can neither be achieved nor denied as such. This is a philosophical point consummately if somewhat obliquely argued by Louis Althusser, for whom there is no getting outside ideology, and Michel Foucault, for whom repression enjoins productivity and freedoms insinuate their own demands. When Bedouin women bought lingerie in the 1980s to add to their wedding trousseaus and scandalize their elders, the anthropologist Lila Abu-Lughod argues, they resisted power in one way only to be sucked further into relations of inequality in another.[24] Lingerie retails for money; the acquisition of money requires someone to sell labor power; the most common venues for wage labor impelled Bedouin away from a sustainable nomadic economy, toward the settled way of life that the state sought to foist upon them. The move that would liberate also ensnares. Likewise in North America, where capitalism has consistently managed to lay claim to its adversaries' finest moments, recycling protest in the form of advertising and other incitements to need.[25]

So long as opposition regularly reinvents itself as hegemony, theorists, like activists, have to keep moving. The alternative is despondency, or an only superficially more sophisticated version of the belief that women are free because tampons now come in five choices that can all be advertised on TV. Liberation denied, liberation achieved; both visions dependent upon an all-or-nothing approach to social change. Both visions dependent *on* vision and an unexamined allegiance to the concept of change. A certain grandiosity prevails in either case, puffed up by generous infusions of time.

To dissolve a paradox is not, however, to dismiss its social effects. It is by no means an easy matter to extricate gender studies from the "seething of words and dreams" that issues from its utopian heritage.[26] How to generate an analytics that will, if only for a time, resist the lure of commodification? How to grasp the resources withheld from women—and which women?—at the self-proclaimed centers of freedom? Shifting between scraps of land claimed by different states, or simply holding hands, remains a life-threatening proposition in many of the sites where modernity's well-schooled voice proclaims that life is uniformly better.

The responses to these questions move with time itself: historical time; sojourns in time; transitions that pass unobserved; time caught between loss and remembrance; a politicoeconomic landscape in ragged motion; the knowledge effects of theories that effectively put a stop to passage. But with gender studies given over to vision, time languishes.

## VISION JUST IN TIME: THE SECOND PARADOX

A politics conceived in terms of social change always entails a "when." Liberation, when? The abolition of gender, when? The invention of egalitarian forms of gender, when? Perhaps things will improve eventually, but what accounts for the delay? When will change (however conceived) extend to this group of women, or that? Tomorrow? Decades? Years? After the next change of government? Following the war? If the answer should come up "never," that, too, implies a passage, into eternity, if nothing else. And for each "when," there must be a waiting. "Never" proffers the longest wait of all.[27]

Of course, there are other sorts of "whens" than the ones prefigured by utopias. The time sense embedded in gender politics is not limited to the rhythm of the drumbeat, the steady march of time associated with progress, or the collapse into infinity that comes with the knowledge that the freedom train will never pull into liberation station. A more historically inclined analyst, rather than speculating about days of reckoning and liberation, might ask about the timing of gendered classifications, say, or the retailing of gender. When and why did people in the United States start speaking of "androgyny," a "Third Gender," "bulldaggers," "unisex," "transgendered"? When and under what sorts of politicoeconomic circumstances did the commodification of gender emerge? At what historical juncture did it become possible to imagine gender as an artifact of performance or a resource for pleasure rather than some dead weight to be thrown off? Could a time without gender lie in unrecognized dimensions of the here and now, rather than some far off, future "then"?

To broach the historical requires some recognition of movement in relation to place and specifically in relation to the "topos" in "utopia." Utopia and dystopia take their names from "topos," or place, which also supplies the root for "topography." At a certain point in history, the mapping of bodies becomes the proper activity of science; the mapping of continents, the proper activity of merchant trade and conquest; the mapping of futures, the proper activity of a politics. It is no accident that Euro-American feminisms once spoke in terms of visions of a genderless world, or for that matter, a world forever "marked" by gender. The horrors awaiting women in the dream space of forever or once-upon-a-time, the wonders of a now space that displaces oppression onto other shoulders and other shores, call out for temporal analysis. You wouldn't know this, however, from reading much contemporary writing on gender. While theorists have acknowledged the importance of history, as well as political economy, their focus remains on various forms of topos—place—and the vision required to take its measure.

Social constructionist "readings" of gender, for example, rely upon the eye as much as most forms of literacy. In Euro-American societies, where many people think of gender as biologically based, people often rely upon visual markers to bring constructions of gender into play. They do not routinely ask new acquaintances to submit to DNA tests or drop their drawers in order to confirm that everyone has gendered their pronouns (he? she?) correctly. Instead, they infer chromosomes and genitalia from cues that are open to visual and, to a lesser extent, auditory or tactile inspection. Hair, dress, posture, stylized ways of calling the muscles to action, all nudge perception down familiar interpretive roads. Passing depends, in part, upon the ability to manipulate such visual signifiers. (Of course, passing also presumes the dangers of enlightenment—being found out—and hence a veiled realness. But that is another matter.)

The early women's and lesbian/gay movements also trafficked heavily in appeals to the eye. Visibility became what theorist Rosemary Hennessy calls a struggle term.[28] Organizers described themselves as bringing invisible aspects of women's lives to light (when they were not otherwise occupied with "breaking the silence"). Feminist scholars, too, set about making the invisible visual: finding publication outlets for lost novels authored by women; chronicling the achievements of women previously judged unworthy of historical attention; casting light on the circumstances of women whose color or poverty or both had pushed them to the margins of conventional accounts; making "room" for the study of same-sex eroticism. These developments are well known, but not especially for their emphasis on seeing and space as metaphors for overcoming oppression.

This "visibility-is-currency economy" did not go unchallenged.[29] To describe women as moving out of the shadows, into the light, is to assume a preformed subject, unfettered by observation or description, unaffected by the glare of newfound interest, which, far from being neutral, was necessarily selective in the aspects of gender it "saw." By the 1990s, most gender theorists had come to recognize that apparently simple acts of description could be constitutive of gender, and inequality as well. They began to regard the project of "making the invisible visible" as politically bankrupt, if not naïve. Yet they continued to rely upon metaphors of vision and space to organize their accounts, usually at the expense of temporality.

In these accounts gendered subjects have to be "located" in space; desire must be "imaged" rather than imagined. Feminist geography has consistently framed research in terms of spatial division, landscape, scales, even "paradoxical space." Psychoanalytic discussions of "the gaze" provide another obvious illustration. The metaphor of the cone of vision, derived from Euclidean geometry, pervades feminist theories of representation. Theories of performativity enlist a wealth of visual markers to describe the production of gender through the repetition of everyday performance. Transnational approaches to gender enlist concepts such as "global visibility." In writing on technoscience, gender often enters the analysis through close scrutiny of visual images, as in discussions of reproductive rights struggles that incorporate highly politicized images of fetuses in the womb. Even the consciousness-raising groups in which North American women gathered during the 1970s took their name from an optical metaphor.[30] The list could be extended, perhaps not ad infinitum, but certainly to a length of several pages.

These developments in gender theory and gender movements can be understood as part of a wider turn to vision in critical theory, cultural studies, and indeed society at large. This at a historical moment when visual anthropology and visual culture emerge as codified fields of inquiry, the very moment when "eye candy" begins to describe a range of visually induced consumer pleasures. Late-twentieth-century business texts began to highlight another, related sort of vision. James Paul Gee and his colleagues in social criticism may overstate the point, but they are not wholly off the mark: "The fast capitalist stress on vision (stemming from charismatic business leaders) is the leading edge of imperialism. Since businesses can no longer be solely about profit, it is said, they are now in competition with churches, governments, and universities in the framing and conduct of social and moral agendas."[31] In a sense it is less surprising than disheartening to notice how little attention temporality has garnered in gender theory, which has tended to follow the fashions of a visual age.

So it is that we come to the paradox of spacetime, in which people paradoxically believe they can speak about space and vision without reference to time (or vice versa). Wherever there is space, there is time. Every vision of gender equality carries its histories as well as the imagery of dreams, not least because historical struggles against colonialism continue to frame narratives of liberation. No gendered space, no utopian vision, exists as a static metaphor unto itself. Chronicles, duration, memory infuse every rallying cry, each picture of a gendered or genderless world.

In calling attention to the paradox of spacetime, my goal is not just to alert gender studies to the importance of time, to the fleeting elements in all that appears to be fixed, to the politicoeconomic histories embedded in imagery and location. I hope, as well, to extricate gender studies from approaches that reduce temporality to a subjective sense of duration. When writers on gender have managed to venture into temporal waters, most have tended to compensate for the visual emphasis of gender theory by focusing on time to the exclusion of space. In so doing they fall into the "vice versa" of the paradox of spacetime: The equally paradoxical belief that time can be studied apart from space. The result is a timeless sort of time that targets subjectivity, as though subjects could be formed without social action or historical developments, much less the (visual) imagery used to conceptualize time as such.

This book does not ask how perceptions of time might vary from Woman to Man, body to body, culture to culture. That is the sort of relativist question that concerned Friedrich Nietzsche and Julia Kristeva, a question that led to endless debates on equality versus difference and bequeathed to feminism the dubious contention that women possess a distinctive experience of time's passage.[32] That is also the stuff of ethnotemporality, which might juxtapose, say, a Mayan conception of cyclical time to a European conception of linear time. (But here, too, is space: The cycle represented as a circle, the narrative conception of history as a line.) Studies of temporal subjectivity can be useful in their own way. There is something to be learned from observing that a cyclical conception of time will not support the linearity of a political demand to abandon the past for the promise of a more glorious future. But for contemporary gender theory, it is the inseparability of time from space that beckons.

This paradox of spacetime might better be described, then, as a paradox within a paradox, a box within a box, in which one paradox opens onto another. For there is certainly something paradoxical about calling gender theory inattentive to matters of temporality, when so many feminists have spilled ink attempting to trace the outlines of something they called "women's time." And there are equal measures of irony to be found in the scattered attempts to bring space into relationship with time, most notably in the work of Elizabeth Grosz, where time and space refuse to coalesce, stubbornly insisting upon separating into two dimensions.

Grosz is the rare student of gender who has attempted to bring time and space into the same scholarly orbit. She utilizes the concept of spacetime in her work and acknowledges a debt to quantum mechanics in her studies of architecture, transgression, and desire. Although time is not the centerpiece of her account, it bears heavily on her primary interest, embodiment, a subject that has received more than its share of attention within feminism. But because space and time make their appearance in Grosz's work as twin but separable dimensions, her insightful analysis ends up more Kantian than Einsteinian, despite assertions to the contrary. The difference is an additive rather than an integrated understanding of spacetime.[33]

Space-plus-time (space and time) is not the same theoretical apparatus as spacetime. Different ways of framing the relationship of space to time generate different types of questions, with major consequences for the study of gender.

An additive understanding (space-plus-time) pictures time and space as two geometric planes that intersect, two streams or dimensions that flow together, with the eye trained on their confluence. The analyst brings the two together after the fact by first imagining them as separate but interdependent, then investigating the effect that one has on the other. How do they operate in conjunction? How do they mix?

This is an example of what used to be known as conflating an internal dialectic with an external dialectic. An external dialectic treats time and space as two discrete entities, later to be joined under the auspices of theory, when it is theory itself that has posited the two as distinct! By proposing to examine the relationship of time to space without acknowledging its own part in separating them out analytically, gender theory creates the problem of bringing them back together again.

An integrated understanding of spacetime offers a better approach. If space and time are aspects of the same phenomenon, they can be said to relate to one another by an internal dialectic. There is no need to explain how they come together (in women's or anyone else's experience) because nothing stands between them. In their naming and their measurement, they are historical products. Anthony Giddens has argued that a tendency to separate space from time is itself characteristic of the period he calls "high modernity."[34] The unified concept of spacetime puts gender back into time by calling attention to what is peculiar to the production of gender under the latest capitalism. The unified concept of spacetime also suggests that even ostensibly visual analyses of gender will have temporal implications that are worth a "look." Space-and-time offers nothing of the sort.

Internal dialectics treats "things as moments in their own development in, with, and through other things."[35] When things (gender, visible) are moments (gender, temporal) conceived in relation to other things, analysis shifts away from congealed gender differences toward shifting relations of power and production. What accounts for the places where gender effects are produced, the reconfiguration of looking and lingering and timing, under this set of historical conditions or that? Who labors, who wanders, who appropriates, who hits, who savors, who endeavors, somehow in the process coming up gendered?

Space-plus-time, then, can never be spacetime as Einstein's successors have known it. To understand why, you do not even need political economy; you have only to consider the celebrated accounts of rocket ships and railway carriages that Einstein used to illustrate his special theory of relativity. As the speed of a rocket approaches the speed of light, an observer stationed on Earth will come up with a shorter measurement for the length of the rocket than she did before the rocket took off (that is, while it was at rest). The same observer will see the hands of a clock on the rocket ship mark time at a slower rate as the rocket approaches light speed. (Conversely, a passenger on the rocket ship will see clocks on Earth slow down.) If the rider and the earthbound observer are twins, the space-traveling twin will be younger than her sibling when she arrives back on earth.

In Einstein's rocket ship scenario, time stretches (dilates) as length contracts. Neither is an absolute dimension, separable from the other. Why should this be so? Remember that speed is defined as distance divided by time ($v = d/t$). A speedometer measures $d/t$: miles or kilometers per hour. Because the speed of light (that is, the speed approached by the rocket) is a constant, distance and time will acquire different values in different reference frames. (A reference frame is simply the platform from which a person makes observations: the Earth frame, the rocket frame.) Although measurements will vary for observers according to frame, they will not vary randomly, precisely because the speed of light does not change. In the special theory of relativity, it's not *all* relative: Measurements and perceptions vary in predictable ways, relative to one's frame of reference.

The combined spacetime separation between two events is called the invariant interval: A quantity that will be identical for all observers of the same events regardless of where they are stationed. While time and space may seem to vary individually from one reference frame to another, so that lightning cannot strike "simultaneously" in two places, the integrated dimension of spacetime (sometimes called the fourth dimension) stays constant.[36] There can be no absolute division between time and space, because each in some sense *is* the (relation to the) other.

Notice in the rocket ship example what happens to vision and light. Light has long been associated with the mechanics of vision and the centuries-old science of optics.[37] Luminous or incandescent, light rays permit a seeing subject to measure and (metaphorically) to take a subject's measure. Move on to a post-Einsteinian universe and light not only illuminates space, it travels. Traveling, light acquires velocity. Velocity, in turn, links light to spacetime, vision to duration.

This excursion into physics may seem to have brought the discussion a long way from genderless utopias and social movements, but here again the length of the journey depends upon the frame. Every allusion to seeing, to observation, incorporates an implicit allusion to time. In physics, as in gender studies.

When there is space, there is time: These not-two exist in a smoke-with-fire sort of relationship. This means that every time a discussion of gender restricts its focus to vision and space, temporal aspects of these topics remain unexplored. Any shift in understandings of time will have implications for visual/spatial analysis, just as research into display and location must inform any analysis that hopes to "begin" with time.

In order to understand how time travels for gender and its analysts, the chapters that follow treat spacetime as a unified phenomenon, rather than two separate (albeit related) dimensions. Tactically this approach allows me to search in some very familiar "places" for my subjects, so that my analysis engages some of the same concerns recently taken up by gender theorists preoccupied with vision: violence, performance, embodiment, historical memory, ambiguity, and commodification.

The social relations that make gender visible, visual, turn out to be drenched in history, time discipline, and duration. Whether it be heated glances exchanged at a checkout counter, flirtation on a dance floor, memories of working in a "man's job," or a brutal attack on a bus, in each case gendered bodies come up temporal.

Visual metaphors and a spatial understanding of social relations tether gender to bodies for a society that already prefers its accounts of gender steeped in hormones and genes. Bodies easily become naturalized in the process, taken out of context, isolated from economies and time. Interactions risk becoming moments unto themselves, whether construed in terms of performativity or roles or some expression of underlying gender traits. "We're here! Invisible no more! Take in the performance! Analyze the imagery! Map out gender relations!" Ironically, all these appeals to the visual emanate from an era in which *invisible* modes of discipline increasingly operate to establish inequalities. Ask the supervisor monitoring your keystrokes, the government agent authorized to listen in on your most intimate electronic conversations.

It comes as no news to street dykes, assembly line workers, or the heirs of Foucault that visual surveillance can foster discipline. Foucault's famous critique of Jeremy Bentham's prison design, the Panopticon, explains how a building's spatial layout can institute control by placing guards in a central observatory where they can watch a prisoner's every move. Observation shades into punishment. Out on the street, passersby scan one another for visual signifiers of belonging, with hostility, avoidance, or camaraderie to follow. Onlookers may expect hair to "give away" race; the cheap cut of a suit to betray class; a butch appearance to mark a queer identity; "Western" clothing to symbolize urban or Christian affiliation.[38] Meanwhile, Western, butch, good hair, bad hair, and what constitutes wealth in textiles all have something less than visible to do with the eye of the beholder.

Workers use vision to fight vision by inventing ways to "look busy" and installing quick-close programs for their computer solitaire games when managers show up without warning. As people go about the business of consumption, one-way mirrors bring the science of optics to bear on light-fingered shoppers, hoping to ensure monetary exchange. And as people go about the business of analysis, they enlist visual techniques indebted to scientific disciplines that do in fact discipline. Measures, maps, instruments, surveys, scales, and the narrative device of an all-seeing "I" (the so-called God's-eye view) subordinate individuals to standards produced under the kind of scientific gaze that regulates its subjects. "Am I normal?" writes the fourteen-year-old to the advice columnist. Not "What is the source of authority for this strange thing called a norm?" Not "Why am I getting beaten up on the way home from school in the name of a social science concept?"

The politics of visibility depend upon certain invisibilities, produced in and through time. Far from this fourteen-year-old in space and time (but not, perhaps, spacetime), the British built a Cellular Jail in the

Andaman Islands. This nineteenth-century compound, originally constructed to house the "better class" of prisoners fighting for independence from British rule, attempted to realize in mortar the systems of visual surveillance built into Bentham's Panopticon design. Satadru Sen describes the ironies associated with this novel prison architecture, promoted in the name of modernity and prison reform, the supervision built into its walls offered as an antidote to punishment by caprice. No more flogging, no more subjection to the whims of brutal wardens, no more public spectacle to keep prisoners in hand. Individual cells allowed the introduction of "humane" punishments such as solitary confinement and dietary restriction, each regulated by codes and certified by physicians.[39]

This new disciplinary regime proved effective precisely to the extent that it simultaneously enlisted and escaped vision, enlisted but denied time. Hours in solitary without human contact took a grave toll; medically supervised dietary restrictions could mean a scientifically protracted starvation. These more insidious effects remained invisible, yet they owed their existence to an architectural layout that called attention to its organization of space. Punishments played out over the course of years passed as humane treatment and achieved legitimacy due to the watchful eyes of guards and physicians.

In a political economy of spacetime, temporality does not replace, complement, or alternate with spatiality. A prison floor plan that highlights visual surveillance permits the debilitating effects of time-enforced disciplines to pass without notice. Imagine it: months locked in a cell; years on a diet of broken bits of rice. The consequences were deadly. The paradox of spacetime serves as a reminder to attend to time as it is implicated in space whenever vision becomes the headliner.

Reconsider, in this light, the calls by women's and GLBT movements for greater visibility as a means to confront oppression.[40] Evelynn Hammonds, a historian of science, has argued that visibility provides, at best, a partial political goal for African-American women, because it works differently for black and white subjects. Visibility elicits recognition, but in a racist society, it can also help define a target. Writes Hammonds, "In overturning the 'politics of silence' the goal cannot be merely to be seen: visibility in and of itself does not erase a history of silence nor does it challenge the structure of power and domination, symbolic and material, that determines what can and cannot be seen."[41] Black and brown women have to negotiate the contradictory aspects of vision as it is taken up into social relations, finding themselves now invisible (jostled as though not even there), now highly visible (object of the averted eye, the handgun, or the stare). Hammonds would have theorists investigate these far from innocuous aspects of the ways that vision is structured in order to understand how space and power articulate with desire and difference. Her appeal to history suggests that the investigation can scarcely begin without attending to time as well.

Rosemary Hennessy has critiqued the effects of the call for greater visibility in queer politics, arguing that "the visibility of sexual identity is often a matter of commodification, a process that invariably depends on the lives and labor of invisible others." Is the only acceptable queer subjectivity a consumer subjectivity, cobbled together with leather jackets, rainbow flags, television footage, freedom rings, real estate in gay neighborhoods, billboards amenable to dual readings, cruise packages, outdoor adventures, evenings out at the club? If so, a queer politics of visibility relies upon a class politics that exploits workers who may themselves be queer, workers in a global economy who often cannot afford the commodities they produce. As the paradox of spacetime works its way through gender and sexuality, becoming visible means "keep[ing] invisible the violent social relations new urban identities depend on."[42]

A political economy of spacetime, rather than simply vision and space, would ask what histories, what travesties, what invisible demands of duration have led to such paradoxical effects. If (some) queers buy now, who pays later? Who has already paid? In what currency? Since when? While people perform gender in capitalist economies, whose weary limbs hold up the stage? What spatiotemporal processes join recognition to forgetting: out of sight, out of mind? What analytic and political tactics offer a hope of intervention?

Once power is taken into account, spacetime relates much more than a story of moving bodies in multiple frames. Gendered bodies move "in" and "through" historically sedimented, power-infused sets of social relations.[43] They bargain, alienate, extract, subordinate, produce, *and* consume. Resources handed over by some appear perpetually available to others. It is all very well to endure, but as whom? With what?

## SURVIVING REPRESENTATION: THE THIRD PARADOX

"How can you stand up there and talk about signs and gender relations when real women are dying!" This passionate denunciation can be heard at almost any conference that takes up the theme of gender and social struggle. Like many such appeals, this one builds upon an all too easily verifiable observation. People *are* murdered, beaten, denigrated, abused, and defrauded on a regular basis, for reasons that have everything to do with gender. Whatever insights the study of representation might yield about the seductions of violence, "deconstructed" is not "disarmed."

Paradox enters the fray only when activists and theorists pit survival against representation, treating the two as though they were mutually exclusive rather than radically intertwined.[44] In scholarship, efforts to split the two generate claims of this sort: "Western feminists" are more concerned with matters of representation (ontologies of gender) because they can afford to be, whereas "African feminism" necessarily concentrates on hunger, education, clean water, infant mortality, and other survival-related issues. In activism, the split often takes the form of a growing impatience with theory.[45]

Attempts to treat survival and representation as antagonistic, or even separate, matters yield paradoxical results. The two cannot be lived or analyzed in isolation, because they occur in and through one another. To explain why this woman rather than that woman is hungry or attends literacy classes or dies requires both. To explain why gender differences can translate into a four-hour walk to the watering hole—or a four-hour wait in the food-stamp line, or for that matter, a four-hour visit to the spa— requires both. Like commodification and alienation, representation and survival are conceptual tools for understanding different aspects of social relations in the latest period of capitalism.

Across from the campus of an East Coast university, where money walks the corridors like ivy covers the walls, a woman sits on the pavement. To all appearances she is white. Day after day, her garments accented with frost or sweat, she calls to passersby and gestures toward her cup. "Spare change, sir?" she intones, with a rising inflection that suggests expectation. "Ma'am, spare change?" Always a gendered appeal. In another year and a shorter haircut, I eddied in the wake of a stream of commuters that channeled out of the subway to flow directly past her post. "Spare change, ma'am? Spare change, sir?" When she got to me, her cadence held. "Spare change, sir-ma'am-sir?" For that gift alone I offered up my coins.

In this twenty-first-century vignette, a woman's survival depends upon calling people into classification. They will be stirred (she hopes) to action through a gendered form of address that in its application invokes class, age, and race as well as gender. Against a moving backdrop of T-shirts and knapsacks, cameras and skateboards, the formality of the language positions the speaker as supplicant. In this context, "ma'am" and "sir" cannot help but carry the inflection of centuries of subordination. These are the terms in which a street theorist hails her walking public.

Her invocations run back and forth—creatively—between culturally fixed possibilities. As with "sir" and "ma'am," "sir-ma'am-sir" rests on a conception of gender that permits only dual options, which may or may not find resonance in the bodies passing by. You are a woman or you are a man, presumed in either case to have deep pockets, or at least deeper pockets than the one calling out. It is an attempt to cover all the bases, offering no offense, assuming that the bases end at two.

Or perhaps not all the bases. The relationship between gender and survival, survival and representation, feeds on more than terms of endearment and terms of address. In their split-second decisions to contribute or pass on, the commuters respond to petitions that exceed words. Hailed as bourgeois, they peer out at her through histories of propriety and suspicion: Is this a beggar shamming? What legitimate circumstance could lead a "good woman" to the streets?

Knowingly or unknowingly, the passersby draw upon ideologies of deserving and undeserving poor, elaborated in debates over welfare reform but heir as well to the centuries of land enclosure and forced settlement that produced "vagrancy" as an offense.[46] Even their estimation of her need transforms commodities into a gauge of time. What does "a woman like her" need to get by? A different set of goods in twenty-first-century Boston, presumably, than fourteenth-century Aztlan. Not for nothing did Karl Marx and Frederick Engels term the production of new needs "the first historical act."[47]

In the process, representation becomes both a means to survival and the thing to be survived. A person may be judged of no account because she's "only" a street person, regardless of what accommodation the long hours of spare-changing allow her to make for the night. As a woman, for safety's sake, she may have to hide by nightfall. As a white woman, she may gain access to the lobbies of stores where people with darker skin are routinely followed. At the same time, she must be able to present herself as convincingly impoverished. To do so, she traffics in meanings and symbols as well as coins, not only in dress or deportment, but in her judgments about whom to hail, and as what.

On the street, this street, an entire political economy passes by. Who finds the cash when she reaches for it? Who gets told to move on? The birthplace of streetcar suburbs has a subway that spits out pedestrians, there to be greeted as benefactor, sir, ma'am, sir. After years of pressure from car manufacturers, not all North American cities can say the same.[48] These historical circumstances, like the lightning-fast assessments demanded by a gendered form of address, pull everyone back into time.

In the chapters that follow, hair-trigger judgments about gender lead to romance as well as lethal exchange. Women out to play with gender at a dance find themselves constrained by economics and racialization, fixed when the theorist finds them most free. Lesbians create a community with a history by traveling imaginatively through time, looking over their shoulders at earlier ways of doing gender. A "modern woman" builds her life upon a series of imagined contrasts with her mother's generation. Kids attack a woman for evading representation, her appearance (to them) gender-race-class ambiguous. The commodification of gender gathers momentum in the United States, where too many paradoxes remain unspoken. What does it mean to come of age in an economy repeatedly described as "booming" when your pet has to downsize to cut-rate dog food, your girlfriend considers marrying for financial security, and your car is repossessed?[49] Survival, meet representation.

## MATTERS MATÉRIEL

Before setting off, a word to the time traveler about the materials used in this book. Like a cat bearing unwanted gifts, gender studies has dragged many objects onto tables and pillowcases over the years, in various states of evisceration. The division of labor, put forward by liberal and socialist feminists as a likely candidate to explain gender inequality, encountered objections that had as much to do with the cold war as matters of evidence. Psychoanalytic explanations foundered on the rocks of historical and cultural difference. Social constructivist explanations stepped into the breach, using history and ethnography to argue that gender is meaning-fully (and thus variably) constituted rather than biologically given. But constructivism, too, proved something of a Trojan horse, carrying a mortal question in the belly of its promise of liberation. If it's all constructed, why are things so difficult to change?[50]

When do-all, be-all explanations for gendered inequality fell out of favor, the quest drifted toward agency, subversion, transgression. Studies of heterosexual marriage, parenting, division of household chores, gendered cosmologies, and distribution of meat after the hunt gave way to research on avant-garde film, transgender movements, queer relationships, and postcolonial resistance, among a host of other topics. Sometimes analysts approached their subjects as limit cases, sometimes as devices used to throw what's taken for granted into relief.[51] All this provided food for thought to the cat, fluff and fad and half-digested guts to her more conservative colleagues, who made a face and worked hard to clean it up.

While I am wary of the romanticism embedded in the emphasis on subversion, I continue to find value in the study of queer materiality for anyone who wants to grasp how gender relations are produced, undermined, transformed, and reproduced. Ambiguously gendered bodies, lesbian relationships, enigmatic friendships, strip joints, skyscrapers, and bars become sites that can help theorize the most recalcitrant inequalities.

Within these pages other things have been queered as well, queered in the sense of rendered unexpected and strange. At various points, as in the preceding discussion of spacetime, I have looked to science and mathematics for inspiration. *Gender in Real Time* owes a debt not only to physics, but also to medieval Arabic/Islamic science, the Buddhist/Hindu conception of zero, evolutionary theory, the mathematics of symmetry, and arithmetical practices associated with counting, each inseparable from the politicoeconomic contexts in which it developed.

In contrast to my earlier books, where theory provided a framework for ethnographic analysis, in this work ethnography dances attendance on theory. Rather than using theory to help make sense of interviews and observations, I have used observations and interviews to illustrate theoretical points. Illustrative evidence serves to breathe life into an argument by fleshing out abstraction. In no sense is excerpt or anecdote expected to carry the weight of the argument.

One need not always travel abroad, shuffle through historical archives, or wait for a utopian redistribution of resources—in other words, look elsewhere—to cast gender relations into critical perspective. By thinking temporally, not just visually, about gender, you as a reader can catch the small shifts that mark its reproduction in a field or a bathroom or a bar, the political and economic concerns that filter histories through the now. By attending to inequalities in time, you can begin to understand how living a gendered life comes to double as both "activity for another and of another" (in other words, alienation) and a source of great satisfaction.[52]

In the chapters that follow I take up selected temporal aspects of gender as part of, not in lieu of, spatial relations mapped out by the eye. The first chapter, "Unsexed: A Zero Concept for Gender Studies," considers how the fetish for enumerating genders that accompanied the expansion of mercantile trade routes contributes to the violence directed at ambiguity today. By drawing upon elements of Arabic/Islamic and Buddhist/Hindu science that provided the wherewithal for global navigation, I develop a zero concept to comprehend the fleeting moments in which gender makes its disappearance on a daily basis. The next chapter, "Do Clothes Make the Woman?" offers a historical materialist critique of the theory of gender performativity. How is it that a theory that highlights the fleeting qualities of ostensibly deeply rooted masculinities and femininities ends up freezing and fixing gender? What accounts for the rapid popularization of performativity as an explanation for gender? The answer lies, in part, in the theory's use of commodities and repetition, concepts with temporal rhythms and "roots" in industrial manufacturing.

"The Ghosts of Gender Past" uses the figure of time travel to complicate recent discussions of labor, memory, modernity, and forgetting. Through a series of imagined historical contrasts in the way gender has been practiced by successive generations (complete with its own Darwinian detour), women create a community with a history and my godmother transforms Alzheimer's into something more meaningful than loss. "The Global Economy Next Time" concludes the book with a brief meditation on time claims and the periodic zeroing out of gender in the current era of globalization. What are the implications of time travel for gender studies? What does it mean for gender studies to do the time?

On the far side of paradox, our time travels open with an investigation into the violence of counting. As industrialization took hold in different areas of the world, an "avalanche of numbers" generated by shining new bureaucracies promised to tame chance by calculating probabilities. First to be aggregated by these technologies were the landless bodies pouring into the city from the countryside.[53] The king's subjects, poorhouse residents, and the dead, all sorted into closed categories and counted. In the current era of nation-states and transnational corporations, number fetishism continues to lend fluid social relations the appearance of fixity and to cloak unjust social arrangements with an aura of the inevitable.

Gender studies maintains an investment in counting just as finely calibrated as the annual reports issued by institutions whose abuses feminists have worked so hard to expose. When it comes to counting, the operations hardly differ, whether they involve a corporate spreadsheet, a tally of paradoxes, or the number sequence implied in the commonplace that there exist but two genders. How to grasp the murderous consequences that this investment continues to visit upon our heads? By learning to tack between present-day injustice and the concept of zero introduced during much earlier periods of globalization.

© Kath Weston

# CHAPTER TWO

# UNSEXED: A ZERO CONCEPT FOR GENDER STUDIES

> The circulation of money takes place in time,
> but it is also time itself.
> —*Carol Greenhouse on Marx's theory of capitalism*

She was handed off from passenger to passenger, like a football, like excrement, like desire.[1] "What . . . is . . . it?" Some looked on with intrigue, with contempt. One stared at her neighbor's shoe, another at the wads of gum calcified between the ridges of the rubber mat that lined the aisle. The bus driver did the only thing he was trained to do: He drove. Past the rows of steel-shuttered buildings. Past the emergency call box that could have saved her. (But with a police force trained as well as the bus driver, and a forty-minute response time to that "bad" section of the city, probably not.) As the minutes passed, the chorus changed: "Give me the slant-eyed bitch." "Maybe he's not a Jap." "Tell us what you are, babe." "Are you a girl or a guy? A faggot? A goddamn dyke?" Her shirt, ripped. Her tormenters, white. Her packages, scattered, like her arms, flailing, then hands bound to sides, then nothing. An African-American passenger interceded: "That's enough." Resolve in his stance, terror in his eyes. And it was enough, because her tanned or saffron body in its leather jacket lay still across one of the seats, folded back into its ambiguities, or whatever certainties her killers proposed and could not find. Gender as a raced reading; death, its corporeal effect.

This story was told to me in San Francisco in the mid-1980s by a multiraced, lesbian-identified woman in her late twenties. Everything is "true" but the ending: A friend who had boarded the same bus fended off her attackers with a can of mace, allowing the two to make their escape. But the ending is also true in its way, because it speaks the nightmare fantasy that hurled this woman back toward consciousness when she tried to sleep in the nights following the attack. It is this alternate ending that left her cursing and sobbing and railing against ghosts she could never dispatch. No escape from that. No escape, either, from the reports compiled by Community United Against Violence (CUAV), a local organization that defined antigay violence as attacks directed at people *presumed* to be queer. In CUAV records both endings appeared, as the story repeated itself (though never in the same way) in altercations at street corner pay phones and grocery store parking lots.[2] Fantasies piece themselves together from deadly truths like these.

Without representation, there is no violence. But without the history of social and material relations for which "violence" provides a comforting shorthand, there is no representation.[3] And so the annals of gay lore house another not-quite-everywoman's story. This time, she lets the door swing closed behind her as she steps into a public restroom. This time, no one asks, "What . . . is . . . it?" But twenty pairs of eyes dart questions. Even a toddler, pushed back to safety, peers out from behind her mother's skirt. Slowly, deliberately, they undress her. An unabashed stare grazes the nipples lying flat beneath her loose-fitting shirt. A sidelong glance gauges the inches from heel to crotch. One look after another strokes the gentle bulge, seemly or unseemly, in her jeans. Their scrutiny laps at her boots, finding ways to resolve them into cowgirl, into "garçonne look," into boy. Their rough gaze, however disapproving, lingers longest where otherwise forbidden.

Then suddenly, a rush to judgment: "I think you're in the wrong place." There are women of different colors and classes in this space, but only the white women speak. What should she say to these self-appointed keepers of gender, this domestic border patrol? Should she turn and walk from the room? Should she drop her jeans, lending credence to the commonplace that the mysteries of gender reside in the genitals, like sexuality in genes of another sort? Should she ignore them? Insist that they look again? Pull out an Uzi and take care of the violation once and for all? Spend the remainder of the day wondering if they would have read her differently had her clothes been more or less expensive, her skin lighter or darker, her arm trailing a three-year-old instead of a suitcase? Spend the remainder of the day attempting to throw off a shame she knows by right is not hers to feel?

Spaces have their histories. In the long and ignoble history of attempts to sort people into manageable (and thus exploitable) class/color/gender combinations in the United States, restrooms occupy prime cultural real estate. Separate facilities for "colored" and "white" became a battleground in the civil rights struggles of the 1950s and 1960s. During the 1970s, unisex bathrooms offered a symbol of liberation  or degeneration (depending) in the fight over equal rights legislation and the entry of women into skilled blue-collar trades. North American workers have spent decades fighting for the right to exercise their most basic bodily functions. Casual laborers in fields and sweatshops find nothing casual about the ongoing resistance to their demands for toilet facilities and the breaks required to use them.[4]

Every identity-based social movement seems to have its bathroom story. Restrooms continue to be classed and raced, with relations of power embedded in location. Airports are not bus terminals, and this side of the tracks is not the other side of town. When a flash of gendered uncertainties prompts onlookers to do whatever they can to set a person at odds with the call of her own body, she walks through a history, not just a door.

Not all gender policing is such an everyday affair. Across the ocean, at a window marked "passport control," a woman stands silent before a uniformed official who speaks to her in Japanese. Receiving no response, his hand hesitates above an array of rubber stamps. With a flourish, he jabs one onto the paper and returns the passport to her, closed. Six days into her trip, she checks the visa page to find that he has marked *otoko* (male) on the immigration form. Apparently the immigration official has been reading across more than his desk. The photo page of the passport proclaims her female, or more precisely, "F." Will she be able to leave the country with this contradictory document, she wonders? A small worry insinuates itself into the rest of her travels.[5]

Back in the United States, at the head of a supermarket checkout line, the customer is waiting. A row of turquoise earrings and a biker jacket adorn her slender, muscled frame. Fluorescent lights bear down on her packages and impart smoothness to her scalp. Feeling good, she smiles. "Nice haircut!" quips the cashier with a grin that says, "Just making conversation." Heads swivel to the tasks of inspection.

Having little to go on by way of hair, patrons scrutinize the conveyor belt for the choice of vegetables, corn chips, dish detergent, in hope of gathering insight into indeterminacies that toy with their already eroding patience. Hmm, no condoms, no makeup, no Tampax. Could this be one of those sex-changing freaks they have heard so much about on TV? Or someone very much like themselves, a not-so-secret sharer in Buddhist practice, or was that sexual identity, someone with whom to make common cause? It wouldn't be . . . no, not Irma's little sister, looking for every possible edge now that she's made the high school swim team? Not Art's prodigal son, barred from the house a year ago for shooting drugs? And what if that bald pate is not shaved at all, but belongs to a chemotherapy patient with a fierce sense of style? This last guess is sobering. Better not to stare, then . . . but the glances come anyway, fast, thick, emphatic enough to prompt the customer to grab her change from the cashier's hand and make her way quickly through the line.

Something is going on in the streets and shops of a globalizing economy, at century's beginning, at century's end, that targets ambiguities as raced and classed as they are gendered.[6] Something is going on in the posts and outposts of power, where gender reasserts itself with each breach of a border. Something is going on that involves more than an inability (and on the part of whom?) to let well enough alone, to let ambiguity remain ambiguity, to let your hesitation double as my knowledge, your verities locked in conflict with my relative interpretation.

## ALL THAT IS FLEETING COMPACTS

There is a moment, an exceedingly liminal moment, a culture- and site-specific moment, when a person can become unsexed. Unsexed does not mean crossing over into male terrain. Unsexed is not what happens when you mistake a butch for a man. Unsexed is not a lifetime proposition. Unsexed has nothing to do with adding a third or fourth or twenty-seventh gender to a heretofore two-gender system. Unsexed is a vanishing, not something you are, a fleeting moment of being "called out of one's sex" before being called into another gendered position.

This is not "unsexed" in the nineteenth-century European sense of a change in status, a fall from grace of the sort that occurred when a woman dirtied herself by laboring in a coal mine or a man in reduced circumstances took up a "feminine" occupation. Nor is this "unsexed" in the early-twentieth-century sense used by white men who refused to share tasks assigned to African-American coworkers. For white workers living out the racist legacies of slavery, such tasks held connotations of "less than manly," if not "'cringing' and 'servile,'" which in turn, according to Robin D. G. Kelley, "meant not only being unsexed, but less than white as well."[7] Older usages of "unsexed" imply crossing over into gendered territory reserved for color/class locations presumed to be of lesser value than one's own. In terms of the beatings and border crossings and grocery store encounters that open this chapter, these older usages describe far too stable a repositioning, much too permanent a fall.

What does "unsexed" mean, then, in the way I have used the term here? Not a loss of womanhood or manhood in the face of transgression. Unsexed is what you become in the moment of doubt before reclassification. Unsexed is what you become in a flash of discomfort before "oh, I get it" sets you back on familiar terrain. Unsexed is the "it" before the "she," the "what" before the "dyke," the "huh?" before the "butch," the "chola," the "society lady," or the "watch out, a weird guy in boots." Unsexed is what can happen when a person—any person—gets thrown up against the question that need not speak its name: "What are you? And what are *you* doing (out of place) here?" Unsexed never lasts. Ambiguity resolves back into certainty, doubt into gendered absolutes.

And what does unsexed begin to explain? Whatever it is that makes someone feel justified or desperate or curious enough to lash out at the woman in the bathroom or the bus, to whittle her down to naked flesh, in public, without touch. Why some people, differently positioned in histories of class and race relations, seldom reach that point. Who is likely to confront, and who will remain silent because her own body carries a legacy of confrontation. (It is not so long, after all, since the abolition of Jim Crow laws that segregated public facilities by race. Which is to say, since the cold hard stare picked up where government agencies left off.)

Although this temporary suspension of gender that I am calling "unsexed" does not define a new gender position, it does have specific social effects that, in the United States, are intricately bound up with color, class, age, race relations. In her essay, "How to Recognize a Lesbian: The Cultural Politics of Looking Like What You Are," Lisa Walker contends that "a butch woman of color might not be recognized as a lesbian because she is not white."[8] For many Anglos in the United States, ultrafemme still turns up blue-eyed blonde, ultramasculine a dark (but not *too* dark) figure, as built as he is handsome. More may be at stake here, however, than the common representation of homosexuality as a "white thing." Who knows how much hyper(hetero)sexualized portrayals of women of color (as Sapphire, as decorative object, as whore) contribute to the tendency to locate lesbians of color beyond the "pale" of queer? And such readings, racist or no, are inevitably complicated by point of view and line of sight: White lesbians who read as "femme" in an African-American woman what African-American lesbians would be more likely to read as "butch"; Chicanas who read gendered ambiguity into Native American bodies in ways that the Indians in question would be hard put to accept.[9]

Consider the situation that faces the stranger—Blackfeet, Diné, or Lakota—who undertakes the simplest of contemporary American moves: stopping at a convenience store. Odds are that the reception will differ if that store is located in downtown Los Angeles, on the rez (whose rez?), or in the hostility-laced atmosphere of a reservation border town. Add to this mix differences in the uses of vision. For most Indians, it's not polite to stare. Many whites look up to seek direct eye contact the minute someone enters a room. Mexicanas, Salvadorans, African Americans, Dominicans . . . people use different parts of the body to indicate or to point. Whatever the method for sizing someone up, the same long hair that marks a body as "ambiguous" in one reading of race/gender can serve as a marker of "traditional" (which is to say, Indian man, appropriately gendered) in another. As the settings and the backgrounds of viewers differ, so do the borders that interpretation has to traverse.

Consider, by way of contrast, the middle-class, one-and-a-half-generation Japanese-American woman who accompanies me on her first trip to the barrio, not as class/race tourist, but as friend. What is this uptown girl, who associates flannel on a woman with pictures of grandmothers or (white) lesbians or (again white) grunge, who can't tell a Pendleton from a J.C. Penney plaid-shirt special, to make of the homeys in a place like Pico Rivera? "Why do they button it like that?" she wonders.

Finally, consider the middle-class white woman who leans over to say of the speaker at a lesbigay event, "How nice, they included a femme on the panel." When I, knowing the speaker to be butch-identified, intimate as much, the woman replies, "But her hair is long!" "Still, look at how she carries herself and the style, not the length, of her dreads." "Those are dreads? I always thought dreads were messy, like a rat's nest." And finally, in the guarded tones that mark racism tightening its grip, "Anyway, *I* think she looks femme." Class backgrounds aside, what separates the woman making these comments from me, three months into my first fieldwork project?

These vignettes raise the possibility—the inevitability—of multiple, conflicting readings. What one reads as "straight" another reads as gender-bending. What one understands as oppressively or scintillatingly real, another takes as parody, a third as failed attempt. Privilege, often unannounced, bolsters claims to a definitive interpretation. And how could such adversarial readings fail to conjure up the phantom figures that haunt renditions of identity in the United States: the black lesbian as bulldagger, the Latina as lover *caliente*, the poor white woman as waitress or truck driver déclassé, the young Asian American as Dragon Lady or China Doll? Each discordant interpretation laden with its own historical legacies of stereotype and struggle.

When readings of gender conflict, it is not because interpretive glitches short-circuit recognition of some freestanding "is-ness" of masculinity or femininity or sexual identification. The girl who barely managed to extricate her bruised and pummeled body from the hands of strangers on a bus did not identify as butch or femme, and for all her attackers knew, she might not have identified as gay. She faced death because she appeared multiply ambiguous, as momentarily unraced and unclassed as she was unsexed.[10] Multiply ambiguous, not to her family or friends or herself, but to her resolutely white and heterosexual antagonists. The vagaries that accosted her grew fat on an apparent absence of signification. Ambiguity coalesced in her adversaries' vacillation between it and she, dyke and he, light brown skin and a tan, an expensive jacket on a poverty route bus. An ambiguity compounded, in other words, from that all-American ensemble, race/class/gender/nation/sexuality.

When one person's femme becomes another's butch or "halfway middler," the interpretive shifts involved are neither arbitrary nor random. They depend upon who's viewing whom, at which historical point and in the context of what sorts of power relations. It is instructive to note that the same folks prepared to unsex someone with their eyes in the shelter of a public restroom generally recast their targets in short order. This very eagerness to move someone out of that moment of becoming unsexed, to arrive at a classification of femme or man or dyke, is the product of an era in which the absence of clear demarcations subjects bodies to desperate measures. Presence turns into passing, and even "deviants" find themselves slotted into neatly tagged categories.

Why should ambiguity, in this time and in this place, elicit the particular fears and fascinations that it does? Put another way, why has ambiguity come to occupy such a key position in fights for social purity and social justice alike? With these questions I attempt to head off the ahistorical orientation that marks many discussions of ambiguity and demarcation in the Mary Douglas vein.[11] Whatever happened in that checkout line or on that bus cannot be explained away with reference to the unsettling effects of blurred boundaries, the inevitability of shadow areas in matters of classification, or purification rituals that endeavor to put things to rights. There is a history to each move to banish doubt, a history to sanctions for violence in the pursuit of clarity. There is a history to "the trumping power of suffering stories" that recount injustice and, with luck, a narrow escape.[12] There is also a history to retail sales that traffic in the markers of identity, a history to the cultivation of ambiguity as a form of social protest, a history to alliances formed between androgyny and particular forms of commodification.

At this last turn of a century, ambiguous identities constituted not only a provocation to violence, but also an incitement to reform and reflection. No doubt, ambiguities can supply a rationale for bloodshed in the service of the kind of restoration project that seeks to bring back a mythical golden age. (Don't you remember the epoch when women were women and men were men, upward mobility called to mind something other than the lottery, and everybody knew their place?) But in recent years, "gender rebels" have also hammered ambiguities into weapons, recognizing categories and hierarchies only long enough to subvert them. Radically different visions, each premised on the belief that ambiguity fosters social change. One locates its utopia in a past that never was, the other in a future that may never be. Two sides of the same torso.

The popular (that is, hegemonic) imagination, which seldom thinks in combination about identities, has harnessed the power of ambiguity to more than transgendered bodies and transgressive sexualities. The 1990s did witness the emergence of "transgender warriors," who saw themselves working for social change each time they marched with pride into a restroom of choice.[13] But with deindustrialization proceeding apace, the same period also saw a spate of reportage in the United States focused on middle-class families that had "passed over" into the working class, into the ranks of the homeless and unemployed. Of particular fascination: the way "those people" managed, at least for a while, to hide their altered circumstances. It has been a time, as well, for the marketing of books on racial ambiguity: phenotypically white bodies that turn out "really" to be black, biracial kids of "mixed" marriages, the effects of light skin and class privilege on racial identification.

All these projects can be considered, in some sense, politically engaged. Yet they vary widely. Some focus on disentangling oppression from betrayal: the problematic alliance of *mestizaje* with Mexican nationalism, the abandonment of "community" associated with class mobility and intermarriage. Others promote ambiguity as an inherently progressive force for change.[14]

For better or worse, the slow dissolve of ambiguity into identity tags dovetails rather neatly with the processes of commodification that permeate life in this latest era of globalization. Tags allow people to enumerate, sort, manage subjectivity, and above all, target it for sale. Insofar as identity tags emerge from an alliance of numbering (bodies) with classification (of bodies), they build upon the distinctive uses of censuses and statistics developed in an earlier period under colonial rule.[15] At the same time, the countable communities produced through strategies of enumeration provide rhetorical sites from which to mount a fight *against* purveyors of arms and dominant ideologies. Enter identity politics, in all its troubling and contradictory glory.

In contemporary political struggles that foreground identity and difference, ambiguity would offer no weapon at all if it merely provoked remembrance or indifference rather than deconstruction and rage. Yet ironically enough, the very activists who would enlist ambiguity often end up bending their politics to the tasks of specification and enumeration. Witness the endless attempts to lay discomfort to rest through a rush to classification. Witness the move to turn identity into a territory, making it subject to land grabs and surveillance. (How "real" are you? Are you in or are you out? Stake your claim.) Witness the demand to trace lines of familiarity into the ashes of everyday encounters. (Tell us what you are, babe: Asian? A guy? A dyke?) Witness the impetus to create new kinds of personhood from the complexities of sociality and desire. (Who am I? Biracial-transgender-half-red-part-brown-ambisexual-class-traitor-hybrid . . .) What does ambiguity compel, so much as its imminent resolution?

## SUNYA, SIFR, ZERO

At such a historical juncture, what are the implications for gender theory of taking into account that fleeting interval of violation and interpretation I have called "unsexed"? Since the feminist movements of the 1970s, analysts have devoted a great deal of thought to developing explanations (not all of them compatible) for the tremendous variability in constructions of gender. Why have women been considered sexually voracious here, lacking in passion there, unsuited to work in one time and place, heavy laborers in another? If the differences that separate men from women are more social and cultural than "natural," why do those differences persist?

Sociologists and psychologists have studied the fine points of interpersonal encounters to understand how individuals learn to categorize others as "women" or "men." Literary critics have examined the part played by imagery and juxtaposition in the reproduction of gender. Economists have studied the institutional mechanisms that slot differently gendered persons into differently gendered jobs. Historians have examined the invention of traditions that attribute certain qualities to women, others to men, perhaps a third set to hermaphrodites. Anthropologists have sought to explain the classificatory propensities that lead human beings to turn all that is vague, overlapping, and uncertain into the arrangements that came to be known as social constructions.[16] In the wake of these investigations, however unfinished, however contentious, it is not so much gender ambiguity or its resolution that cries out for analysis, but the vanishing before something much more substantial takes hold.

To think about how to accommodate "unsexed" within the conventions of gender theory is to draw attention to the temporality of the processes involved in classification. Social constructions imply a degree of fixity, whereas in the case of becoming unsexed, transience beckons. Unsexed is an attempt to describe a fluctuation in the spacetime of everyday life. Unsexed engages less with the presence already presupposed in a question ("What are you?"), and more with the ways that time travels to produce a hiatus in which gender momentarily slips away. Unsexed refers to that passing glimmer of an instant just before an acceleration into meaning gives way to what is commonly called "gender."

Because "unsexed" in this sense represents neither a new gender nor a newly gendered position, it is a concept that is not so easily commodified and recapitulated as identity, at least for the purposes of analytic exchange. Its transient character sets up a different, if not singular, vantage point on the social processes that meld gender with class, race, age, nation, sexuality—that is to say, a vantage point on the work of identity in the political economy of the day. To consider the implications of this confluence of gender, time, and capitalism, I want to lead gender theory into unexpected waters: the history of mathematics.

Ask a person on the street in New York, Wichita, or Santa Ana for an accounting of gender, and you are likely to hear gender described as a sum of discrete variables. There's woman (call her x) and man (call him y), with maybe just enough imagination left over to cover claims to a transgender identity, special cases from New Guinea, or unforeseen occasions. "Man" and "Woman" are fixed positions that can be added—two genders, two—with little reference to historical change or time passing. In the rare case where history enters, it generally intercedes in the form of a new tallying. Such is the case, for example, in the work of Thomas Laqueur, who has argued that the ancient Greeks inhabited a world in which "two genders correspond to but one sex."[17] According to Laqueur, women and men were thought to possess a common set of bodily organs, albeit differently positioned. The cultural symbolism placed on genitalia as a referent for gender by contemporary North Americans would hardly have been enough to prompt the Greeks to split the world into halves. Extremely valuable scholarship, but a very different project than an examination of the ways that counting itself may have hindered development of a historically sensitive gender theory.

To theorize gender and identity anew, a person needs something qualitatively different than a number that can be counted. To represent what it means to become unsexed, she needs something more than an operation of addition or subtraction applied to identities already conceived as things or positions. (Let $x$ = Woman. Let $y$ = Man. Let $t$ = Transgender. $x + y + t = 3z$, where $z$ represents the number of genders in a "cultural system.") A gender theory with any critical perspective on time, economy, and motion requires much, much more than another spook to set beside the door of the genders (Woman plus Man) people think they already know. That something, I would submit, is the zero.

In his book *Signifying Nothing*, Brian Rotman chronicles the introduction of zero into European systems of counting and accounting.[18] Hindu/Arabic numerals, including a zero, traveled to Europe from the Middle East via Arabic/Islamic institutions in Spain and port cities in what would one day become Italy. Algebra discovered Europe in the twelfth and thirteenth centuries, not only through the move to translate manuscripts from Arabic into Latin, but also through a more generalized exchange of traders and travelers. One such was Leonardo Pisano, who came of age in North Africa, where his father managed a customs house. Pisano's *Liber abbaci* (1202) introduced the work of Arabic/Islamic mathematicians to a nascently "Italian" audience.

By the late thirteenth century the study of algebra in Italy centered not in universities but in the abacus schools where merchants sent their sons to train under *maestri d'abbaco*. The existence of a merchant and commercial class in Italy (but not France) during this period may explain the much later "arrival" of algebra in western portions of Europe. Yet the utilization of mathematical innovations such as algebra and the zero was by no means economically determined.[19] Algebra initially developed through the patronage not of merchants but of caliphs who gave scholars a place at court. Pre-Mayan peoples utilized a type of zero hundreds of years before their first encounters with missionaries, conquistadors, and colonialism. Early Christian interest in Buddhist/Hindu numeration had less to do with nascent capitalism and more to do with problems involved in the calculation of a religious calendar.[20]

Muhammad ibn Musa al-Khwarizmi's foundational algebra text, *Kitab al-Jabr wa al-Muqabala* (The Book of Restoring and Balancing), continued to be used in Europe as late as the sixteenth century. Yet despite the tremendous influence of al-Khwarizmi's work on European modes of reckoning, attempts to shift European economies from Roman numerals to a system of calculation that included the zero initially encountered massive resistance.

Those who feared or scorned the zero did not seem to have utilitarian concerns in mind. In combination with a theory of place value, a zero could have facilitated all sorts of transactions. Like Muslims, who looked to algebra to settle questions of inheritance (*fara'id*), European Christians also needed to divide estates, albeit according to different cultural logics. Like Muslims, who used trigonometry to calculate the mobile dates of holy days, Christians looked to the heavens for guidance, though the occasion might be Easter rather than Ramadan.[21] Still the Europeans dragged their feet, captivated by and apprehensive about the implications of Arabic/Islamic science.

According to Ali Abdullah Al-Daffá, "the concept of a mathematical representation that appeared to have no content of its own made no sense to European mathematicians." Rotman points to something more: a deepseated response of ambivalence, if not horror, to the nothingness zero seemed to represent. Much of ancient Greek philosophy recoiled from the void, while early Christian theology associated nothingness with evil, Satan, and the absence of God. Resistance notwithstanding, the zero, "that eerie Hindu-Arabic sign indicating something that is not," would help usher in the quantitative revolution that Alfred Crosby identifies as a precursor to global colonization.[22]

Like any shift, the adoption of a zero did not occur uniformly. From the tenth to the thirteenth centuries, abacists wrote in Roman numerals and (true to their name) calculated with an abacus; algorists wrote *and* calculated with so-called Hindu numerals. Scholars in search of a way to index the Christian scriptures produced concordances that employed Hindu-Arabic numerals long before merchants and financiers adopted the "new" signs. Rotman examines the eventual European acceptance of zero in conjunction with what he considers related, and roughly contemporaneous, developments: the invention of the vanishing point in perspectival painting and the introduction of imaginary money into exchange relations (as a counterpoint to the "realness" associated with gold or silver bullion). To this list, Crosby might add the invention of the rest, a sign for the absence of sound, by musicians whose notation for the polyphonic type of composition called *ars antiqua* provided a novel way to divide sound and silence into measurable units.[23]

Throughout, Rotman never lapses into the orientalist cadence of so many American and European historians of mathematics who, on the rare occasions when they give more than passing notice to mathematics outside "the West," tend to register amazement at its historical depth and sophistication. Yet his otherwise discerning analysis approaches history from a resolutely European perspective, tracing the migration of mathematical practices and concepts onto the continent from somewhere else. In classic ethnographic fashion, Europe supplies Rotman's "here," South Asia and the Middle East his "there."

The result is a sort of arithmetical import-export narrative. Students, traders, and scholars travel from the Middle East to pick up astronomy and mathematics on the South Asian subcontinent. They bring back what first becomes known as Arabic, then Hindu-Arabic, numerals, including the concept of a zero. In alternative accounts, intellectuals in Baghdad learn about the numerals from a delegation of visiting scholars who journey from Sindh (now part of Pakistan) to the court of the caliph al-Mansur about 780 CE.[24] In either case, the Middle East exports the "Indian" numeric system to Europe through Sicily and Spain. (Notice how the incendiary markers of regional and communal identity are lost as Sindhi slides into "Indian," a multireligious batch of astronomers collapses into "Hindu," and so on.) Those who tie the meaning of zero directly to South Asia by deriving zero from the Sanskrit word *sunya*, commonly translated as "emptiness" or "void," minimize the interplay of meanings produced by this complex legacy of cultural and geographic mediation.

In contrast, an account of the zero centered in South Asia, China, North America, or the Middle East would focus in each case on different historical periods and different diasporas. If one were to take South Asia as a point of departure, for example, Buddhist-Hindu debates about concepts such as *sunyata* would assume more prominence, with astronomers, religious leaders, traders, and notational systems shown engaging with Islam and embarking from a different geographic nexus. Numerals and dating systems developed on the subcontinent would follow the propagation of Buddhist and Hindu teachings to locales throughout the Pacific and Southeast Asia.[25] A recent meditation on the zero by Robert Kaplan, which locates Sumeria as point of origin, shares with most other accounts of the sign a tendency to borrow heavily from the genre of travelogue ("travelers' tales," "zero's path through time and thought") to establish its argument.[26]

Any narrative of the zero's development centered in the political economy of North America would emphasize Mayan discoveries. Inscriptions from the eighth century show Mayans using glyphs to represent the absence of time units of a certain order. Those glyphs mark the space of an absence which, if left blank, might have brought confusion to the reader. (Was the space intentional or an artifact of hasty writing? How many spaces does a blank represent? Should the number read 8–3, 8–0–3, or 8–0–0–3?) Ifrah calls this system "a remarkable place-value written numeration with a genuine zero."[27]

Yet Maya-centered accounts of the zero remain relatively uncommon. Not only have the indigenous peoples of the Americas been marginalized, along with their creations, but Mayan glyphs, unlike Hindu-Arabic numerals, reputedly were used more for ritual than for daily calculations or trade. This form of zero never attained universal currency; the arrival of the conquistadors saw to that. From the arrogant perspective of today's global commerce, the Mayan zero can appear to be "a one-step affair; and, moreover, one that led to nothing."[28] The same has been said for the zero invented by the Babylonians, whose sexagesimal (base-sixty) system lingers in the contemporary division of hours into 60 minutes and circles into 360 degrees, but whose cuneiform notation was discarded along the way to double-entry bookkeeping and *portolano* charts for navigation."[29]

Alternatively, Islam can provide a nongeographic center for a story of the zero's travels, given the reach of Muslim thought and practice. From the ninth through the eleventh centuries, leaders such as the caliph al-Ma'mun established centers of learning in cities such as Baghdad. With merchant vessels regularly plying the waters from South Asia to the Persian Gulf and the port of Basra, scholars working in Arabic were bound to learn about "Indian" numerals. A history of global trade was implicit in the medieval Arabic term for the study of optics, mathematics, and the like: "the foreign sciences," which would only later and in European retrospect come to be known as "Islamic science." As Scott Montgomery points out, the "foreign" in "foreign sciences" would eventually court a satiric usage, as study outside the *madrasas* became common enough to attract its share of critics.[30]

With the benefit of court patronage, al-Ma'mun's *Bait al-Hikma* (House of Wisdom), founded around 800 CE, rivaled the famous library at Alexandria. Over the years such institutions attracted the likes of al-Khwarizmi, al-Battani ("the Ptolemy of Baghdad"), Thabit ibn Qurra (translator of Archimedes and an expert on irrational numbers), and Ibn al-Haytham (author of *Kitab al-Manazir* [Book of Mirrors], an influential treatise on optics). As these thinkers translated and elaborated upon Alexandrian, South Asian, and Greek texts, they were quick to incorporate the zero into the emerging arts of algebra and trigonometry.[31] Perhaps it would be more accurate to say that they incorporated "a" zero, since the meanings carried by the concept fluctuated over the course of travel and translation.

*Sifr*, the Arabic rendering of the Sanskrit *sunya*, is often rendered (like *sunya*) as "nothing" or "emptiness," but it can also mean "vacating" or "emptying," an important distinction to which I will return below. The symbols used to indicate *sifr* also varied, ranging from a dot, to a dot within a circle, to the circle used in international finance today.[32]

Even the customary terminology of Hindu-Arabic numerals, intended to credit the originators of contemporary arithmetical notation, oversimplifies the zero's history, for it reflects nothing of regional or religious contributions beyond Hinduism and Islam. In the eighth and ninth centuries, the scientific center that was Baghdad sheltered a mix of Muslims, Nestorian Christians, Jews, and Parsis, not to mention the visiting delegation of scholars from Sindh. The "Chinese" author of *Khai-Yuan Chan Ching*, which included a chapter on numeric systems of South Asia, was actually an Indian Buddhist, Chhüthan Hsi-Ta, who had relocated to the T'ang capital. Jain astronomers joined Buddhist stargazers in the perusal of the night skies. Jewish, Christian, Muslim, and Sabian intellectuals collaborated to produce translations of classical texts, while experts on the Kabbalah developed an arguably zero-like conception of their own. Even al-Khwarizmi, the "father" of algebra and author of *The Book of Addition and Subtraction According to the Hindu Calculation*, was Muslim but not Arab, in the contemporary sense of the term, since he migrated to Baghdad from Central Asia.[33]

The complexities of this intellectual diaspora were not sufficient to immunize mathematics from the excesses of contemporary identity politics. Seidenberg revives an old debate that opposes diffusion to independent invention in order to argue that Mayans may have derived "their" zero from Asia. Al-Daffá distinguishes between a "Muslim zero" and a "Hindu example of a zero," then allows these two fictions to vie for the earliest date of invention, even though the leading contenders remain separated by as little as three years. A long line of European humanists, in their turn, have done everything possible by way of historical conjecture to bypass South Asia and the Middle East in order to claim the zero for ancient Greece.[34]

What, then, does the intricate history of this remarkable sign have to do with gender? Several interesting things happen once you begin to think in conjunction about the place occupied by "zero" (with respect to numbers) and the place occupied by "unsexed" (with respect to genders). And you must think about zero and unsexed in conjunction, for the two are joined by the ongoing commodification of "things" and "not-things," including gender, as scholars have ventured, traders have traded, and capitalism has continued to wend its way through the centuries. The emptying out of gender into that flash of uncertainty that I have called unsexed gives gender theory a sign that, like zero, allows for certain types of operations. As a zero concept, "unsexed" opens new possibilities for reckoning the effects of buying and selling on the reproduction of gender, and new technologies of accounting for gendered relations of power. How is it that a flux of signifiers keeps regrouping into those stubbornly substantive categories Woman and Man, with all their associated disciplinary effects? A zero hurls gender back into time, in pursuit of just such questions.

To understand the zero's implications for gender theory, you need first to understand what this sign promotes and permits. Zero is qualitatively different from a number. It does not pretend to make reference to something countable, something there, in any ontological sense. Zero does not denote a thing. Zero marks absence and (perhaps) nothingness at the same time as it holds open a place for—represents the potential for—signification.

Of course, a case can be made that numbers, too, are nonreferential in the sense that they need not refer to objects. As many mathematicians have argued, the work that numbers do in the world is not reducible to counting sheep or other items that can be assumed to exist somewhere "out there," if only in one's dreams.[35] Negative numbers provide a key example of a kind of number that is not concrete in the sense that it cannot be counted through pointing or touch. Yet nonreferential approaches in mathematics are themselves historically indebted to the introduction of a zero, which allowed scholars to distinguish between counting and the measurement of things available to count.

In a twenty-first-century sense, zero is not just another number among numbers or a sign among signs. Instead, as Rotman makes clear, zero operates as a meta-sign: both a sign *about* signs, and a sign for the *absence* of other signs. If zero is there, seven is not there; in the place where zero stands, two and forty-seven are not. As such, zero signifies not only an absence, but also the potential for later occupation. Movement is thus implicit in the sign.

Zero also keeps other numerals in their place, so to speak. By occupying a position in a certain order, a zero endows that position with value, while changing the value of adjoining numbers accordingly. The two in "2," written identically to the two in "20," acquires the value of $2 \times 10$ through the mechanics of place value in a base-ten system. There are other ways to signify orders of magnitude, of course (for example, finger joints, Chinese "hybrid numeration"), but zero represents a particularly ingenious one.[36] Why? In a word: calculation.

Division, subtraction, multiplication, addition, square roots, tangents, cosines: These are the operations (or their products) that have combined to make so-called Hindu-Arabic numerals the global standard for all manner of reckoning. To take a contrasting example, Roman numerals "do not lend themselves to calculation because of the static nature of their basic numerals, which are essentially only abbreviations for recording the results of calculations already done by means of a counting board or abacus."[37] Try arranging XLVIII, XXXI, and MCLX in columns to calculate their sum, and the logic of Ifrah's statement will quickly become apparent. When used together with Hindu-Arabic numerals arranged in a place-value system, the zero becomes an operator as well as a signifier.

Like zero, unsexed does not refer to something that is there—"a" gender—in any ontological sense. Like zero, unsexed operates as a meta-sign, a sign about that ephemeral instant in which someone perceives an absence of gendered signification. In the instant before "what?" changes to "she," the person momentarily unsexed appears to embody Judith Butler's now classic point about the nonontological status of genders. According to Butler, the reification of "woman" and "man," "masculine" and "feminine," implies essence where none exists, and existence when essence is nowhere to be found. A person "is" not feminine, apart from the play of eyeliner and fingernails that points to an interior essence and makes it seem so.

Performativity theories work against the reification of gender by attempting to explain how the impression of substantively existing masculinities and femininities emerges from essentially nothing. In contrast, the critique developed here of gender theory's ill-fated fascination with counting concerns itself with much more than ontology. The zero concept of unsexed draws attention to a movement in and out of gender that occurs under very specific historical conditions, conditions that have everything to do with shifting relations of power and production that performativity theories can acknowledge, but otherwise fail to engage. As we shall see in the following chapter, the temporalities involved far exceed the processual time of performativity.

As with genders, so with numbers: "Two" and "three" are not referential notations for countable objects, like fingers or toes, but signs defined in relationship to other signs and in relationship to a political economy that has shaped the practices of geometry and merchant trade, not to mention the latest in actuarial tables or flexible inventory accounting. So the instant when a person becomes unsexed is not a misrecognition of some real thing: a gender lying in wait to be accurately perceived or radically misconstrued. Rather, that flash of confusion calls attention to the social relations (reeking as they do of power, infused as they are with signification) that constitute gender.

To echo Rotman's organizing question: "What can be said through the agency of such a sign [as zero, as unsexed] that could not be said, was unsayable, without it?"[38] For one, unsexed unsettles the presumption that discussions of gender must ultimately refer back to genders—something countable and enumerable, however culturally constituted that something may be. Like zero, unsexed does not stand alone, but acquires meaning in relation to a number sequence, whether that sequence extends to two (Man, Woman) or three (Man, Woman, Third Gender) or some number of genders yet to be determined, potentially infinite in its extension. Yet, as a zero concept, unsexed is no androgyne. It cannot represent a quasi-gender in its own right, but only gender's temporary lapse.

Unsexed no more signifies arrival in that one-time utopia—a genderless world—than zero indicates that we have put the nasty business of ones, twos, and forty-eights behind us, thank you very much. To become unsexed is not to transcend or "opt out" of gender, any more than zero can acquire meaning apart from the numerals for which it reserves a place. People pass through moments of becoming unsexed as they pass on to those apparently fixed, quantifiable, and culturally recognizable states known as genders. What the concept of unsexed contributes is an opportunity to notice the passing, and with it, the process by which the fullness of gendered signification depends on this movement and this emptying. In so doing, the concept of unsexed allows people to formulate questions that the recent ethnographic voyages of discovery to bring back a third (or fourth, or fifth) gender foreclose.

## THE CALL OF THE THIRD

There is a relationship of longstanding between counting and commodification. As business expands, corporations, publishers, even academic departments have to keep track of what they sell, producing the intangibles of service or scent in the form of units subject to charge. Knowledge begins to retail in the form of student credit hours (SCH), yours for a modest fee. There was a time when college courses (count: three SCH) conveyed two staple quantities to its students: Woman and Man, sometimes relating to one another, sometimes not. As the possessors of fixed and discrete gender "roles," these two shadow figures were easily recorded in the ledger books that double as class notes. Once placed in a one-to-one correspondence with their respective "roles," these figures had little option but to acquiesce or rebel against larger social forces that continued to define them as gendered beings, even in rebellion. Genders—however reconfigured in an allegedly postfeminist world—seemed irretrievably naturalized, as commodities tend to be. There are women and there are men—anyone can see that, right? How then to get people to think outside the lines, the givens, to imagine gender as something other than a thing, to imagine a world in which gender would not become a nexus for inequality and oppression?

At some point binaries were identified as the culprit. Woman plus

Man yields a sum of two genders. But "two" too often translated into social life as one up, one down, so a quest began for a way to break up this cozy yet hierarchically inclined couple. The search ranged across cultural borderlands and rode roughshod through historical periods. Various candidates for the job emerged, most prominently The Third Gender, The Butch, and The Transgendered. In recent scholarship, these spectral figures symbolize the Last Best Hope for disrupting the stability of what analysts have generally conceived as a two-gender order.

Are societies divisible into two-gender and multiple-gender systems? Many anthropologists and historians have come to think so. By extending Gayle Rubin's path-breaking concept of a sex/gender system a bit farther down the number line, they have identified Third (and Fourth, and Fifth) Genders from India to Oman, from Sambia villages in New Guinea to wind-blown stretches of the Zuñi reservation. In his widely read book, *Making Sex*, Thomas Laqueur went "back in time" to reverse the directionality of this movement along the number line by characterizing ancient Greece as a "single-gender" system. Up for analysis in most cases is not the presumption of systematicity or the notion of enumeration per se, but rather the reproduction and disruption of variously numbered gender systems.[39]

In its geographic application, the notion of a Third Gender has traveled faster if not farther than the zero. One of the concept's leading critics accordingly notes its abstraction from social context.[40] The Third has gathered together, under the same rubric, *hijras*, transsexuals, *guevedoche*, butches, eunuchs, *xanith*, sapphists, *kwolu-aatmwol*, "Balkan virgins," and more, not to mention garden-variety gays. These are "local" categories that describe everything from castrated bodies to community membership to identities that require no bodily modification. One could argue that Third Gender has become a catch-all term for anomalies and residue produced by the categorical division between Woman and Man. The effect is to equate a certain way of styling oneself lesbian in the United States ("butch") with 5–alpha reductase hermaphroditism in the Dominican Republic (*guevedoche*), at least to the extent that each term occupies an intermediary position between The Second and The First. As to whether Woman or Man comes in First, I leave that to the reader's imagination.

Much of the writing on The Third Gender shares the celebratory tone common to contemporary treatments of transgression. But of course, The Third transgresses only in the comparison: What looks radical to an aficionado of two fixed genders may look like everyday observation to people who use the term "*guevedoche*." Even then, there is more to understand before evaluating claims that The Third Gender overturns gender-as-"we"-know-it.[41] The multiple genders that have insinuated their way into monographs as analytic as well as descriptive devices are signs arrayed alongside other signs. *They are not meta-signs like zero, but signs of the same order.* Ethnographies continue to string genders together like numbers on a number line, like suspects in a lineup, like ducks in a row. Even the naming practices emphasize enumeration: "the two sexes," "the five sexes," "the third gender."

In the hands of academics and advertising executives, this retailing of gender in the form of countable, shrink-wrapped units obscures transitional moments of becoming unsexed by abstracting gender from political and economic relationships and taking gender out of time. Without the *dis*traction of that kind of *ab*straction, one might begin to suspect that the onset of scholarly fascination with the notion of a Third Gender coincided with shifts in more generalized social processes of commodification.[42] And look who does and does not qualify as a fourth or a third. From "the *hijras* of India" to "the *xanith* of Oman," Third Genders have added a bit of color to gender theory through a bit of neocolonialist artifice. Only the rare scholar asks why *hijras* qualify as gender celebrities in ethnographic writing while, say, *jankhas* have never been asked to audition for the part.[43] There has still been no serious attempt to find a place for domestic race/class/color combinations in this adamantly Othered but overseas collection.

Except for American Indians, whose *nadles* and *winktes* can pull down a part so long as they play the colonized within, almost the entire cast of Third Genders performs on a "Third World" stage, sometimes, it seems, against painted harem and South Sea island backdrops. Genders that come up multiple in "the (white) West's" portrayals of "the Rest" live at a comfortable distance, where they can be exoticized in ways fully compatible with the colonialist penchant for new nomenclature and classification.

Historians rallying to the call of a Third have tended to focus on Europe and, to a lesser degree, the United States. Often they proceed with minimal or no reflection on the continuities between their work and the nineteenth-century European project of qualifying homosexuals as a Third Sex. In the collection *Third Sex, Third Gender: Beyond Sexual Dimorphism in Culture and History*, the historical essays discuss Europe, while the ethnographic essays tend to participate in the trophy sport of bringing "back" (from where, to where?) a Third.[44] So-called Third Genders abroad tend to be conceived in static, "species," terms, even for regions where historical documents are available and history and political economy are, as always, of the essence.

Packaging gender into the calculable bundles that are genders—even in culturally or historically relative terms—paves the way for disciplinary practices that subject bodies to tallying and sorting. Without this kind of makeover, there are no guessing games about who is and who is not, no medical interventions to sort "intersexed" people (hermaphrodites) into numbered slots, no controversies over chromosome testing in international sports, no heated discussions about where to place someone when "it" walks through the door of a bathroom or a bus.[45] Without the mutual entanglement of gender and race that historically has informed this kind of makeover in the United States, Pansy Weasel Bear would not have had to comfort her daughter after officials disqualified the ten-year-old's basketball team from a regional YMCA tournament. Accused by off-reservation opponents of "playing boys," the Indian team's victory on the court was nullified after officials made players drop their gym shorts in order to check for bra straps and panties. "They thought we were boys," another member of the team reported. Parents responded with anger and charges of racial and gender discrimination.[46]

The search for genders—be they First, Second, or Third—fixes as it nominalizes, encouraging people to look once again to bodies, to the visual, as gender's ultimate referent. Bodies can be racked up, ordered, totaled in a way that the power relations involved in a moment of unsexing cannot. Three, Two, One: For the impoverished gender theory that results, it's back to the body count.[47]

Where there's commodification, there's fetishization. So it should not be surprising that just as quickly as gender is packaged into genders, ambiguity becomes reified in theory by conflating "unsexed" with another gendered category, The Butch. The Butch in queer theory, like The Third Gender in ethnographic writing, was widely assumed to operate as a meta-sign.[48] As a character recently brought in from the wings and repositioned under the spotlight of academic writing, The Butch is the celebrated one who disrupts, critiques, subverts—all those moves near and dear to the hearts of scholar/activists. Queer theory set her up as the paradigmatic gender rebel who dismantles gender with her every transgression of prescriptions for femininity. Who better to foreground the constructedness of gender than this woman in wolf's clothing?[49]

But if you can get past the hopeless romanticism associated with this phantom figure, it quickly becomes evident that The Butch, like The Third Gender, is no meta-sign. Far from operating as a sign (like zero) that points to the absence of the signs that help constitute gender, The Butch is just another number on the number line, another gendered category like "Woman" or "Man" that fixes as much as it subverts. I am speaking here, of course, of The Butch *as a representation*, quite apart from the diversity of individuals who use the term or claim it as an identity. The reification of The Butch in gender theory as a signifier of a certain anti-gender order effectively lays to rest and puts to past the fleeting moment of becoming unsexed that constitutes gender's disruption. Paradoxically enough, this gender rebel without a pause brings semiotic closure to the very process of unsexing that begins to break apart gender.

"Don't you know, Mama?" says the child, following the question in her mother's eyes to the other side of the street. "That's a *butch!* They had some on Oprah." As a practiced representation, The Butch may sometimes turn out to be less visually anomalous than her theorists might think. Every time a discerning audience arrives at a judgment of Bimbo, Jock, Housewife, Nerd, Third Gender, Gangbanger, Butch, the timelessly gendered qualities ascribed to each figure, rebel or no, effectively stop the motion. The apparent solidity of such categories, derived in turn from a predominantly visual diagnosis, obscures the possibility that gender must and does, on occasion, "zero out." Once "it" becomes "Butch," the questions stop, the interrogation of gender (via race, via class) comes to a grinding halt, and people rally to the humdrum tasks of evisceration or eviction.

And what of the disappearance of "femininity" produced by the sleight of hand that moves a passing moment of "it" into "masculine," or "huh" into "butch"? Other writers have tempered the romanticism attached to the figure of The Butch by idolizing The Femme as a gender hero in her own right.[50] Like celebrations of The Butch, however, these accounts tend to equate acts of transgression with social subversion and to place their bets for social change on a fixed subject position, rather than attending to the power relations embedded in fleeting moments of displacement.[51]

What's more, if race and class inevitably complicate the readings of gender in the United States, transforming one woman's Femme into another's Butch, then it becomes perfectly possible for feminized lesbians, not to mention heterosexual grandmothers of four, to experience challenges on the bus and strip searches at the border. Judgments based on "looks" formulate themselves in the looking as well as the presentation. Clearly, then, the butch-identified are not the only ones ever to have had their access to sex-segregated space challenged by those bathroom fixtures of another order, the gender sentries who patrol the porcelain. After twenty years of gender theory, it should go without saying—although it probably bears repeating—that physical features gain meaning only through context. In the harrowing narrative that opens this chapter, there is no way to know for sure how blue eyes would have played against the same complexion, hairstyle, or jacket. Bodies assuredly go to their reckoning, but not without interpretation.

Once the pronouns start, once the "he's" and "she's" replace the "its" and "huhs," can other sorts of gendered identities be far behind? Alternative gender identities such as femme and butch tend to downplay the complexities of their own racing and classing, much as they obscure the instant of becoming unsexed that occurs betwixt and between fixed signification.[52] In the process, they line out that zero moment that orders a running commentary on the historical and material processes bound up with signification.

So "butch" may turn out to be more effective as an erotic identity than a political weapon. Why? Because the semiotic closure produced by fixed gender categories plays right into the processes of commodification featured in today's economy. Those processes cast gender as a collection of discrete things (masculine, feminine, androgynous "traits"), visually detectable, all the better to buy and sell with. Rather than breaking dichotomies wide open, these identity tags shut down the not-so-free play of signification more commonly dubbed "ambiguity."

That leaves only The Transgendered on our list of latter-day gender outlaws and gender heroes. What could be better calculated to set received gender categories in motion than a figure that refuses to be boxed? As an analytic device, The Transgendered attempts to give arbitrary categories the slip, yet can end up replicating the very gender divisions it would contest.

The popular formulations FTM (female-to-male) and MTF (male-to-female) have all the limitations associated with any fixed gender position, because they preserve male and female as two discrete locations. All that is left to The Transgendered is to "cross over." No serious challenge to the number line here. More intriguingly for gender theory, some activists have shifted the focus away from transgender identity toward transgendering, a movement that tacks betwixt and between socially recognized classifications.[53] High heels, bracelets, and a beard will disrupt traffic—as well as assumptions—on most days in most cities in North America. Five-car pileups aside, transgendering remains an activity in which only certain bodies engage. However disruptive, it employs signifiers that appear stable, at least with respect to their ambiguity. In this sense, "transgender," for all its attractions, no more eludes fixity or commodification than older conceptions such as androgyny.[54]

Writing on transgendering does employ a slightly more advanced mathematics; to wit, an exercise in fractions. The eye slides from goatee to painted fingernails and back to breasts, without necessarily becoming any the wiser about surgery, injections, or genitalia. These bodies "mix" traits customarily parceled out between two sexes. Yet a move to mix aspects of Woman together with fractional qualities of Man, in proportions that keep passersby guessing, is not the same thing as unsettling a number system altogether. The entire operation remains organized by gender*s*, now splintered into qualities that may be added or subtracted in minute amounts assigned to any given body. Alongside those genders, no zero sign marks the vacating instant, the potential for their absence. A "mix" of gendered attributes in a single body bears little resemblance to what occurs when someone becomes temporarily unsexed, signification undone, identities askew, in a moment that can erupt into anyone's and everyone's lives.

Perhaps the problem for gender theory lies not so much in binaries or the number of genders available for study, but instead in the very focus on quantities and counting that produces those numbers in the first place. As long as people continue to traffic primarily in measurable units called genders (or gender traits), they miss the analytic significance of the fleeting moment that I have been calling "unsexed," while playing right into the forces of commodification. Shooting down dichotomies, that eminently feminist sport, can never carry the weight of social change. At least not as an additive enterprise.

Why? Because reckoning in an additional term—be it Transgendered, Third, or Butch—does nothing to address the theoretical impasses reached by those who have struggled with the question of how to represent the compounding of gender with class and race and a host of other social relations. Likewise, adding a term of the same order to a series does little to undercut the processes of counting or commodification. The Third Gender, like The Fourth and The Fifth, will continue to be subject to packaging and tallying as a social position and an identity. To the extent that the figure of The Transgendered relies upon formulations such as shifting from one gender to another, or a mix of enumerable gendered attributes, the result is the same.

How extensive the subversion, how meaningful the transgression, if scholars follow passersby in naming the transgressor as mannish, masculine, profoundly troubled, diesel femme, or even another exemplary figure out to set gender dichotomies on their head? Adding genders and gendered icons to an already available lexicon of the same is a fight-fire-with-fire approach that leaves everybody wondering what happened when the theoretical edifice goes up in flames. How can reified figures such as The Androgyne or The Femme or The Third Gender or The Butch ever undercut reification? I would argue, on the contrary, that they are eminently suited to the marketing of gender and the recuperation of trangression back into a two-sex system. Back, that is, to a future of "explanations" that cast lesbianism as inversion, back to cultural or genetic determinism, back to assumptions about the existence of a gendered something that is there and knowable, if not known.

## DECIPHERING

Zero (unsexed) holds open the place, theoretically, that multiple genders (numbers) foreclose. Its power lies, in part, in its ability to enable nonreferential operations. With zero people learned to multiply and divide in the absence of collections of visible objects. Without it, they had to resort to finger-counting or its symbolic equivalents. Only zero allowed people to employ numerical symbols with reference to one another, rather than to an observable world.[55] No zero, no quadratic equation, no analytic geometry, no calculations for mortgages or falling real wages or gross domestic product.

Zero is "the origin of ordering, the position which excludes the possibility of predecessors."[56] As such, zero endows numbers with place value; its mark of absence affects the meaning of all associated signs. Place-value systems derived from South Asia employ numerals as "signs with no direct visual reference," in contrast, say, to the rod numerals used in China or Japan.[57] The invisible distinction that place value permits between cardinal and ordinal numbers bears special relevance for gender theory.

As a meta-sign, zero allows analysts to distinguish between the social effects of speaking about three genders and a third. "Three" is a cardinal number that makes reference to a collection arranged in no particular order. A number system that lacked a zero could still speak meaningfully about three (or five, or two) genders. In contrast, the "third" in Third Gender is an ordinal number that sets up a rank order by attributing a sequenced position to each object or sign. Looking for three seats in a sports stadium instead of interpreting the number stamped on your ticket as a sign for the third row could leave you wandering miles of aisles. Grabbing five cookies off a plate will precipitate a very different response in the United States than helping yourself to a fifth after the plate has made several rounds, especially if there's no more money for dessert until payday.

Instead of racking up additional genders, the refiguring of "unsexed" as a zero concept calls attention to the ranking and sequencing of genders already in circulation. More is at stake here than the formal property of providing a starting point for enumeration (one, two, three). Ordinal numbers can indicate power differentials through positioning. On this point Simone de Beauvoir proved wiser than many of those eager to celebrate the "discovery" of a Third Sex today. Beauvoir's title, *The Second Sex*, incorporates a clear sense of protest at the use of ordinal numbers to demarcate privilege: Woman second, Man first.

So go ahead, allocate those multiple genders a position on the number line: First Sex/Gender, Second Sex/Gender, Third Sex/Gender, Fourth Sex/Gender. . . . Say all you want about the importance of disrupting dichotomies by arriving at a number greater than two. Then flip that number line vertical and note its resemblance to an evolutionary scale or a Great (White) Chain of Gendered Being with button-down-shirt-suited Man on top.

Where power is concerned, it makes all the difference in the world that what has attracted all the attention is not just the idea of three sexes, but the notion of a third. Gender theory has set up The Third Gender, like The Transgendered and The Butch, to mediate between Woman and Man. Rank ordered into an ancillary position after one and two, s/he alters the First and Second Genders not a whit, while allowing them to continue to occupy the priority positions. All the more reason to look further for analytic concepts such as unsexed that can challenge facile conceptualizations of genders across the board. Only then will gender theory begin to meet the challenge of the feminist critique developed in the 1980s by women of color, who denounced the racism and classism that slapped them in the face each time white theorists deployed Woman and Man as one-size-fits-all concepts.[58]

When not conceived as a number line with the potential to extend multiple genders into infinity, gender in the United States tends to be modeled as a continuum from feminine to masculine, Woman to Man, with figures like The Butch located in the middle as go between.[59] The poles of any continuum necessarily remain fixed at two, but which two? Defined by what criteria? Hair—"good" or "bad," skin—"dark" or "light," deportment—"trashy" or "refined"? Depending upon who's doing the looking, ultrafeminine can turn up long-haired brown and "cultural," blue-eyed blond seductress, or honey-colored society lady. These are scales that tend to class and race gender in predictable and predictably offensive ways, continua that establish fixed positions where onlookers might otherwise construe ambiguities and shifting alliances. Gender materializes as a ruler, a single axis divided into mathematically precise segments (fractions) that establish degrees of distance from each of the poles or extremes. (Note the use of a base-ten numerical system in the resulting ten-point scale.) If "one" is "feminine" and "ten" is "masculine," the only question can be: How does the girl measure up?

Zero cannot refer to what is measurable or countable, regardless of whether an operation involves moving along a number line or sliding along a continuum. The flash of an instant in which gender zeroes out to become unsexed does not linger in the realm of the visible. The eye's search for the familiarly gendered reassurance of boots, stance, or jewelry: all this comes later, with reinscription into a gendered order.

Through its very nonreferentiality, a zero concept makes it possible for gender theory to move past an inventory of genders, gender traits, gender roles, gender norms, and gendered positions to consider temporality, shifts in power, and commodification. Through its very nonreferentiality, a zero concept opens a critical perspective on contemporary society's tendency to produce every social relation, including gender, as a commodity: just another saleable, countable "thing." This is not to pass judgment on commodification itself as good or bad, as a desirable, reprehensible, or merely short-sighted mode for producing social relations. Clearly a zero, if not the zero, remains thoroughly implicated in histories of finance, commodification, and exchange. What a zero concept contributes to social theory is a certain analytic purchase, if you will, on some of the very social relations that it enables, and thus on the contingency of their production.

Ubiquitous slips into referentiality by gender theory only underscore the need for the nonreferential zero concept that I have called unsexed. What do I mean by "slips into referentiality"? Even The Butch gets defined with reference to genitalia; with different equipment she would be The Transgendered or The Man. However socially constructed theorists have asserted gender to be, however separable from the biological "facts" of sex, they have continued to anchor gender to aspects of bodies that can be watched, inferred, and counted.

To draw upon mathematics in order to develop a nonreferential analytic concept is not necessarily to move gender theory in the direction of an idealist analysis. In times such as these, that would be dangerous. Certainly the violence and the violation that can accompany being called out of one's sex are material enough, as are the circumstances in which hatreds fester. But the cracking of bones, the hair set afire, the endless interrogatory can also be understood as attempts to force reference by coercing ambiguous bodies into providing audible, visible signs of gender for those about to dispense summary injustice.

Although anyone can become unsexed/unraced/unclassed—undone—at any given moment, the process is not random.[60] However equal people may or may not have been created, they are seldom counted and treated as such. But the ability to discern this in the carnage requires a concept that is disembodied, without visual reference, and for that very reason, all the more intimately bearing on the concrete.

As a person becomes undone, s/he becomes a cipher. "Cipher" is, after all, just another word for zero, for the Arabic *sifr*, newly minted after its passage through Spain and France.[61] In the glaring light of the customs booth, s/he fills a place before s/he puzzles—but not a place susceptible to representation on any immigration form. However short-lived, the value endowed on the place that the cipher holds open is the potential for gendered signification. With it comes the potential for reflection.

Although I focus here on gender, by way of rethinking gender theory, the cipher represents a more general undoing of identities in which gender may have melded with class, race, age, religion, or any of the classifiers used for social sorting. Unsexing is a process too instantaneous, too ephemeral, and too complex to call only gender in and out of play. What at first appears to be a passing absence of signification turns out to involve a plethora of signs, none of them referenced, none of them fixed. Whatever onlookers perceive, it is not what they expected. A cipher emerges in the rare instance when perceptions lead expectations. In the instant that is *sifr*, the radical arbitrariness of the sign becomes visceral: arbitrary, visceral, but never free-floating. There is no necessary connection between nail polish and femininity, no necessary link between ambiguity and peril. Why the cipher that exposes these disjunctures should resolve into threat can be explained only by calling upon wider sets of social relations: national loyalties, racialized betrayal, global economy, the privatization of public space that is the restroom.

Embedded within any momentary absence of *expected* signification is an enticement to resolution. Unsexed gives way in judgment to the cultural categories of Professional Woman, Real Man, Cancer Patient, Church Lady, Butch, Cowboy, Freak. The very ordering and sorting operations that zero permits imply that this should be so. Unsexed is neither an idealized nor a dystopian state, nor yet a tourist destination: A zero remains meaningful only as it gives way, on occasion, to numbers. The place unsexed holds open is a place held open *for*. But when gender *theory* is too quick to lay the cipher to rest, it is another matter. Analysts with an appetite for certainties begin to approach the cipher as a code to be cracked rather than an enigma. Inevitably, they miss something in the rush to decipher. Their search for hidden fixities—the key to the code—nudges discussion back toward reified gender constructs (norms, genders, roles). "What are you?" becomes a question with a palpable answer.

Left to signify after their own fashion, the enigmatics of zero moments can clarify what keeps the narrative of stable, fixed genders in place. When the expected fails to appear, the cipher that marks its absence serves as "a signified non-presence of certain signs."[62] Man surely defines itself relative to Woman, Femme relative to Butch, Third Gender from its position alongside a Second and a First, Night in terms of Dawn and Dusk and Day. But genders also acquire their meaning from the cryptic flashes in which identities unravel. The zero puts gender back into history, into movement, into time, in a way that carries analysis past any impulse to genuflect before the altar of a strictly visual presentation.

Let $x$ stand for the number of locally recognized genders. Popular models ask a simple $x$-gender system—or continuum—to represent what are, after all, intricately classed/raced/sexualized/gendered relations. All the more reason that those who would understand gender cannot limit themselves to the task of deciphering local meanings. What would it mean to decipher the gendered social "distance" between me, my middle-class Japanese-American friend, the homegirls from Pico Rivera, and a white Boston born-to-money society matron, while reifying the gendered "divide" between said matron and her golf-club-toting husband? What would you miss by arraying us on somebody's, anybody's, dual-gender axis? About our differences and identities and relative privilege, enumeration—six Women, one Man—tells you next to nothing.

## VACATING THE VOID

Next to . . . nothing? Historically there has been no little tension between interpretations that treat zero as a meta-sign or mark of absence, and interpretations that treat zero as a sign of some more substantively conceived "thing": emptiness, nothingness, the void, the abyss. For Rotman, "the mathematical sign zero points to the absence of certain other mathematical signs, and not to the non-presence of any real 'things' that are supposedly independent of or prior to signs which represent them."[63] Likewise, in ancient Babylon, writes Ifrah, "the zero sign did not signify 'the number zero'":

> Although it [zero] was used with the meaning of "empty," (that is, "an empty place in a written number"), it does not seem to have been given the meaning of "nothing," as in "10 minus 10," for example; those two concepts were still regarded as distinct. In a mathematical text from Susa, the scribe, obviously not knowing how to express the result of subtracting 20 from 20, concluded in this way: "20 minus 20 . . . you see."[64]

Kushyar bin Labban's *Principles of Hindu Reckoning*, in its time a standard text on arithmetic in the Arabic-speaking world, introduces zero as "the symbol to be placed in a position 'where there is no number'": a very different matter from representing something as spatial in its vacuity as a void.[65] Even the dot used in some regions to symbolize the zero resulted from a process of "making the [open] circular sign smaller and smaller, until finally the space inside it disappeared."[66] Vacating the void, indeed!

Yet it is equally well possible to dethrone a meta-sign such as zero by treating it as just another sign among signs. By way of contrast, ancient Indian astronomy used symbolic number words from Sanskrit to indicate whole numbers, of which *sunya* is only one. Bhaskara I, writing about 629 CE, used symbolic number words to express 4,320,000 as "viyadambaraakaasasasasunyayamaraamaveda."[67] Roughly and a bit woodenly translated, the term becomes:

sky/atmosphere/space/void/primordial couple/Rama/Veda
0 /　　0 　/ 0 / 0 /　　　2　　　/ 3 / 4

The values of each number word are listed below that word as Hindu-Arabic numerals. In this example, "sky," "atmosphere," "space," and "void" all come out "zero."[68] It is not hard to discern the outlines of the visual, the "thing" that is nothing, in contours of space and sky. This is not vacating; this approaches reification. The Abyss.

A distinction between absence and nothingness, like the oscillation of *sifr* between vacating and vacancy, emptying and empty, is of the utmost significance for gender theory under late capitalism. In the earliest Buddhist interpretations, *sunya* signifies neither-existence-nor-nonexistence: a kind of latency that can only be understood with reference to what is, potentially, to come. In the meaning shift from this *relation* of absence/potential presence, on the one hand, to the *thing* that is a void, on the other, something is lost: A singular vantage point on processes of commodification. For what is commodification, if not a mystification that renders social relations in the form of a thing?

This tension explains why ambiguity alone cannot subvert the order of things. Retailers eagerly recast ambiguity as androgyny: a fixed look, an attribute, a condition, even an identity.[69] Just as zero can transform into nothingness—a fixed state rather than an absence—so ambiguity becomes susceptible to commodification, especially in the guise of mixture. When market relations recuperate the zero concept of "unsexed" as androgyny (or what have you), a process of reification and naturalization begins, very similar to the one described by Rotman in which "meta-signs are denied their status as signs of signs and appear as mere signs: Zero becomes just another number among the infinity of numbers."[70]

Which is to say that the "meta" qualities of zero—like the transient "zeroing out" of gender—do not protect it from what used to be called co-optation. The flash of expectation denied that is "unsexed" can just as easily give way to Androgynous, Transgendered, or Neuter, as to Woman, Man, or Butch. In the process, not only is gender reified, so are you as the tabulating subject. In the act of counting off the possibilities for interpretation, you end up "traversing what will become a sequence of counted positions," becoming an enumerator of things rather than an analyst of gendered relations.[71]

One might think that androgyny, with its air of indeterminacy, would depart somewhat from these adventures in tabulation. Yes and no. No, to the extent that people understand androgyny as a mixture of preconceived gender attributes. Yes, in the sense that the gendered indeterminacies of androgyny borrow a lesson from algebra. In the hands of al-Khwarizmi, algebra "transformed the concept of a number from its earlier arithmetic character as a fixed quantity into that of a variable element in an equation."[72] But numbers those variables remained. Algebraic variables such as

$x$ and $y$, which stand for unknowns, still manage to bring semiotic closure by assigning some definite value to whatever position they occupy. Thus the medieval Italian term for algebra—*regola della cosa*, or rule of the thing.[73] Unlike "unsexed," androgyny shifts the cipher away from its meaning as a meta-sign for absence, a riot of signification, and toward the cipher as a given, a sign, a puzzle waiting to be solved.

As a zero concept, "unsexed" remains qualitatively different from $x$ or $y$, from Woman (one) or Man (two), and as such less easily accommodated to activities such as finger-counting and gender tallying, not to mention merchandising. A zero concept offers better possibilities for putting ever-changing social relations into perspective. (Perspective itself constituting an artistic innovation that depended upon the invention of a vanishing point, which in turn coincided with the introduction of zero.)[74]

Interpreted as a meta-sign, the zero that is "unsexed" encourages theorists to examine the temporal aspects of gender relations, especially the respects in which time informs the dynamics of space and vision that have classically served to focus gender studies. Interpreted as a meta-sign, zero offers a new set of analytic tools to reflect upon power, ranking, racing, and classing in theoretical models of gender. To explore how ambiguity comes to double as a vector of threat and an agent for change. To spot attempts to pass off fixity (The Third Gender, The Transgendered, The Butch) as the subversion of classification. To analyze the processes that insistently transform what are, after all, exceedingly complex social negotiations back into rock-solid, oven-baked identities.

By calling attention to the blink of an eye in which a person gets called out of gender, "unsexed" also directs attention to the specific sites where people labor to produce certainties from more everyday fare. By calling forth its own critique of mathematical muddles in the gender models, "unsexed" helps explain what, besides malice or ignorance or a blind spot the size of a barn door, disposes otherwise well-meaning theorists to continue declassing and whiting out their subjects with every "new" theoretical turn.[75]

A global economy binds remuneration ever closer to enumeration. It is in this sense that a zero concept invites a closer examination of the marketing of race, gender, sexuality, care, memory, love, nationality, greed, desire . . . a veritable service economy that trades in what some used to call the soul.[76] And what would that examination entail? Tracing out links between, say, the historical moment when I can sit at my computer and generate a paper on something called "unsexed," and the historical moment when electronic money has begun to replace the imaginary money embodied in bills or coins. Paper notes (xenomoney) appeared only with the invention of double-entry bookkeeping, itself an artifact of the introduction of the zero into mercantile trade.[77] The instruments of exchange that have resulted from the contemporary shift toward electronic money lend themselves a bit less to counting and a bit more to accountability. Zero is to the introduction of imaginary money as unsexed is to . . . data flows? Plastic? After all, in many sectors of the sex industry, a middle-class "you" already has the ability to "put her on your card."

The zero changed mathematics and economies forever. Europe's resistance to looking into the abyss that this sign seemed to represent was part and parcel of the social struggles that ushered in a mercantile economy. Although that economy predated by centuries what we now call global capitalism, it was no less global in its aspirations. After all, the zero was carried into Europe in the packs of "Arab" and "Italian" merchants, who had already adapted the Hindu/Buddhist concept of *sunya* to the exigencies of trade. The history of mathematics is a history of the movements of people as well as ships, ledgers, concepts, and texts.

Like mathematics, gender theory requires a meta-sign to denote the presence, temporal sequence, and position of absence. That it should derive such a sign through histories of commerce only sweetens the irony. Such is the impure world of late capitalism, where gender (together with those who would take its tally) has become increasingly commodified. The Man in the Stetson sells cigarettes; the Woman Welder, exuding androgyny, sells trucks.[78] A few clicks at an on-line brokerage seal your investment in technologies that herald prenatal sex selection. It is precisely at this historical juncture that ambiguity transmutes into an incitement and a provocation: to buy, to kill, to conquer. Gender as a classed/raced reading; death, only one of its corporeal effects.

Anyone interested in holding open a place for the resignification of gender, including the ability to take note of gender's absence (which is to say, its constructedness), or gender's profitability, needs to pay attention to those transitory moments when gender "zeros out." They are moments steeped in conflict and the violence of representation. They are moments that exact a toll in blood, sleeplessness, and shame. As with genders, so with numbers: The zero's passage into common currency bears a lesson for later, and equally diasporic, times.

© Judi Weston, reprinted by permission

# CHAPTER THREE

# DO CLOTHES MAKE THE WOMAN?: PERFORMING IN AND OUT OF INDUSTRIAL TIME

We are never as steeped in history as when we pretend not to be.
—*Michel-Rolph Trouillot*

Imagine an encounter that calls you temporarily out of classification. It might be a moment of danger set in motion by the border guard who detains you because he cannot quite "place" you, in a country (the United States) where noncitizens can be detained indefinitely. It might be a moment of promise inaugurated by the gently inquiring glance that meets your eyes from across a crowded room. Both the glance and the detention involve interrogations that will force sense from bodies, however willing or recalcitrant. In both instances, ephemeral instants of uncertainty, when gender ( . . . /nation/race/class/sexuality/ . . . ) zeroes out, quickly give way to provisional identifications. Such moments partake of all that is fleeting, but they are never random.

Bodies that appear ambiguous, the sites and occasions on which meanings begin to fray, the "obvious" response to uncertainty (violence? fascination? malaise?), the materials used in the scramble to arrive at a comfortably gendered interpretation, the scrambling itself: All turn out to be historically and culturally informed. Not everyone is pulled over. Not everyone is singled out. Not always is gender construed as a matter of such importance that a vaguely gendered body evokes frantic attempts at signification.

In the late-twentieth century a new theory arose that attempted to explain the counterpart of the zero moment in which gender temporarily comes undone: the process of gender's meaningful creation. Writers on performativity (also known as performance theory) concluded that when it comes to gender, there is no "there" there, no natural underlying essence of masculinity or femininity waiting to be expressed or repressed. Relying heavily on the work of Judith Butler, they offered a fairly novel explanation for how people nevertheless can come to perceive gender as a collection of recognizable attributes or traits, individually possessed. Like wildfire, the concept of performativity jumped disciplines, transforming the landscape in fields as diverse as literary criticism, sociology, and legal studies.

To all appearances, performance theory *looks* like it might rely upon a zero concept, in the sense developed in the previous chapter. After all, it begins from the premise that nothing like gender really exists, at least until performance makes it so, and "nothing" sounds a lot like zero. The performatively gendered world rests on the back of a turtle, which rests on the back of another turtle, which rests on another . . . well, suffice it to say that with performativity, it's turtles all the way down. Performance gives the impression, through repetition, that masculinities and femininities are there to be perceived and that they are foundational. Performing gender over and over creates the illusion that gender is somehow basic to the person I know myself to be.

Repetition is all about time. To repeat means, by definition, to do the "same" things again, in sequence, one after the other. *Yet the movement and sequencing of time embedded in performativity's account of gender bears very little resemblance to the lightning-quick shifts characteristic of the zero moment in which a person becomes unsexed.* An endlessly repeated performance of gender is not a coming undone, much less an instantaneous event, although it has much to teach about the processes that call or drag a body back through meaning. Repetition encodes a very different temporality than a transitory unraveling and enjoys a very different relationship with the political economy of the day.

Like other popular schools of gender theory, performativity tarries with the visual without exploring the temporal implications of vision and space.[1] Each performance of gender requires an observant gaze in order to present its culturally gendered cues—eyeliner, thick-soled boots, hands on hips—for visual inspection. Even in the process of disputing Enlightenment precepts, performance theory still requires that its subjects be en-light-ened, illuminated by the eye if not always by reason.

With both proponents and critics of performativity otherwise optically engaged, the temporal dimensions of performativity have elicited almost no comment. Analysts of performativity acknowledge that historical change and economic circumstances shape gender performances, but these aspects of time remain peripheral to the workings of the theory. The temporal cycles implicit in the concept of repetition go unremarked. The irony of building a theory of gender's production atop repetition, that hallmark of assembly-line mass production, at a moment when assembly lines are rapidly disappearing from the United States, has managed to escape notice altogether.[2]

Before traveling through the hidden temporalities of the late twentieth century's most celebrated approach to the understanding of gender, it's worth taking a closer look at performance theory's account of the social makeover through which people learn to regard one another as belonging to discrete genders. Our journey begins with a reprise of some of the controversies that shook the foundations of gender theory during the 1980s, controversies to which performance theory implicitly responds. Next stop will be a Prom Nite dance, where gendered performances demand more historical, political, and economic accountability than a theory of performativity can provide. Then it's back to the future to discuss the limitations of analyzing gender with a toolkit geared more to the rhythms of factory work than a global economy that segregates manufacturing from the production of "service" and "information." The latest movements of global capital raise questions about commodification, inequality, and time that ought to trouble previous theories of gender trouble.

## DANCE AND STANCE

From the time the women's movement first began to carve out a place for itself within the academy, "gender relations" served, oddly enough, as a code phrase for male-female relations.[3] On the face of it, this was a curious development. After all, social constructionists had long argued that gender is at least partially the product of culture. Societies may symbolically incorporate genitalia and other elements of anatomy into gender constructs, but bodies and biology in no way determine those interpretive leaps. Research across borders and boundaries lent validity to this claim by demonstrating the sheer variability, from time to time and place to place, of phenomena that Euro-American observers had studied under the rubrics of gender and sexuality.[4]

What happens, then, when an analysis pushes social construction to its limits by factoring anatomy—"sex differences," in the Euro-American sense—out of the equation? Same-sex relations can also be gendered, and gendered differently according to circumstance. Gendered differences might as well characterize the way that women on a soccer team describe one another or the way that two men in a couple divide household chores as relations between men and women per se.

Initially this shift in focus from looking at gender*s* (man and woman) to the gender*ing* of all social relations would seem to threaten the very project of gender studies. What would gender mean once displaced from the contrast drawn between female and male? Yet the epistemological foundation for gender studies has proved none too secure in recent years, regardless.

In the 1980s, women of color active in movements for social change began to protest the exclusionary effects of overarching generalizations about women's specialized capacity to nurture, feel, and intuit. The "nurturing" demanded of African-American women forced to breast-feed white infants under slavery (or play "Mammy" roles in movies today) cannot be compared to the "nurturing" celebrated by the free white women who elevated motherhood to the realm of the sacred. Accordingly, these critics insisted that feminism and gender theory account for the ways race, class, nation, and sexuality have differentiated women's experiences by privileging certain women in certain respects while simultaneously oppressing others.[5] The politics of difference that emerged in response to their critique distinguishes *Woman*—the unitary and illusory subject, represented as possessing a set of qualities largely derived from white middle-class experience—from *women*, the concrete historical beings who find themselves caught up in gendered relations but manage to go about their everyday affairs, with or without the benefit of gender theory.

But if Woman were dead, would gender studies be forced to abandon theory to resume the projects of its younger days, collecting data about innumerable individual women's (and men's) lives? Could any aspect of women's experience be characterized collectively? What prospects for organizing are offered by a radical relativism that finds women's experiences less and less comparable across lines of race, class, nation, religion, or sexuality? Gendered differences among women, like these more established distinctions, position women within fields of social relations that are also, of course, power relations.

It was precisely this challenge of how to comprehend the differences that divide women, without denying the complexity of those differences or lapsing into essentialism, that led Teresa de Lauretis to call for a reexamination of marginalized sexualities positioned "outside the heterosexual social contract."[6] Historically the sites where gender intersects with sexual identities have produced and disseminated a wealth of cultural categories that combine gendered meanings with nuances of class and race, generation and place. Not only femme and butch, but also androgynous and ki-ki, swish and queen, lipstick lesbians, kids, and bulldaggers represent classifications that have emerged from close to a century of queer community building in North America.

When I first began to study the gendering of relationships among lesbians in the San Francisco Bay Area in 1985, I focused on "femme" and "butch" as categories with the potential to cut across a series of debates on gender identity.[7] I wanted to know how these terms figured in the lives of lesbians who condemned them or used them only in jest as well as those who called themselves butch or femme. I also assumed the possibility that such categories represent a creative transformation, rather than a straightforward reproduction, of the old opposition between male and female.

My approach broke decisively with the earliest lesbian-feminist treatments of butch/femme, which portrayed "roles" as a regrettable imitation of oppressive power relations derived from heterosexuality. For writers such as Sheila Jeffreys (1987), femme and butch lesbians had, at best, capitulated to pressures to conform to a stereotype of what a lesbian couple should be. At worst, butches and femmes were misguided carryovers from the "old gay" days when lesbians allegedly had become "male-identified" because they lacked models for nonhierarchical relationships. In other words, according to these writers, lesbians didn't know any better until feminism arrived to offer an alternative. Looking back, the condescension that frames this critique seems palpable. At the time, few lesbian-feminists were interested in what femme and butch meant to the women who claimed the terms.

Then came the 1980s, with the sex debates about sadomasochism and "role-playing," accompanied by a revival of butch/femme in large urban areas on the East and West Coasts. A new set of theories emerged that promised to expand the meaning of gender by rehabilitating butch/femme in the context of postmodernist feminisms. Older depictions of "roles" as an outgrowth of false consciousness yielded to novel perspectives that associated butch/femme with an intensified awareness of gender.[8]

Perhaps the most famous, and certainly the most widely utilized, of these revisionist perspectives on butch/femme emerged from the theory of gender performativity. Many accounts of gender as performance portray butch/femme as the ultimate in self-reflection, a resistance waged by lesbian "actors" who are specially, if not uniquely, positioned to see through the illusion of gender as a coherent, core identity. In this new thinking, butch/femme represents a subversive practice not so much because of its innovative content but because it exposes gender as a social construct: something historically, collectively, and rather arbitrarily made rather than naturally and definitively given.

In the rush to "prove" first that lesbians really want to be men, then that lesbians are just as feminine as heterosexual women, and more recently that the practice of butch/femme offers a revolutionary subject position capable of subverting oppressive gender relations, analysts have paid little attention to how queer women themselves have interpreted gender in their relationships. How do attempts to theorize gender in literary studies, theater/film criticism, and philosophy stack up against an ethnographic analysis that examines what lesbians of different back-

grounds and political persuasions have been doing and saying while scholars debate gender's fate?

The 1985 Prom Nite dance at the Women's Building of the Bay Area
was one of several events I attended in the course of my research that
highlighted the possibility—perhaps the inevitability—of gendering
same-sex relationships. While Rachel Becker was getting ready to go to
the dance, styling and restyling her collar-length hair in the mirror,
another woman in our group came into the bathroom to offer her opinion
on the overall effect.[9] "It looks good," she said, "only you've got it parted
on the girls' side." "Is there anything that gender doesn't permeate in this
society?" I wondered, still grappling with its complexities after a year of
the close attention to detail and compulsive note-taking that characterize
anthropological fieldwork.

On several previous occasions Rachel had insisted that she seldom
thought of herself in terms of what she called "roles." When other lesbians
categorized her, she believed they tended to see her as femme; that had
certainly been the case with her last girlfriend. Like many lesbians who
claimed that the categories butch and femme had little to do with their
self-perception, however, Rachel was prepared to accept the classification
others attributed to her, "if I have to choose." For the dance she had
decided to add her new leather vest to a tailored shirt, dress pants, and a
pair of shoes that everyone agreed sent out "mixed messages." On our way
over to San Francisco's Mission District, she tried to enlist the group's
support for her (re)gendering project, saying with a laugh, "You guys
remind me to act butch, okay?"

The auditorium, one of the few rooms in the Women's Building large
enough to hold a gathering of hundreds, resembled a high school gym
enough to provide the perfect setting for the evening's event. Volunteers
from the local clean-and-sober organization sponsoring the dance had
spent hours decorating the space to invoke lesbian identity and carry
through the prom night motif. On one wall a slide show created a montage of images of women from different cultures. Here and there posters
proclaimed "Sappho Lives" or "Dyke of Earl" in a graffiti scrawl. In a corner I spotted Brook Luzio celebrating her birthday at the head of a long
table filled with friends. Paulette Ducharme was there; so was Marta
Rosales. After searching in vain for Carolyn Fisher, I asked Charlyne
Harris to dance, then settled back to survey the scene.

When our group had originally walked in the door, the first people we
encountered were a woman in a black sheath dress escorted by another in
a white pleated shirt and bow tie. Behind me someone exclaimed with
delight, "Oh, good, I'm glad people dressed!" It took us several minutes to
work our way into the auditorium, where pink, yellow, and black helium-

filled balloons drifted slowly across the ceiling, trailing ribbons that threaded their way through a room packed with dancers. On one side of the floor a woman in a pinstriped shirt and red tie leaned against the stage, hair slicked back, with just a few strands falling—carelessly? artfully?—over her forehead. In her arms was a woman in a sleeveless gold top that glittered under the lights, her outfit accented with lipstick, fishnets, and costume jewelry. Someone had on a full set of leathers; another wore handcuffs hooked through a belt loop. More than a few were clad in the natural fibers usually attributed to the lesbians known as "East Bay dykes" or "crunchy granola types" (depending on one's perspective).

On some women earrings dangling neatly, symmetrically, while women without jewelry turned their heads to reveal a row of earrings arrayed on one side. There were those who had created their own version of "gender fuck" drag by juxtaposing symbols of femme and butch: long earrings with a flashy tie or nylons with combat boots. As women in jeans and button-down shirts kissed one another in the hallways, women in short skirts paired off for a song or two. Lesbians in ball gowns, all tulle and satin, joined partners in tuxes with red cummerbunds or suspenders and bow ties. Some of the women could have danced their way unobtrusively through any school prom in the state—unobtrusively, that is, unless they had walked in together, hand in hand.

An hour or so later, Rachel found me in the crowd and confided, "It's amazing what dressing butch will do for you. I already asked three women to dance! And I'm saying the most incredible things." What sorts of things? "Well, you know . . . flirting. And here I was worried I'd be a wall-flower!" "Wallflower—now there's a term I haven't heard since junior high," I thought to myself. If I remembered correctly, it was a term reserved for the girls, not the boys. Objects of pity or desire, the girls who sat out the dances came under the boys' scrutiny at the very moment they seemed most marginalized.

After a few dances, I wasn't the only one eyeing the carrot cake that stood, still uncut, amid the remnants of Brook's birthday potluck. By ten-thirty the place was jammed and sweat began to mingle with the scents of perfume. More and more people were eager to move their bodies to the beat, with less and less room left to work out that energy on the dance floor. Following through on the prom night theme, the DJ began to mix in hits from the 1950s and early 1960s. Little Richard screamed "Lucille" until Ritchie Valens cut in with "La Bamba." During the slow dances, the floor hardly cleared. Cornrows and perms rested on shoulders beneath flattops and dreds, wedges and buzz cuts. When "I Love How You Love Me" came over the speakers, I shouted, "It's the Paris Sisters!" to a new acquaintance sitting across the table. "The who?" she yelled back. Judging from appearances, half the women in the room had not been born when that single was released in 1961. Given the noise that both enveloped and elevated the crowd, appearances were about all anyone had to go on.

## GENDER IS AS GENDER DOES?

Although I had grown up in the United States, I had assiduously avoided my own high school prom, believing it to be someone else's event: neither for me nor about me. Had I, as a teenager, been more preoccupied with boys and less preoccupied with class mobility and coming out, perhaps Prom Nite would have stirred memories. As it was, I awoke the morning after the dance contemplating questions about parody, play, nostalgia, time, exclusion, and the melding of gender with desire.

In the search for a theoretical framework that could illuminate what had transpired at the Prom Nite dance, I turned first to the theories of gender performativity that were beginning to achieve currency in the early 1990s. Performance theory has been elaborated most notably by Judith Butler in a very sophisticated critique of psychoanalytic approaches to gender theory, and explored in a specifically lesbian context by Sue-Ellen Case. Both Butler and Case argue that practices such as butch/femme and drag have the potential to frame a cultural politics that can step in where a politics grounded in identity has failed, since both practices undermine the illusion of a coherently gendered self. Although many insights developed by performance theory are useful for ethnographic analysis, ultimately this analytic framework falls short, because it cannot account for the ways that the changing historical and material conditions under which people live and love help constitute gender. A cyclical notion of time embedded in the theory has combined with an unacknowledged debt to commodity culture to shield these limitations from scrutiny.

Performance theories of gender, which weave together strands of postmodernist, speech act, and feminist theory, grew out of a stalemate in the debate between social constructivist accounts of gender and essentialist accounts that explain gender differentiation as a direct outgrowth of biology or culture. Because determinism of any sort attempts to isolate a foundation for a fixed identity that is subsequently expressed, essentialist accounts afforded little insight into the *production* of gendered subjectivity, much less its anomalies, contradictions, and discontinuities.[10]

According to Butler, gender is not a core identity or essence that precedes expression, but rather a social product created through the *practice* of relating to other people. As people perform gender, they orchestrate the play of gendered symbols upon and through the body's surface to create an illusion of a fixed interior reality. This play of signifiers not only performs gender, in the sense of staging its nuances, the practice also performs the act of calling gender into being, in the way that certain classes of speech acts can be considered performative. The statement, "I promise," conveys the sense of future obligation even as it creates such an obligation through the very act of making the statement.[11] Likewise with gender performances, which convey gendered meanings even as they gender the contours of social life.

One way to characterize Prom Nite would be as an event that takes the volume and "pumps it up," an image that condenses several aspects of postmodernist accounts of gender. In the first sense of "volume," the music, dance, and encompassing sound of urban nightlife created a social arena for the people in attendance to create gendered presentations through movement, dress, and interaction. The "loudness" of their displays drew attention to this process of cultural construction through parody, humor, and an overall accentuation of gendered signification. As the volume of performances picked up, the possibilities multiplied for gendering relations in ways that some would argue offer an alternative to the restrictions of a two-gender system.

At an event such as Prom Nite, performance theory would say that people play with—as they play on—cultural representations of gender by juxtaposing certain styles of hair, makeup, stance, scent, clothing, and even the long-term reconfiguration of musculature through bodybuilding or sport. Rachel Becker's sense that the gendering of her body was largely a matter of presentation allowed her to believe in the possibility of moving between femme and butch personae. With respect to other people's perceptions, Sarah Voss agreed: "Gender is so ritualized that the most phony gestures in either direction are enough to make you present [as a woman or a man]. I get called 'sir' all the time, and I do not have a 'sir' shape."[12]

Performance theory grants no ontological status to the psychic space that many people in the United States image as the locus of a "true" or core self. The spectacle created by the constant play of gendered signification across the body's surface implies an inner substance, but the fixed gender of that "real me" simply does not exist. In Butler's analysis, "gender is precisely the fantasy enacted by and through the corporeal styles that constitute bodily significations."[13] The hands in the pockets and the bouffant hairdo point to the possession of a substantive identity as surely as they mask its absence. For performance theorists, it's all in the act—not the essence.

According to Butler, practices such as butch/femme are radicalizing precisely because they expose and break apart the fiction of a neat, natural correspondence among anatomy, gender identity, and desire. In this respect, Butler's analysis can be grouped with postmodernisms of resistance. Unlike variants of postmodernism that depict people as passive consumers of "prefabricated images of power and desire," postmodernisms of resistance grant human beings the capacity to recast the circumstances in which they find themselves by engaging in a cultural politics that draws attention to the process of fabrication.[14]

Lesbians have every reason to be critical of the putative correspondence of gender to genitalia and eroticism. In Euro-American societies where gender inversion theories of homosexuality prevail, heterosexuals often confuse homosexuality with "cross-gender" identification. Popular stereotypes continue to associate lesbianism with masculinity and male homosexuality with effeminacy. On occasion after occasion, lesbians and gay men are subjected to searches for the gendered signs inscribed in bodies (the low-pitched voice, the limp wrist) that people in the United States use to infer gay identity. Because passing for straight requires the careful management of symbols that are more specifically linked to gender than to sexuality per se, coming out to oneself as a gay person generally entails coming *into* a heightened consciousness of gender.[15]

"The closet has given us the lie," wrote Sue-Ellen Case in 1989, "and the lie has given us camp."[16] Many accounts of gender as performance rely heavily upon an analogy between butch/femme and gay male drag, or more precisely, on an analysis that interprets butch/femme as an instance of drag or camp style. A year later, Butler drew upon Esther Newton's classic study of female impersonators to argue that "drag fully subverts the distinction between inner and outer psychic space." In her 1979 book *Mother Camp*, Esther Newton discussed the paradox of the man in drag, who overlays symbols of femininity upon a masculinity assumed to be more essential while simultaneously signaling masculinity with his anatomical "outside," even as the practice of impersonation imputes a feminine orientation to his "inner" self. "Both claims to truth contradict one another and so displace the entire enactment of gender significations from the discourse of truth and falsity."[17]

Well before writers on performativity took up the topic of butch/femme, Marilyn Frye, herself no friend of drag, arrived at a remarkably similar analysis that likened butch/femme to drag, and linked drag to the maintenance of a binary gender system:

> It is quite a spectacle, really, once one sees it, these humans so
> devoted to dressing up and acting out and "fixing" one another
> so everyone lives up to and lives out the theory that there are
> two sharply distinct sexes and never the twain shall overlap or
> be confused or conflated. . . . It is wonderful that homosexuals
> and lesbians are mocked and judged for "playing butch-femme

roles" and for dressing in "butch-femme drag," for nobody goes about in full public view as thoroughly decked out in butch and femme drag as respectable heterosexuals when they are dressed up to go out in the evening, or to go to church, or to go to the office. Heterosexual critics of queers' "role-playing" ought to look at themselves in the mirror on their way out for a night on the town to see who's in drag. The answer is, everybody is. Perhaps the main difference between heterosexuals and queers is that when queers go forth in drag, they know they are engaged in theater—they are playing and they know they are playing. Heterosexuals usually are taking it all perfectly seriously.[18]

While I was in the Bay Area, someone had written in large letters on a wall where Castro Street turns into Divisadero: "There are no women—there are only drag queens." If a feminist version of performance theory were to add anything to the writing on the wall, it would be that there are also no men—only stone butches and diesel dykes. By this logic no performer exists, no fixed subject, no authentic femininity or masculinity waiting to be learned or recovered. Each performance refers to other performances, rather than to some originating standard of femaleness and maleness. It is in this sense that Butler calls gender a "citational practice." The performance offers but an "imitation" of an "imitation," like a remake of a movie that never had its first release.

As an exposé of the gendering of social relations, performance theories of gender can be very seductive. Most of their tenets initially seemed applicable to the way I saw lesbians gendering their relationships. Prom Nite, for instance, combined many elements customarily mentioned in attempts to distinguish the postmodern era from its modernist predecessor: nostalgia; a fragmentation that isolates artifacts (earrings, boots, hair) and presses them into the service of parody or pastiche; an overriding emphasis on fashion and style; and the distanced approach to gender epitomized by Rachel's sense of playing a part.[19] Like performance theorists, ethnographers have recognized the image of an atomized, inner self as the product of a peculiarly Euro-American way of ordering experience. Performance theory's focus on the social significance of bodily movement and adornment is quite compatible with anthropological studies of how people use ritual, work style, and dance to produce culturally specific notions of gender and selfhood.[20]

More troubling is the question of whether butch/femme and drag work to denaturalize and subvert because they help viewers (including analysts) "see through" identity, or whether their political merits are supposed to reside in an altered consciousness that people acquire through "doing" gender. As Butler herself notes, drag's ambivalent implication in power relations, its willingness to borrow literally and figuratively from the trappings that cloak inequalities of all sorts, means that drag can just as easily shore up gendered hegemonies as make a case for sedition.[21] Only context can tell. In everyday life butch/femme may sometimes be associated with a playful, irreverent, anti-essentialist approach to gender, but this association has been confined to a limited number of "players" in relatively specialized historical circumstances.

## BEHIND THE SCENES WITH PERFORMATIVITY

Prom Nite cannot legitimately be isolated and reduced to a setting for a string of gendered performances; it must also be understood as an activity that took shape in a distinctive context. Organizers staged the dance as a one-time celebration invoking a theme that encouraged women to participate in a spirit of satire and costume. Clearly no one interpreted the advance advertisements as invitations to an actual school prom. As a result, many women attended who probably would not have systematically integrated the sorts of gendered representations they made visible at the dance into other arenas of their lives.

The gendering of language, clothing, and posture was much more marked at Prom Nite than at most other gatherings of lesbians I attended in the Bay Area. Several of the people I encountered that night mentioned that having people dress up made the experience fun, outrageous, "a kick": precisely the sorts of words gay men use when they're camping it up. None of the women I knew who went to the dance considered herself "seriously into" butch/femme (with the possible exception of Paulette Ducharme, who once described herself as "more butch and more femme than most").

This broader context for the representations of femme and butch observed at Prom Nite hints at significant changes that separate the butch/femme of the 1980s and 1990s from that of the 1920s through 1950s. For some lesbians, "eighties butch-femme—if it accurately can be termed as such—is a self-conscious aesthetic that plays with style and power, rather than an embrace of one's 'true' nature against the constraints of straight society."[22] Many felt free to style themselves femme or butch, perhaps for an evening, perhaps for the duration, without necessarily following through in bed, without claiming femme or butch as identities, and without adhering to any particular logic for dividing up the chores. Herein lies the novelty, relative to past decades.

To the extent that theories of gender performativity ignore these historical shifts, they do not differentiate phenomena specific to the butch/femme of the 1980s and 1990s from the gendered practices of earlier periods. Insightful though applications of the concept of performativity to the gendering of lesbian relationships might be, they can also be considered period pieces in the sense that they could only have been written in the wake of butch/femme's second wave. By the late twentieth century it had become possible for at least some lesbians to pursue butch/femme as a fashion statement without the expectation that other aspects of daily life would be gendered accordingly. Roberta Osabe, for instance, left a lover in the 1980s because the woman had an "old-fashioned" idea of how femmes were supposed to conduct themselves. As Roberta explained, "I only wanted to do it, really, through looks, and certain small little behavior things. . . . I didn't want to do all the dishes!"

The focus on style and presentation, as well as the resistance to using gender as a scaffolding for inequality, makes the second wave of butch/femme well-suited to an analysis of gender as performance. Yet this congenial fit between theory and practice emerges from relatively recent historical developments that have sundered any presumed congruence among the ways that a woman genders herself (butch, femme, what have you) in different domains (dress, behavior, sex).[23]

The current marginalization of women who call themselves femme or butch lesbians also contrasts sharply with prefeminist working-class lesbian communities in which women generally adopted one or another of these categories as a persona, if not always as an identity.[24] By the 1980s, the crucial question had become not "Which are you?" but "Are you into it?" To characterize butch/femme as a paradigm for resistance to essentialist models of gender collapses a multitude of meanings, contexts, uses, and practices into "the butch/femme couple." The Femme and The Butch cannot stand for the entire range of lesbians who have employed these categories any more than Woman can adequately represent the concrete women who have peopled the planet.

Even within the present period, it is dangerous to mistake a small, though eye-catching, segment of lesbian nightlife for the totality of the gendering of lesbian relations. Although bodies may be culturally malleable, it is important to remember that not all people experience them as such. A study of gay women conducted as early as the mid-1970s found that while some approached butch/femme with playfulness or irony, others considered femme and butch unalterable personal attributes.[25] In the Bay Area during the 1980s, notions of a coherently gendered self were alive and well. Complaints about facades and calls to "drop the act" are usually voiced because a person expects that something will be there to enjoy once the mask has been ripped away. For both the women who embraced butch or femme as identities and the ones who flirted with these categories in a more limited way, essentialism could exist in conjunction with the very practice that performance theory expected to undermine it.

While Sarah Voss believed that she could, to a degree, control others' perceptions of her gender and sexual identity, she could not conceive how a new suit of clothes or a shortened stride could ever touch her sense of herself as a butch. One day Sarah decided to trade clothes with a friend she placed "on the femme side of the scale":

> We were having one of those arguments about, "Well, if you walked a mile in my shoes." And here they are! Right, let's do it! Her immediate hit on my clothes is that they were uncomfortable, and mine was that hers were vulnerable. They made me sexually vulnerable in ways I didn't like, like these loose, flowing pants that could fall off at any time, and this loose, flowing blouse. . . . Clothing, especially on a motorcycle, has got to be armor in some sense. You know, skin is expensive. Also, it didn't work, but it may not have worked because all the people we hung out with all day were people who already knew us in our roles. So, of course, their immediate take on seeing us wearing each other's clothes was to lie down on the floor and throw up laughing so hard. I still don't think we could have passed, though. You can say it's body language; you could say it's attitude.

Compare Vicki Turner's comments on her former roommate, a self-described butch: "She's worn skirts and things like that. But I couldn't see her in these [gestures at her spandex pants] and carrying it off to be really this ultra–Jessica Rabbit kind of thing. Sorry, girlfriend! It's like me being the daddy butch. They'd look at me and go, 'Sorry, hon. You just don't have it.'" Drawing on notions of fit and coherence, some women claimed that wearing any outfit can feel like putting on drag if it is not "right for you." Like many of the lesbians I interviewed, Vicki used autobiographical anecdotes to establish the "naturalness" or "rightness" of gendered traits that she attributed to herself. "I was bred to primp," she explained, so identifying as a femme offered "an easier way to live."

For Vicki, style was the *least* important part of being a femme, although she enjoyed getting ready to go out in dresses and pumps: "I'm not one of those halfway middlers, that 'go in between' kind of thing. I really am feminine in poofy stuff. And I can dress up to the epitome of feminine. I mean, I can go *all* the way. Which some women can't, because they can't carry it off." Many butch- and femme-identified women described clothes, hairstyles, and other aspects of visual presentation becoming less important to them as they grew older and came to feel "secure" in their identities. These self-portraits were not incompatible with performance theory's emphasis on vision and aesthetics, since performative gestures that appealed to the eye sometimes preceded the consolidation of identity. Yet the same accounts also demonstrated how essentialist interpretations of identity can reassert themselves even for those whose practice fractures any naturalized correspondence between gender(ing) and action or desire.

Vicki, who worked as a stripper, drew upon the experience of playing a part on a literal stage to make a distinction between acting and "real life." Significantly, she considered her femme identity and her partnership with a butch-identified woman to be part of that reality, rather than just another act. By rejecting the language of "roles" as inadequate to describe the complexity of their everyday lives, other femme- and butch-identified women also distinguished between act and essence. "Roles" in this formulation came to represent something false and prepackaged; something readily adopted and just as easily cast off. Both these concepts were at odds with their conceptualization of butch and femme as authentic extensions of a core self.

Another way women reinstated the notion of a gendered identity waiting to be expressed was through imagery of the butch who "goes overboard" and the "ultra-femme." "When you've got a scale, you always have the people who are over here off the scale . . . like overly femme and kind of false, and the same for butch," explained Marilyn Daniels, who described herself as "two and a half" on a scale from one (femme) to ten (butch). According to Jeanne Riley, who disliked the whole notion of butch/femme, "I know [lesbians] who actually have long red fingernails and mince around in skirts and do all those right things. And I can sort of see it as a drag queen, effectively. For me to do that, that's what I would have to be." Interestingly, Jeanne's account was not very different from how Vicki said she felt after she had spent an hour "grooming" for a night out: "flamboyant, like more of a drag queen." Although Jeanne condemned the practice and Vicki reveled in it, both used the "ultra" category to distinguish between gendering as artifice and gendering as an extension of self. Not all femmes "foreground cultural femininity" in such a way as to expose its social construction, and of those who do, not all do so consistently.[26]

Of course, not everyone who participates in butch/femme finds herself invested in creating coherence. Like Rachel Becker, Louise Romero (who told me, "They all call me femme, so I go as femme") accepted the attribution contextually but did not construct "femme" as a personal identity. Other women seemed quite comfortable with incongruities, relocating themselves up and down an imaginary butch/femme scale as they moved from one relationship or one cultural domain to another. Teresa Ramirez associated butch/femme with style and superficiality—"it's more on the surface, more of a front"—but that did not prevent her from drawing a second-order contrast between butch/femme and what she called her "feminine and masculine sides."

> You change depending on your mood, on the situation. I don't know if you feel this way, but with certain people I feel very vulnerable, and the vulnerability brings out my feminine qualities and I want to be very giving and I want to take care of the person and I want to kiss them, I want to hug them, I want to feed them, I want to do all this stuff, right? And with . . . certain other people, I feel very in control. Like, hey, I'm cool, I got it, and I'm gonna take care of this person: sort of like this other attitude. I think it's partly chemistry that you have with people, that certain people bring out something, a part of your life that is beyond words. . . . So with certain people I'm much more feminine than with other people.

The variety in these women's conceptions of how their relationships were gendered should not come as a great surprise to anyone familiar with the many paths that lead to the adoption of an identity such as lesbian or gay. Although coming out does facilitate—perhaps even demand—a reflective approach to gender (as theorists of performativity contend), it can also incorporate an essentialist model of self-discovery in which an individual arrives at the final "truth" of her or his sexual identity.[27] That person may or may not incorporate such a model into a politics of resistance. Jonathan Dollimore, for one, has argued that any analysis of the politics of essentialism is incomplete without an understanding of history as well as "the ways essentialism has signified differently for subordinated as distinct from dominant groups."[28]

In *Bodies That Matter*, Judith Butler responded to critiques of *Gender Trouble* with an ambitious inquiry into the materiality inscribed in and ascribed to bodies as "power's most productive effect."[29] Following Michel Foucault, she attributed a history to nature and sex. Despite this nod to history and the emphasis on the material, the result is not a historical materialism. Butler's material is more corporeal than economic, her bodies glimpsed as they move through subjective but not identifiably historic time. Rather than helping to generate her controversial reading of the film *Paris Is Burning*, histories of economic dislocation and racial oppression remain in the background, sedimented, assumed, and acknowledged, but not integral to the analysis.

Performance theory elaborates an extended theatrical and contractual metaphor that works very well to illuminate the mechanics and demystify the organics of gender's production. (Contractual in the sense that the promise John Searle used to illustrate what the performative *does*—establish an agreement that looks to a future—is heir to the histories of merchant trade explored in the last chapter, including the innovation of the promissory note.) Yet metaphor cannot carry the weight of all that theory leaves unexamined. Despite an overt commitment to attend to the specificities of race, class, history, material conditions, and culture, performance theory's restricted focus on process leaves little room for the complexities and contradictions that appear as soon as an event like Prom Nite is firmly located in context. As a result, theories of gender performativity rest their political aspirations on a foundation as ethereal as the groundwork believed to prop up gender.

## A DIFFERENT KIND OF CLOSET

It is one thing to understand the limitations of performance theory; it is another to comprehend its appeal. Accounts of performativity tend to cast femmes and butches as "spin doctors" of gender, actors whose performances may be limited by contingency, but who nevertheless enjoy great interpretive leeway to manipulate their audiences.[30] Who wouldn't be attracted to the competence implicit in this image of the "new lesbian," whose savvy approach to gender allows her to orchestrate self-presentation so as to create others' perceptions in the image of her own phantasmatic?

The same decade that produced "dress for success" also generated "the butch/femme aesthetic." Not coincidentally, the illustrations used to explain performance theory have focused on visual display, often by featuring gesture, clothing, and bodily adornment to the exclusion of other phenomena associated with butch/femme, such as gendered divisions of labor and sexual acts. Makeup more readily becomes subject to individual manipulation (and thus more easily incorporated into theories of performativity) than work hierarchies or other aspects of daily life that must be socially negotiated and historically explained. The marketing and mass production of clothing and accessories yield artifacts that are not only gendered, but also infused with nuances of race, age, class, religion, and other markers of identity, depending on location.[31] If not every lesbian is prepared to become a biker, *chola*, soccer mom, prom queen, or video vamp, she can at least assume the trappings. Or so consumer capitalism seems to promise.

Of course I am not arguing, in reductionist fashion, that people perform gender primarily through clothing or fashion, as some readers of an earlier, abbreviated version of this essay concluded.[32] What I find striking is the recourse to visual imagery, especially descriptions of clothing and other accoutrements that are both observable and easily commodified, in so many accounts of gender and performativity. Why should this be so, when in theory and in practice people can conjure gender through the delicacy of scent, the timbre of voice, a lingering touch, each accomplished with eyes closed? To ask whether clothes make the woman is to pose a rhetorical question that opens onto a broader set of issues about the relationship of gendering to commodification, history, spatiotemporal modes of apprehension, and political economies of desire.

The particular version of butch/femme, circa 1990, that attracted the attention of performance theorists incorporates a culturally and historically specific (if problematic) notion of personhood that is rooted in bourgeois individualism. Like the worker under capitalism who is formally free to sell her labor (or free to die for lack of the wages to buy food and shelter), practitioners of this kind of butch/femme are apparently free to present gendered representations of self that they assemble, according to personal taste, from repertoires of commodities. With ties and tunics, heels and haircuts, they freeze and then fragment gender so that it appears not as the product of an oppressive power relation (Man over Woman), but as a cultural resource that can empower without oppressing—a resource utilizable by all, regardless of anatomical differences.

Historically debates on butch/femme have oscillated between the poles of the deluded and the self-created lesbian. Contradictory models of same-sex relations are quite capable of coexisting. Even if Case is correct in claiming that (some) lesbians practice butch/femme in a way that denaturalizes gender, which in turn prevents them from becoming "impaled on the poles of sexual difference," I suspect that they may yet find themselves caught between the rock of structure and the hard place of agency. Without further specification of why butch/femme should represent a potentially subversive activity for its practitioners and its audiences, as opposed to its theorists, its political implications remain indeterminate and subject to romanticization.[33]

Certainly there have been queer events framed to encourage the reflective, even satirical, stance that can turn gender performances into gender critiques. On April Fool's Day, for example, an organization in San Francisco sponsored a Butch/Femme Soirée, billing it as "A Night of Gender Confusion." Activities included "Wrench and Rose Awards" for the winners of competitions such as the "Recombinant Queer Contest," which sought "the best butch and femme rolled into one contestant; a genetic engineer's nightmare."[34] Camp humor is hardly the exclusive province of gay men (the lesbian who described a restaurant's decor as "tastefully overdone," and the one who introduced her rusting Datsun as "a Porsche in drag," come immediately to mind). In its most recent incarnations, butch/femme has incorporated, in certain settings, some of the artifice customarily attributed to camp. Yet drag and camp themselves do not occupy the utopian space of pure performance. Gay men that I interviewed in San Francisco such as Jorge Quintana, who were more familiar with drag than many lesbians, contended that one person's imaginary could become another's virtual reality:

> If one day you want to dress up in a beautiful gown, you have
> the right to do so. Like if I want to go out in a black tie, I have
> the right to do so. But that doesn't mean I'm going to believe the
> role I'm playing. . . . It's only for one night [that] I will become
> Cinderella. You don't wake up in the morning with the dia-
> monds all day long and think that you are queen of the world.
> Or that, if I wear a black tie one night . . . I'm going to come
> back here to my studio and think I'm rich. Well, there's no way!
> I look at my bankbook! But a lot of people believe in that fan-
> tasy. You see, they don't think of it as a fantasy.

For a good number of the women I met, gender and sexuality inhered in traits they understood to be possessed, rather than presentations enacted. They considered those perceived traits to be subject to verification not by bank account or social context, but through visual inspection of the body. Commenting on the gendering of a physique that she believed prevented her from passing for straight, Lourdes Alcantara explained, "You can't hide that [your lesbian identity]. It's on your face, in your walking, your eyes, through your gestures. It's all over you." While some women thought they could alter their gendered presentations at will, "like a chameleon," the majority did not. "If I was bald, I'd still look feminine," claimed Vicki Turner. Paula Nevins, a barber with a large lesbian clientele, described the limitations she perceived in being able to contribute to the gendering her clients desired:

> I've gotten some heavy-duty dykes—I mean real masculine,
> cock-of-the-walk type, bottom-line dykes—that will sit down in
> my chair, and have the clothes and the attitude to be just the
> butchest thing in town, and say that they want a haircut and
> they want it real short, but they don't want to look butch. Well,
> there's nothing you can do for a person like that. If you're butch,
> you're butch.

Actions and "body language," which many women found more difficult to control than clothing or hairstyle, could also interfere with the
desired effect. Craig Galloway, a gay man who had moved to the Bay Area
from the East Coast in the 1970s, told me about a classificatory schema
he had invented to account for some of these incongruities. I include his
categories here because they rely upon a distinction many lesbians also
embraced between act and appearance.

> I made this conceptual breakdown of gay men into four classes
> once when I was riding the bus. Looks butch, acts femme: that's
> where most of the people fall, into that category. Most gay men
> [in the 1980s] fall into the LBAF category. . . . And then there's
> a small category of people who look femme and act butch. I'm
> sure that you find this, too: people who are butch with friends,
> but get them home and close the door and they're the ones who
> act femme. And then of course there are the people who look
> butch and act butch, and the people who look femme and act
> femme.

A practice such as "gender fuck" drag, which combined signifiers of masculinity and femininity (for example, wearing a beard with a ball gown),
represented a deliberate attempt to disconcert viewers by denaturalizing
gender. In contrast, the humor of the LBAF category (as well as much jok-
ing about butch/femme) derives at least in part from inadvertent discrepancies that can disrupt gendered presentations.

Some of the reasons that people do not always experience themselves
as being in control of gender performances involve their immersion in
social and material relations. The same idealism that makes performance
theory so appealing, with its hope for personal/political empowerment,
cannot explain how or why the content and significance of gendered presentations shift over time. Neither can performativity's idealist inclina-
tions account for the circumstances leading up to a given presentation, the
reasons (and constraints) that lead a person to assemble one type of bodily montage rather than another, or what a given presentation means to the
women who engage in gendering.

At first glance, performance theory would seem to represent the
antithesis of an idealist approach: What could be more material than *corporeal* signification, bodies made socially salient through the use of artifacts that are visible to all who care to see? Yet there is no such thing as
the "free" play of signification. In a material world, bodies are not passively
inscribed by signs; they are inscribed by people who select and reconfigure
items of material culture from a restricted range of options, displaying

them according to imaginations that are shaped by historical developments. And as Franco Moretti has argued in a commentary on modernist literature, the use of irony and fragmentation may no longer operate to subvert the established order, due in part to "a complicity between modernist irony and indifference to history."[35]

When a lesbian opens the closet door to put together an outfit for the evening, the size of a paycheck limits the choices she finds available. In a material world, the individuals performing gender are never identically positioned with respect to relations of power. However carefully crafted a woman's presentation may be, once she brings it out into the street, her performance can be jarred into a different interpretive framework by the teenager who tears her face open with a rock and calls her "dyke." Likewise for the new acquaintance who enlists much more than observation to beckon her toward the erotic. In a material world, gender performances do not confine themselves to the visible, or the cognitive tasks of deconstruction.

Nor is our hypothetical lesbian's situation one of voluntarism constrained.[36] She may have (far from free) "choices" about how she performs gender, but the materials she uses and the imbrication of gender with other aspects of social relations (race, religion, class, advertising, social struggle) lie well outside individual deliberation or control. At the time of the Prom nite dance, dress and braids and buzz cuts were hardly the only things that had become commodified in North America. Politics and experience have their own histories of commodification as culture and as style. In "Sensible Shoes," to take just one example, Anne Brydon describes how the marketing of heavy-soled Doc Marten boots in the 1990s depended upon the commodification of rebellion, "making it [rebellion] a consumer object rather than a social movement, a safe means of transgression sanctioned by middle-class shops."[37]

When performativity does away with the gendered subject, it does not look to sociohistorical processes such as commodification. Instead, it inadvertently displaces and fetishizes gender by relocating gender in the hair, beads, muscles, trousers, mascara, set of the shoulders, fingernails, even the stories that people draw on to call gender into being through performance. What this tendency to perceive gender as a property of possessions—or as a product of the significance culturally attributed to possessions—obscures is gender's character as an aspect of social relations.

## GOOD TO THINK OR GOOD TO EAT?

Because social relations are structured through time, they entail more than is immediately apparent in the give-and-take of everyday interactions. I now want to look at an aspect of those relations that is crucial for understanding the emergence of a second wave of butch/femme: lesbian eroticism as it had been shaped and reshaped over previous decades. My initial description of Prom Nite depicts the occasion with an emphasis on the gendering, rather than the erotics, of lesbian relationships. For all that a reader can tell from this account, the women in the halls outside the auditorium may have been kissing for reasons that had nothing to do with presentation or attire. Reflecting back upon the events of that night, I remembered that Rachel Becker worried about ending up a wallflower for multiple reasons. Not only was she concerned that her butch presentation would lack credibility, she also wanted other women to find her attractive, to dance with her, and perhaps to accompany her home. For Rachel, how she looked remained inseparable from the responses she hoped to receive. As we walked into the Women's Building, what struck all the women in our group was the playful atmosphere, but also its "erotic charge."

Most of the lesbians I met in the Bay Area associated gendered performances—both their own and the ones they observed others create—with a sense of themselves as sexual beings. In a setting such as Prom Nite, attraction as well as gendering is the name of the game. Often enough that means moving beyond a primarily visual orientation to style and appearance, in order to engage the other senses of hearing, smell, touch, and (yes) taste. If gender appeared to some lesbians in commodified form as a cultural resource, it had become a resource from which many derived sexual pleasure. When I asked one woman how she would describe butch/femme, her answer situated her experience squarely at the intersection of gender, sexuality, and identity. "It's just who you are and how you like it," she replied.

The gendering of lesbian relationships has its own distinctive history, and that history is tied up with the development of lesbian communities.[38] When the second wave of butch/femme began to gather force in the early 1980s, some saw it as a passing fad, while others described it as a return to "cultural roots" derived from an earlier period. By 1990, with "gender fuck" fashion becoming more prevalent, and butch/butch and femme/femme couples appearing alongside more "traditional" butch/femme pairs, this second wave appeared to me (and to many lesbians in San Francisco) in a somewhat different light. Even women who had hardly participated in butch/femme started to credit "roles" with bringing sexuality back into lesbian relationships. To understand why requires some background about the dominant mode for the eroticization and gendering of lesbian relationships during the preceding decade.

One way to characterize the 1970s with respect to the gendering of relations among lesbians would be as an androgynous interlude between the first and second waves of butch/femme. During this period, the women's movement exerted considerable influence on the wider lesbian population. In the "women-loving-women" years of lesbian-feminism, many feminists (especially middle-class white feminists) tended to assume that gender was an identity, perhaps even an essence, held in common by all women. Lesbian lovers might be distinguished from one another by race, class, age, or ability, but their differences were not supposed to have anything to do with gender. Many feminists also regarded classically-feminine dress as impractical, uncomfortable attire that objectified women and rendered them vulnerable to sexual attack. When they went out at night, they began to minimize gendered differentiation in appearance. Skirts, heels, long hair, and makeup were the first to go. A woman who walked into a lesbian bar in a dress during this period was likely to have her lesbian identity questioned, and unlikely to have anyone ask her to dance.[39]

By the late 1970s, some women had begun to speak disparagingly of jeans and flannel shirts as the lesbian "uniform." Flannel and work boots became the symbolic targets of a growing grassroots resistance to pressures to conform to a set of perceived community standards, not only in dress, but also in sexual activities. Some rejected "vanilla" sex for its limited range of options and its romantic idealization of the simultaneous orgasm. Others derided lesbian-feminists for considering sex practices such as penetration "male-identified." If anything was male-identified, these critics contended, it was the ostensibly androgynous clothing and hairstyles that had been all but mandatory for over a decade.[40]

Of course, the new interest in butch/femme and sadomasochism associated with this critique was not solely the product of political and historical developments internal to lesbian communities. In the larger world, garment manufacturers had begun to mass-produce conspicuously gender-differentiated attire for marketing to North America. Dresses became de rigueur for women in the corporate workplace, while MTV promoted, glamorized, and sexualized explicitly gender-coded fashions and styles. Slowly but surely, the androgynous look became discredited as nothing more than a modified version of working-class male attire—a style of presentation that turned out to be gendered after all. In the eyes of many, this failed attempt to *neutralize* gender was equivalent to an attempt to *neuter* sexuality.[41]

It is as a successor to androgyny that the second wave of butch/femme became interpretively linked to a renewed eroticization of lesbian relationships. But eroticism, like gender, is mediated by "the practices of differently situated and positioned actors within contradictory social relations."[42] In addition to the symbolics of class, race, and age that inform gendered presentations (remember the biker, the soccer mom, and the prom queen), how would such differences enter into a revised account of Prom Nite? Just because differences become commodified and incorporated into the aesthetics of butch/femme does not put an end to the ways these differences, when institutionalized, can affect the gendering and eroticizing of relationships. What sorts of questions might break through Prom Nite's insular framework, following social relations not only back through history, but as they connect outward to relations of power in the wider society?

Aesthetics cannot begin to explain why the dance should have attracted a crowd of younger women fascinated with the 1950s; why working-class styles of clothing predominated, apart from the gowns and tuxes linked directly to the prom motif; or why Charlyne Harris insisted that she was preoccupied with more than gender and attraction when she thought about "roles," because every time she asked a white woman to dance, she could be choosing a partner who would type her as butch just because she was black. Performances are negotiated not only in the act, but also in the wake of historical legacies that shape interpretation.

Although the meaning of dress and dance, invitation and stance at the prom was never fixed, the range of possible interpretations emerged from historically conditioned relations of inequality as well as desire. Nothing can be seen without its temporal dimension. The precise meanings, in Heisenbergian fashion, may be impossible to pinpoint without the act of observation altering whatever it is you wish to grasp. Significance shifts like the position of an electron: Once you can see it, you know that it is gone. Yet from that observation you can also infer a near-past in which the electron has occupied some indeterminate space, along with a measurably uncertain relationship between yourself and the movements of whatever it is you wish to understand.[43] Timing is everything, and nothing when it comes to mastery.

Take the power relations embedded in my own presence as an ethnographer who found herself simultaneously "natived" and "othered," desiring and desired, observing and observed. How to depict my participation? In the Prom Nite narrative I appear as a split subject, albeit of a different sort than the one Sue-Ellen Case had in mind: marked as the narrating anthropologist and unremarked as "the native" in the pinstriped shirt, the two equally riveted by the vision of a woman in fishnets and gold lamé. Observing, narrating, or theorizing alone cannot trace out the unstable, nonlinear connections that link power to gender and gender to performance, which is to say, to violence, attraction, color, money, and days gone by.

Did the woman who stormed out in the middle of the dance leave for a reason that had anything to do with difference or identity? Outside the door, was the one busy revving up her motorcycle climbing aboard a Honda because she couldn't afford a Harley, or was the Honda part of an image she wanted to project? When two women got into their car across the street, was one of them driving because she owned the car, because it was the right thing to do as a butch, or because driving and cooking represented her chores for the week?

Without asking, who would have known that Lourdes Alcantara, only recently arrived from Latin America, was absorbed in unraveling the mysteries of attracting a partner in a country where "all that matters is what brand of pants you wear!" Who would suspect that Marta Rosales had developed a critique of butch/femme as facade, yet decided to come to Prom Nite anyway? Who would realize that the woman at the edge of the dance floor, who had lived through the first wave of butch/femme, was puzzling over the phenomenon of a couple in which both women wore tuxes? "If they stay on the floor during the slow songs," she asked me with a smile, "how will they decide who will lead?" And why was Paulette Ducharme wearing a skirt tailored in vinyl rather than leather? Was her "choice" dictated by income, or was she trying to take her presentation to another level of sleaze? In which case the historical consolidation of whiteness, the resignification of leather products from rural self-sufficiency to urban avant-garde, the global reorganization of the fashion industry, the styles her mama wore, and thirty years of bad-girl movies might have to be taken into account.

Butch/femme defies analysis in terms of simple polarities, gendered or otherwise. Like most practices in this society traversed by differences and shot through with hierarchical relations, particular renditions of femme and butch are suffused with aspects of class, race, age, and sexual desire. In a world where even gender is subject to commodification, "you might look like Radclyffe Hall (if you want to), but will you ever be able to keep yourself in the style to which she was accustomed?" In a world where members of the audience can leave a performance of *The Mikado* convinced that "you can become Japanese in drag," anyone might be able to adopt a prefabricated version of *chola* femme or bulldagger butch, but the act itself will implicate you in a legacy of race relations whose violence depends upon this ability to re-create and then appropriate the Other.[44] Butch/femme may sometimes supply the "moment of critical reflection" necessary to expose gender as a cultural creation, but its radical potential cannot be evaluated apart from specific historical and material contexts.[45] To destabilize is not always to subvert.

If gender can no longer be reduced to self-evident identities (Woman or Man), neither can it be conjured away as the compelling but ultimately illusory product of performance. Gender no more resides in gesture or apparel than it lies buried in bodies and psyches. Look beyond the historically specific logic of gender-as-commodity that lends plausibility to the theory of gender-as-performance, and gender theory finds another object. Just outside the circle of the spotlight are inequalities, historical developments, and differences that structure (without determining) the presentations that people variously interpret as masculine or feminine, androgynous or ambiguous, butch or femme. *Social relations* are gendered, not persons or things, and those relations can incorporate pain and oppression as easily as the pleasures of a Prom Nite.

## NOTHING, REPEAT, NOTHING

With its visual emphasis and temporal rhythms, however tacit those rhythms remain, performativity seems to take gender theory from zero to infinity all over again. Performatively gendered bodies are like onions whose layers peel back to reveal no core truths, no seeds of authenticity, no deeply buried masculinity, femininity, or for that matter, hermaphroditic sensibility.[46] "Onionness" does not lie buried beneath the surface any more than a true gender identity lies in wait to be discovered, or a natural correspondence between gender and desire waits to be put right. There is no "there" there; the layering, like the performance, is the thing. At the center of the onion, at the innermost reaches of the gendered body, lies nothing. And nothing sounds a lot like zero.

Yet this is not zero in the sense of "unsexed," the concept developed in the last chapter. Butler's interest, for example, focuses on how genders without a fixed or given referent can be called into existence through performative acts and naturalized along the way. From an understanding of this process, new insights into the possibilities for resisting injurious gender "norms" and subverting inequitable social arrangements should follow. Social change comes about, at least in part, through "resignification against the aims of violation."[47] This is a key contribution to gender theory, but not one that carefully considers temporality.

Although the call is for change, the exchange here is static: A new signification substitutes for the old, however preferable the new might be. Signification and resignification—even in excess of a referent—substitute for one another like numbers in an equation, but nothing like zero. They can be meaningfully arrayed in sequence, counted and commodified, all the while flying the temporal banner of change. Resignification continues to rely heavily upon visual displays in its efforts to destabilize gender. Left unexamined are the temporal qualities associated with repetition, the engine that makes performativity go. History enters primarily as background or context for changing "norms," rather than being constitutive of gender in its own right. "We may mention a historical context," Nicholas Thomas cautions, "but does that necessarily mean that it in any way animates the analysis?"[48] While it could be argued that, in matters of historical specificity, the devil is in the details, the articulated emphasis of performance theory lies elsewhere, and distinctively not elsewhen.

When performance theorists begin to attend to time, they have a tendency to revert to space. In *Bodies That Matter*, for instance, Butler explains how "the temporal structure of such a[n interpellated] subject is chiasmic in this sense: in the place of a substantial or self-determining 'subject,' this juncture of discursive demands is something like a 'crossroads,' to use Gloria Anzaldúa's phrase."[49] Notice in this dense passage how "temporal" modifies "structure," a resolutely spatialized term that displays amplitude but no periodicity, giving the phrase something of the character of a mixed metaphor. "Structure," in turn, allies itself not only with the geometric convergence of "juncture" and "crossroads," but also with chiasma: a crossing over used to describe the meeting of the two optic nerves. These visual metaphors are followed shortly by "the space of this ambivalence," "the non-space of cultural collision," and the like.

The zero concept of unsexed, in contrast, concerns itself with the *interval* between signification and resignification, the fleeting instant after received wisdom begins to crumble and no convincing "interpellation" has yet arisen to take its place. Like the disruptive repetition of performance theory, the zero that calls itself unsexed describes conditions under which the notion of fixed and referential signification fails to hold. But the temporal concept of an interval is very different from an appeal to chiasmic subjectivities or resignification. When identity and subjectivity come ever so momentarily undone in the interval when someone becomes unsexed, there is a temporary vacating of meaning that, when attended to, exposes the ruthless niceties of power and the arbitrariness of reference. Zeroing effects elude reification as subjects, objects, or norms, hegemonic or otherwise. They cannot be counted or accumulated, indeed they can oftentimes scarcely be credited. Yet there is value for anyone interested in social justice in attending to this movement in and out of signification that, in its daily passage, is always already with us.

Zero in the sense of interval is a thoroughly spatiotemporal concept, capable of being represented visually by the rest in sheet music or durationally by a measured silence. Zero in this sense is also a politicoeconomic and historic concept, emerging out of the developments in science, conquest, and trade chronicled in earlier pages. Its deployment in theory, its rejection in the violence recently directed at ambiguity, mark a very particular moment in the acceleration of global economic relations, the invention of new forms of money, and the consolidation of that abstraction called "the market." Performance theory may not do the work of moving its own conceptual apparatus into historical time, but its phenomenal popularity at the turn of the new century is indebted, in its turn, to a nostalgia for politicoeconomic formations that are rapidly passing from view.

Nowhere is this more evident than in the temporal anchor of performance theory, repetition. For performativity theorists, repetition creates gender. Repetition engenders a sense of reference. Repetition is what entices people to believe their eyes. Repetition leads them to conclude that bodies manifest deep-seated inner truths (in this case, regarding gendered differences). Repetition naturalizes through its very insistence. To reiterate, often as not, is to reify.[50] Citation piles upon citation, until a "new infinity" (in the Deleuzian sense of an anticipated sequence or coherence) opens up.

What is it that repeats? Not only the chinos and the makeup, the number of restrooms on offer, the timbre of voice and gesture, but also (for Butler) "norms," that most reified of sociological constructs, formulated to explain the seemingly heavy hand of the social. When "the norm" appears in writing on performativity, it arrives unaccompanied by irony or any sense that "the norm" is a historical invention, generated via all the headcounts, surveys, and censuses attendant upon the fixing of a "population" through statistics.[51]

At the same time (as it were), performance theorists understand full well that nothing repeats as itself without bringing about some sort of difference.[52] "Difference inhabits repetition," Gilles Deleuze asserts, if only because "the paradox of repetition lie[s] in the fact that one can speak of repetition only by virtue of the change or difference that it introduces into the mind which contemplates it. . . . When A appears, we expect B with a force corresponding to the qualitative impression of all the [repeated and] contracted ABs."[53] Contracted, in this case, over a lifetime of experience with a gendered social landscape. However invariably tick follows tock, the *expectation* that tick will follow tock is something else again, produced through repetition but hardly identical with it. This is why a transgendered person with an ample amount of facial hair can move with relatively little complication through a door marked "Gentlemen." (What lies in wait on the other side of the door may be another matter.) This is also why a body or a film can stage a "disruptive repetition of its own terms" with the potential to lead to resignification.[54]

To be sure, repetition is a temporal concept, but not an adequately historicized one. Even the tick-tock of the Bergsonian clock echoes quaintly in a digital age. Because repetition moves in cycles, its regularities yield generalities, not developments or events: "Women do X, men do Y." "S/he sure looks like a drag queen." "Don't wear that suit, it makes you look trashy." "That's just about would you'd expect from 'those people.'" Whatever hope repetition may entertain of disrupting these sedimented "truths" through the difference it carries, its disruptions always labor under the threat, perhaps the inevitability, of co-optation.[55] And so there ensues a new cycle of mutually reinforcing citations.

Put another way, repetition in performativity theory provides a mechanism not only for the constitution of gender, but also for the constitution of time, or at least a certain modality of time. This cyclic time wields no explanatory power regarding historical change.[56] At best, it can import externally conceived accounts of historical developments into its analysis, acknowledging, for example, that the gendered conventions reified through repetition do change, or that they altered in such-and-such a way around such-and-such a date. A cyclic conception of time lacks the specificity required to explain why certain commodities have a symbolic value that works to gender bodies in the here-and-now, or indeed why bodies themselves should have become commodified in particular ways at a certain point in linear time.

In all fairness, this is not performativity theory's project. Those who have benefited from its insights often voice respect for the difference that history makes, but by and large they have not concerned themselves with how or why gendered performances change. Their attention is more likely to go to the innovative understandings of repetition introduced by Sigmund Freud, through his concept of repetition compulsion, than the forms of repetition that proliferated once Henry Ford assigned a series of recurring motions to workers stationed along the length of a rotating rubber belt.

This turn toward psychoanalysis at the expense of political economy makes it difficult for performance theory to gauge the limits of its own applicability. Lacking any historical perspective of its own, performativity can scarcely attend to the historical circumstances of its own production. Easy enough to forget that Freud was a contemporary of Ford, the two attempting to make sense (and money) from a world given over to imperialist expansion, labor organizing, the reification of markets, reorganized work and family relations, a newly denominated "business cycle," and the wars attendant upon colonization.

Just as zero emerged from a history of mercantile trade and conquest, so the kind of repetition that girds gender with performativity emerged from a history of industrialization and novel fiduciary arrangements. Repetition's deployment in gender theory as an analytic tool coincides with the United States's move into a postindustrial epoch, when the bulk of factory production shifts from Northern to Southern countries, when the bankbook gives way to electronic and other "imaginary" forms of exchange. The majority of jobs in "rich countries" remain stultifying, to be sure, but they are no longer so heavily reiterative. Word processors, cashiers, fry cooks, customer service representatives, even computer programmers produce endless but varied combinations of keystrokes, greetings, fast food orders, strings of text. However patterned and circumscribed those combinations might be, they demand "flexible bodies" to perform them.[57]

This shift from the rhythmic rush of the assembly line to the mind-numbing improvisation demanded by a service-and-information economy begins to expose the repetitive, performative aspects of the production of gender in and through bodies. These are the conditions under which the arbitrary relationship of gender to embodiment, like the arbitrariness of tethering currency to the tangible qualities of gold or silver, becomes evident. (The very era when "repetitive strain injury" acquires its name and enters the pantheon of occupational hazards.) Performance theory stakes its claim in North America just as the rat-a-tat-tat of the riveting gun, the anchoring thud of the stamping machine, the relentless hiss of ball bearings in their races, fade away into someone else's present. Another example of what the philosopher Ian Hacking calls "a common pattern in the history of thought: an idea becomes sharply formulated, and even named, . . . at exactly the moment that it is being put under pressure."[58]

One could go further. It may be that the kind of repetitions performance theory describes are not characteristic of the production of gender per se, but rather of the production of gender in what was, until recently, a Fordist economy.[59] At its most convincing, performance theory offers an account of how gender is made in a timeplace where mechanical reproduction prevails. Walter Benjamin famously described for the work of art how mechanical reproduction erodes the meaningfulness and prestige of an original. What aura of authenticity illuminates the machine-produced copy of a copy of a copy of a Hiroshige or Vermeer? Even more so in the case of art created in and for a time of mass production, when "to an ever greater degree the work of art reproduced becomes the work of art designed for reproducibility."[60] Exhibition value comes to override the value placed on uniqueness.

For the work of gender under similar conditions, it may be that femininities and masculinities, too, modulate with respect to authenticity. As the commodification of gender proceeds apace, gendered accessories and purchased accoutrements do more than their share of the work of signification, in precisely the ways identified by performativity theorists. Bodies are clothed and adorned, scented and displayed, using goods and services that must be bought. From the Harley to the cummerbund to the gold lamé, people gender themselves as copies of copies of copies through a pronounced reliance on machine-produced goods that are copies them-selves. No one has to search for the original goddess braids or punk hair-style, the very first pair of Doc Martens, for these commodities to promise to "express" something about the kind of man or woman you really are.

Of course, there are still aspects of a gendered body that corporations haven't managed to retail . . . yet. Even stance can be bought and taught through gyms, charm schools, weight-loss programs, meditation classes, moving to the latest music, practicing before the mirror (a standard house-hold item now in North America, but also one with a price tag). Eva Illouz has described a similar progression in the commodification of the signi-fiers of romance. Earlier in the century, a romantic evening entailed the purchase of relatively inexpensive items: a touch of cologne, say, or beeswax for a candlelight dinner, newly eroticized in the wake of electrifi-cation. Earlier still, courtship might have rested upon an artfully turned phrase. Today people are just as apt to gauge a suitor's commitment by the high-ticket items on offer: the diamond ring, the concert tickets, the weekend getaway.[61] Any fool can still stand under a balcony and sing to her beloved without exchanging labor power for cash, but such gestures repre-sent a severely weakened currency when commodities increasingly set the international standard for romance.

Under commodity capitalism, a gendered body does not have to be a test tube baby to be mechanically reproduced. The society that generates this particular spectacle, through cocktail dresses, through liposuction, through tattoos, emphasizes the body's exhibition value in classically Benjaminian fashion. Performance takes gender center stage, sometimes as a matter of self-styled production, sometimes in ways available only to the discerning analytic eye. Performativity constitutes theorist and partic-ipant alike as spectators, as a seeing I, as viewers of the visual, very much in the way that the enumeration of a fixed number of genders constitutes a subject as s/he-who-counts. In both cases, the visuality embedded in exhibition value draws attention away from the temporal relations involved. Like counting, performativity requires acts of repetition, though not identical ones. Add a zero—the only number that Gottlob Frege asso-ciated with the concept "not identical with itself"—and the social equa-tion yields difference, not as the inevitable by-product of citation, but through fleeting encounters that unsex bodies and, in so doing, move them in and out of signification.[62] All such acts of tabulation occur in specific historical conditions that may grant or withhold from repetition the power of reification.

When historical conditions are such that workers become separated from the products of their labor, the result is the kind of separation that Guy Debord calls "the alpha and omega of the spectacle."[63] When a global economy develops that not only alienates them from their own labor, but also insulates them from the labor of others congealed in the products that mystically appear on store shelves, something unexpected happens with regard to gender. As mechanical reproduction passes from the lived experience of most North American workers, who use their off-hours to procure packaged goods from retailers, then repackage their own labor from a more generalized servitude into "service," they begin to "see" through some of repetition's effects. Improvising rather than repeating themselves, or at best repeating a series of improvisations wielding keys or telephone headset, their work life comes to be marked by an attentiveness to performativity's effects, as well as a new set of mystifications.

Employers are the first to explain that they're out to evaluate employee "performance": performance in the sense of the tallying that shores up measures of productivity, but also increasingly in the sense of the flexibility to meet demands of an economy now conceived, like the military, in terms of rapid response. Flexibility can mean the opportunity to work at home or acquire new skills, but it is more likely to translate into part-time hours, temporary jobs, retraining at individual expense, benefits cuts, falling real wages, and bodies that must assume very different positions as they cycle through multiple jobs over the course of a lifetime.

The endless modification required by a global economy can lead people to overestimate and overemphasize the malleability of bodies, including their own. It becomes easy to mystify the degree of freedom implicit in the metamorphoses encouraged, nay, demanded at work (and consequently in other arenas to accommodate changes on the job). It becomes easy to succumb to the promise that commodities will set a person free, a promise that has lost none of its allure for having been so often exposed. For some, commodities bequeath chameleonlike qualities to their bodies, allowing them to shape-shift into variously gendered, racialized, and classed locations. For others, commodities enhance "realness." For others still—or perhaps the same people on another day—commodities supply the materials for marking parody. Mystification indeed.

Note that all this occurs not because mechanical reproduction has been consigned to a place called "the past."[64] The old economy of nuts, bolts, and Erector sets was not so much superseded by a new economy as displaced. So long as mascara sells for so many cents a tube, rest assured that a cosmetics factory has been sited in one of the more impoverished areas of the world, where labor is highly exploitable and the reiteration of inequality enforced. Performativity is in no way "out of date" as a theory, fatally linked to what Karl Marx would have termed an earlier, now passing, mode of production. It is merely that performance theory describes best what begins to become evident with hindsight, or the view from afar.

With the onset of mechanical reproduction, the work of gender, like the work of art, comes to feature reproducibility. A person real-izes gender not just through repetition, but through the use of mass-produced commodities that augur gender as they augment the body. These performances turn profits. Makeup costs. Hair coloring costs. The medical care necessary to recover from a thrashing for looking too "ambiguous" costs. Even the weapons that inflicted the damage cost. The more you become convinced that you can bend gender, choose gender, or muscle someone else's body back into the gendered conventions that bring you comfort, the more you must buy.

Zero opens a wormhole of sorts, an unexpected rent in the fabric of meaning and time that allows theory to traverse some of the ways in which gender, along with the explanations that would account for it, can become embedded in commodity aesthetics and commodity production.[65] This happens not by subscribing to the romantic myths of free agency associated with subversion and resistance, counter-hegemonies, utopias, or alternate constructs, but by attending to certain zeroing effects that are by definition forever passing from the scene. In this sense, the zero that is unsexed portends much more than a temporal, temporarily inassimilable instant. But why such an undoing should occur here-now rather than there-then, or even here-then rather than there-now, requires historical explanation. Moving gender into historical time, the time of globalization, enlists a linear accounting produced after the happening, if not after the fact. This sort of time goes one way. Historical memory, in contrast, follows Alice down the rabbit hole to divest time of at least some of its directionality. What happens to gender when time's arrow doubles back upon itself in unexpected ways?

Irene "Rene" Heidenway, the author's godmother (right), with her friend Trudy, circa 1932.
© Kath Weston

# CHAPTER FOUR

# THE GHOSTS OF GENDER PAST: TIME CLAIMS, MEMORY, AND MODERNITY

[The living] are obliged to prepare a banquet for the past.
—*Walter Benjamin*

The ghostliness was merely the absence of time and distance—for that is all that a ghost is, a presence displaced in time.
—*Amitav Ghosh,* The Shadow Lines

My hands etch circles into each small pane of glass, abrading evenings of water spots, long hours of dust.[1] Neon-blue cleaning fluid, rubbed through to transparency, brings the snapshots forward to meet their frames. In this residential facility for Alzheimer's patients, the administration encourages photographs. Family pictures are supposed to usher "confused" residents back to familiarity, allow them to retrace their steps, recognize their rooms. More than scraps of paper, more than reminiscence, these photographs purport to be guides.

My godmother, Irene, watches me through the whole procedure, now impatient, now thoughtful, now perplexed. "Leave that," she says, wishing to spare me work—a feminized sort of work—on this, her first day in a nursing home. "Let the other one do that when she comes." She means my heterosexually married sister. I set the photographs down one by one, expecting time to yield to the ministrations of Windex.

In the largest photograph, my godmother sits stiffly in eighth-grade-graduation best, a huge bow askew in her hair, rows of schoolboys alternating with rows of girls. A film-enforced patience. To the left, her sister at ninety floats in a canoe, orange life jacket radiant as a halo. A studio portrait fixes their father, cuffs too short, shirt too worn, knuckles gripping a straight-backed chair, aging into yellow.

On the print that survives from a brother's double wedding, the women slouch in their beaded dresses, terribly compact beneath a painted Ottoman arch. Next comes a portrait of my godmother at twenty, looking good in her "boyish bob." In a stray snapshot, a lady friend flirts with my godmother's camera on the rooftop of a long-demolished building, fingers grazing the old coal-fired chimneys of Chicago. Then my godmother at thirty in a professional pose: phone to ear, pen to hand, elbow on desk. World War II the invisible background here, the oak of the desk exchanged by its previous tenant for the mud of a trench.

I let my thoughts wander "backward" through the photographs, only to have them emerge—paradoxically, it seems—into the future's worrying light. "Ahead" lie the preoccupations of my unknowns: Will my god-mother outlast this move? Will the harsh routines of institutional life turn out for better, if not best? Better than isolation at home, accompanied only by fading knowledge of how to wash, eat, dress? Is there any room in this new life for touch? Will my godmother's health hold out? Will the money run out? Will tonight's dinner resemble anything either of us would call food?

Viewed against this backdrop of fugitive questions, photographs bring me comfort. The camera seems to encode certainties: people named, rela-tionships well-established, days long done. Yet somehow that very comfort has sent me hurtling toward the receding horizon I call "tomorrow," scrambling after the reassurance of prediction. Each certainty becomes a reverie, unanswered. Only my godmother's voice, curiously softened, brings me back to the room where I already stand. I watch her take in the row of photographs at a glance. "Wouldn't it be nice," she ventures, search-ing my eyes, "if you could see the past?"

For my godmother the unknowable, the unknown, lies as much "behind" as "ahead," the work of memory displaced from vision and any particular sense of direction. To speak is to search. "Now wait a minute here," she says every so often, casting about for an ordered understanding. In her day—perhaps this day—she has known herself as sister's sister, mother's daughter, sister's daughter, the undiscovered tomboy who set a tack in Mrs. Dahnke's classroom chair. A cosmopolitan woman in a sky-scraper city. A white girl moving up into a white man's job. Lucky in war, heartbroken in love. Willing to wrangle with bosses, fighting to mother her nieces. Another old woman on a hallway of women, abandoned to the recognition of fear. To speak is to search, and to come up gendered. But in her fall from linearity, is my godmother so different from me? Are our pasts any more or any less elusive than the conclusions we draw from each "what if . . . " and "what next"? Our presents, yes, of course, present, but with reference to what?

Every claim on a present, much less a future, much less a past, takes practice. One does not automatically "see" events in temporal dimensions. There is a kind of work (to use the ever-expanding metaphor) involved in any attempt, however "confused," to cast a molten world into the contours of time. Although the specific practices vary tremendously from one social location to another, temporalities generally require some method of delineating and ordering artifacts, events, what have you, into sequenced frameworks.[2] The study of historical memory represents an effort to understand precisely how it's done. As a term of art, "historical memory" encompasses the devices people use to conceptualize the past, the different valuations they place on that past, as well as the processes through which they come to believe that they *have* a past: a past which they claim and which they imagine in turn exerts its claims upon them.

In the United States, gender is constituted—partially, but significantly—from such time claims. Gender constructs develop in and through people's understandings of the way that relationships were gendered before they ever arrived on the scene. People explain current circumstances with reference to arrangements that they believe prevailed "back in the day," including the masculinities and femininities of a bygone era. They are quick to contrast the "now" of bikinis with the "then" of button-downs and high-neck collars, today's allegedly expanding job possibilities with yesterday's restriction to janitorial work or domestic service, contemporary *cholo* styles with "old school" *pachuco* sensibilities, the respect offered great-grandparents with the back talk they endure from their own daughters.[3] A rough-and-ready division of time into historical periods often frames such contrasts. Only by traveling the imaginary circuit of historical developments that have ushered me to this place do I begin to live, as apparently I must, in a gendered condition. And the understandings of gendered change embedded in each tenuously historicized statement are, from the very start, configured in terms of race, class, culture, sexuality, nation.

To say that gender in North America is intimately bound up with the work of historical memory is to set aside the theoretical tools most commonly wielded in gender studies. There is scarcely any historical edge built into classic analytic concepts such as gender roles, psychoanalytics, performativity, or socialization. Theorists from otherwise contending schools are happy to acknowledge historical change, but their theories have offered little by way of mechanisms to account for it, much less an appreciation of gender's dependence upon historical narration. Surprisingly, inquiries into historical consciousness have offered no supplement for this lack. Despite the recent explosion of scholarship on historical memory, the literature as a whole is much more concerned with questions of trauma, belonging, and nationalism than questions of how suppositions about what made a man a man in 1934 have something to do with making men and women today. (Of course, the two sorts of queries must be, in multiple senses, related).[4] If gender theory remains historically bereft, attempts to theorize historical memory have been effectively neutered.

In this chapter, I draw upon family history and ethnography to illustrate some of the ways in which gender is temporally produced and to examine the implications of time claims for gender theory. I approach historical memory not only via some of the usual sites and suspects—photographs, monuments, landscapes, commemorations—but also through bodies. What kind of bodies? Variously classed, raced, aged, gendered, and otherwise socially located bodies. Not necessarily bodies breathing in the same space as their interlocutors, but remembered bodies, heard and smelled and pictured through stories. Bodies assigned to represent specific historical periods, and thus to operate as measures of distance or attachment. Bodies as an opening onto a past.[5]

At issue is not only remembering, but forgetting. At issue is not only forgetting, but a kind of time-travel in which yesterday builds on the debris of the future, the present comes out past, and travelers find themselves dumped unceremoniously into memories of days that may never go by. This movement becomes integral to the processes through which any awareness of political economy falls away. Ossification sets in, freezing social relations by giving them the appearance of things. Gender solidifies into a set of learned roles or repeat performances; memories become fixed as possessions. No one asks who is in a position to capitalize on these developments. Time-traveling tethers history to gender to bodies with a certainty that obscures the moments when gender zeroes out, the circumstances of narration, and the inequalities that give oppression its sting. Historical developments appear set in stone, historical changes inexorable. Gender becomes, if not the last bastion of modernity, then key terrain for the reproduction of far from superseded beliefs in betterment, accumulation, and progress.

## FORGETTING: MOMMY NEAREST

Leaves fall from a tree. This Euro-American model of forgetting conceives of memory as a diaphanous material that floats away on the winds of time, sometimes retrievable, more often lost. Leaves scent the air with gentle decay: after eighty, autumn bears no promise of spring. A less pastoral model pictures forgetfulness as a matter of misplaced possessions. Memories fall away like car keys inadvertently dropped into the gutter, never to reappear; like glasses that turn up awkwardly perched on the crown of the searcher's head; like coins secreted in the cracks of upholstery, if only one could remember which couch, and where. This imagery establishes a mental economy of warehouses and inventory, of capitalism and control. "Confusion" results when the markers disappear: memories no longer cling to the branch, the car with the lost keys was consigned to the junkyard long ago, or perhaps you are just searching for change in the wrong sofa.[6]

Spend time with someone whose memory has begun to "fail," and you will begin to realize the inadequacy of these metaphors. Theirs is not a falling away, not amnesia, not loss, at least not in any straightforward sense. Especially it is not a growing tally of discrete memories mysteriously gone missing.[7] When relatives remind my godmother to stop speaking of her sister Elsie in the present tense because Elsie has passed away, my godmother responds as though to a fresh wound: "That's right, I hadn't thought of that." Never one to let things go quietly, she adds, "How come every time I talk about Elsie like she's alive everyone has to say that: 'She's dead'?" Here is the forgetting, the reminder, the painful visitation of memory, but also sudden insight into previous episodes of forgetting. It is not just that forgetting, as the flip side of memory, must necessarily be uneven and selective; it is that the jagged contours of forgetfulness cannot be traced through tropes of senility and loss.[8] If I did not know this before, I would have known it standing there in the nursing home in my godmother's half-furnished room the moment I began to set up the last photograph.

In this final picture my godmother sits at the bottom of a flight of wooden porch steps. A woman has tucked herself into the curve of my godmother's body, not exactly sitting in her lap but not exactly sitting alongside, either. I recognize the woman as my godmother's friend Gertrude—Trudy—the one she has wanted to forget, the one who refuses all forgetting. Arm bent tenaciously around my godmother's young neck, stockings crossed at an angle that suggests elegance, the polished fabric of her dress threatening to forsake her shoulder, muscles taut beneath hands that cup wrist and thigh. My godmother's hands. The two are locked forever in a backyard embrace, forehead inclined to forehead, falling into an intensity of eyes, the unwinding tendrils of Trudy's hair echoing a yearning in the lengthening grass. Before this embrace, "dementia" yields.

A glimpse is enough. "Put that away," my godmother says sharply. "I don't want to see it." She who, on the worst and sometimes even the best of days, cannot place faces. She who no longer matches the dailiness of my presence to my image in a frame. She who has come to treat photographs as clutter to be dusted, not some window onto a past. "Put that away!" And I do.

My godmother always considered herself a modern woman.[9] She once said that she knew this as soon as she decided to risk her father's wrath by exchanging "the thickest hair in all of Forest Park" for the provocation of a bob. But she also marked her modernity by everything that her mother was not. Although my godmother remembered not a single detail of her mother's life, she knew that her mother was the opposite of a modern woman. She knew this by the very forgetting that licenses imagination.

The year is 1977. My godmother drives a car. Her mother, she says, barely knew horses. My godmother speeds through the world. *Her* mother knew nothing of rumble seats, elevators, deadlines. My godmother retired after years of waged work in shadowy urban canyons. *Her* mother stayed home to wash, cook, manage the paychecks turned over by her children, and care for a husband too sick to hold down a job. My godmother knows a man who knows a man who could get you a porterhouse steak when steaks were hard to come by. *Her* mother would have made do, never entertained the thought. My godmother has followed the hands of the clock past many a midnight into dance halls, alleyways, bars. Her immigrant mother must have stayed home nights, in a semblance of Old World isolation. How does my godmother know this? Dressed in long skirts and apron, her mother was an old-fashioned woman. Look at her in the photograph! Yes, she crossed the seas in the hold of a stinking boat, braved an Atlantic viewed once by my godmother from the safety of a boardwalk. But her mother knew nothing about stage shows or girlfriends or fashion. That woman lived a more restricted life. Should have. Must have.

For my godmother, forgetting begins at age seven with her mother's death. Her memories of childhood start then, there, shivering in a hospital waiting room. "Pernicious anemia," they tell her after. The baby of the family, she has to ask her brother Walter what "nishus aneema" means. Mama never returns, remembrance of a time before that waiting room never returns, and my godmother grows up with a parent more specter than memory. This originary forgetting precedes my godmother's "loss of her faculties" by the better part of a life. It is a forgetting long acknowledged, until its memory, too, goes the way of time.

There are women who become "like mothers" in my godmother's stories, and she exiles them just as readily from the shores of the now. "Mama, a lovely woman," reads the caption in her album under the picture of Trudy's mother. Apron, welcoming smile, unapologetically hefty body, home for a backdrop, serviceable shoes. The caption might as well read, "Taking a break from the chores." Trudy's family was wealthier than my godmother's, their house filled with cabinets of books, tastefully done. Her mother's apron probably entered circuits of exchange at a shop in the Loop rather than the local dime store, but it's an apron, just the same. My godmother uses photography to project this woman's rendition of gender through class and age and kinship ("Mama"), back into a less liberated past. One could read some dissonance into the resultant portrait (bows on serviceable shoes?), but my godmother does nothing of the sort.

In my godmother's accounting, her sisters cannot qualify as cosmopolitan women, either. They are women, to be sure, but like Gertrude's mother and the mother she remembers only in absence, they are women of another era and thus women of another kind. "Like a mother" to her they are, and like a mother with respect to modernity.

Ten and twenty years older than my godmother, respectively, her sisters never learned to drive. It is true that the eldest worked for wages, and the middle one as well. They have clerked in department stores and downtown offices; they have shopped for mass-produced clothing in stores; they have attended any number of urban entertainments. These are hallmarks of a working-class white women's modernity put forward by all the leading scholars.[10] But the roller derby is not a nightclub—my godmother is very clear on this point—so it does not qualify her sisters as worldly wise in quite the same sense.

My godmother likes to imagine a chasm with her and her friends on one side, and all the women of preceding generations (her mother, Trudy's mother, her older sisters) gathered together on the other. That chasm is as racialized and sexualized as it is gendered. It calls itself progress.[11]

Back in the days when my godmother had access to narrative (or perhaps I should say, when I had better access to the paths taken by hers), she indulged me by speaking into a tape recorder. The year is now 1982. I am twenty-five; she is seventy-one. "You always used to say, 'I've seen a thing or two in my life,'" I prompt. (Usually to shut your sisters up, I think to myself, but resist the temptation to add.) "What did you mean when you said that?" Her answer takes the form of a story set during the war years, when she took over a "man's job" to work as a printing manager for Marshall Field's, the premier Chicago-area department store:

> [A client] says, "Do you want to see a gay revue?" I said, "Sure.
> I'd like to see it." Of the men, you know. I went in there with
> him [on north Clark Street] and had some beers and watched it.
> They had just like a girls' dancing revue on the stage, only they
> were men dressed up. . . . That didn't impress me *one bit*. But I
> got to all the joints, you know.

"Ach, what do you know about it?" interrupts her middle sister, who has been listening in on the story. ("It" apparently means sex.) "After all, Irene," says the sister, "I'm the only one of us who's been married." "But *you* haven't been to all the joints," my godmother responds dismissively, and to bolster her point, begins another story. Same client, different evening:

A [topless] place on south State Street, he wanted to take me. He said, "You don't want to go there." I said sure I wanted to go there. And they had this heavyset girl, you know, and her busts would swing—she'd swing 'em around, twirl [them] around, you know. And he thought that was nothing for me to see. But then after that was over, I got to know that girl. We talked about it. She has so much strength in there that she can just make 'em go around, or anything she wants to do with them.

At this point my godmother's sister, age eighty-one, tries unsuccessfully to duplicate the feat. "I can't get them to go around," she complains, giving up. "Maybe it's easier with tassels." Try as she might, this sister cannot, will not, encroach upon my godmother's time claims. Like their mother, this like-a-mother will never qualify for modernity. My godmother knows this because her sister has never talked to a stripper. She knows because her sister has never seen women's clothing on a man. She knows because her sister has no idea how to control her tits. She knows (but does not say) because her sister has no photographs like the one she shares with Trudy.

And there is something else. My godmother genders herself cosmopolitan by taking part in a division of labor, not only in the great city that is Chicago, but also around the house. She remembers painting, mowing the lawn, watering the tomato patch, cleaning out the garage, trimming the hedges, falling off ladders while her sisters dusted and washed and cooked. The hard-won license to perform these activities qualifies her as a modern woman (she thinks) even as it distances her from fantasies of "the traditional."

Trudy (of course?) mows no lawns, and my godmother genders herself, in part, by a series of contrasts that distinguish her from the woman to whom she feels such attraction. But these contrasts cannot be reduced to the flatness of feminine versus masculine or butch versus femme, for they, too, are dependent upon notions of departures from a very particularly conceived past.[12] Trudy may haul laundry or cook the occasional evening meal like her mother, but she does so often as a precursor to an evening's paid entertainment, which she will attend (unlike her mother) unchaperoned, in fashions sewn from the very fabric of a modernity in which the future always, always beckons.

In each narrative, each telling of a photographic image, time claims gain substance through a series of historical contrasts. Fragments of a daily journey by elevated train into the Loop array themselves against the imagined stasis of a mother's life in a European village. Older sisters, though still putting food on the table and thus presumably alive, come to represent a time surpassed, which is to say, gone by. Their bodies, weighted less with flesh than film and story, give gendered definition to retreat and advance, to the superseded old and the surely unprecedented new.

Time claims sediment not just through such remembered (albeit constructed) contrasts, but also—and equally so—through forgetting. As the one remembered in name but forgotten in flesh, my godmother's mother serves as the perfect screen, the forever-absent body onto which my godmother can project her difference. The bodies of sisters, Trudy's mother, even Trudy, also serve as screens in their way, especially in the ghost forms of images exposed in a photograph. Onto each my godmother has written her presumptive, and presumptively gendered, histories.

At issue here is more than a personal history of friendship and lilac cologne; more than a family history of death outside this doctor's waiting room, or that; more than a cultural history of beaded dresses and bonnets. At issue is a kind of historical memory that both informs interpersonal relationships and exceeds them. What begins as a boast about working better than a man in a "man's job" becomes, in the details, a story of coping with paper shortages and printers' strikes: all historical events, all datable. For that matter, the shift in clerical work from a male to a female occupation is a relatively recent historical development that had neared completion by the 1930s: just in time for my godmother to use clerical work as a gender marker to differentiate the kind of labor she performed from the lower-paid occupations that engaged her sisters.[13] The pride my godmother took in procuring a steak for a client remains incomprehensible without some knowledge of class-based access to resources, steak as a symbol of virility and wealth, the rationing system that prevailed during the Second World War. Mass production of automobiles and government licensure preceded the skewed demographics associated with the early years of driving and decades of jokes about women behind the wheel. Even specific entertainments have their location in the historical record. Once attendance waned, there would be no more stories about sisterly excursions to the vaudeville stage, no more odes to the joys of watching skaters slam one another up against the boards. A hardening of residential racial segregation in response to the Great Migration of African Americans from the South accounts for changes in the color of the faces that do and do not appear in photographs of the neighborhood where my godmother grew up.[14] Economic necessity explains much about 1920s fashions worn by fashion-conscious women years into the Depression. More than kinship, more than romantic attachment, this is history at work: making narrative from memory and an equally historicized forgetting.

And what is the time claim on which all else depends? That the world has gotten better for women. What are the materials out of which my godmother fashioned her allegiance to progress? Entrée to "all the joints," knowledge of sexualities that eluded her sisters, glamour, shopping, "non-traditional" employment, urban sophistication all herald her entry into things she considered beyond the experience of previous generations. Newly minted commodities, cityscapes with the hubris to reach for the clouds, shifting divisions of labor and novel forms of exchange: These are the steel-frame skeletons that support narratives of gendered modernities. To learn more about these building materials, one might as well ask: What do they exclude?

Using paycheck and purchase and narrative, my godmother managed to usher herself, along with Trudy, into a white modernity, although not one marked as such. The back rooms and basements they frequented staged whites-only entertainment. The passersby she greeted when she mowed the grass were mostly white, too. While the racial homogeneity of urban and suburban neighborhoods in the twentieth century has some-times been overstated, it remains the case that the only Chinese character in her stories works in a laundry and becomes a moving target for chil-dren's rocks. The sole black student in her sister's grade school graduation photograph looks back at the camera from an expanse of white that is only accentuated by rows of ivory-bleached dresses. They are characters set apart by violence, by a restricted range of occupations, by what narrative remembers and what narrative resolutely forgets.

The urban space of Chicago was not the same space for women of all hues and finances. Even the signified freedoms of the city reconfigured themselves according to race and class locations that proved inseparable from gender. The clerical jobs that marked my godmother's sisters as "tra-ditional" in her stories represented, for many Mexican-American women, just the sort of class mobility that qualified as betterment, as advance. The bobbed hair that signified daring and a certain insubordination to my god-mother's father symbolized ethnic betrayal and Americanization (not just generational conflict) to older Chicanos.[15] Different and overlapping meanings, though drawing upon the same commodity culture.

When my godmother cited her adventures in after-hours Chicago as evidence of a cosmopolitan desire, she denied modernity not only to an older generation of mothers and like-mothers, but to scores of her con-temporaries as well. By barring African Americans, the new public amusements became instrumental in creating whiteness as a category that downplayed ethnic and class differences. An innocent (or guilt-ridden) night's entertainment for a forward-looking woman like my godmother subtly contributed to the construction of a public face for "America" as a normatively Caucasian nation that reserved its best rights for whites. Of course, the Bronzeville neighborhood of Chicago hosted its own dance halls and cabarets, where African Americans could circumvent racist door policies for a time and a dime. Still, young working-class black women had to weigh the cost. The same evening on the town that represented an advance for white women was regularly held up by middle-class commentators as evidence of prostitution, moral deficit, and "loose sexuality" when the person in question was black. Social service agencies that took little notice of my godmother or Trudy heavily policed these women's behavior, offering them urban narratives of redemption, not liberation.[16]

Nor can my godmother's freedom to accompany a married client to a drag show compare, in any sensible terms, with the "freedom" to use an unsegregated bathroom or to "choose" paid employment opportunities restricted to domestic service. If commercialism supplied a common ground, city streets a common venue, families the raw material for contrast, and generational consciousness a bridge to historical memory, young women had inherited racialized histories that placed them in very different relationships to progress. "The" modern woman emerged from the negotiation of a plethora of separate and unequal compacts. If this was the Promised Land, then modernity drove a hard bargain.

Could my godmother and Trudy have made their case for cumulative progress without the strapless pumps and silk-lined dresses, without the rotary lawn mower, without the price of innumerable admissions, without automobiles? Given all the privilege accorded to rosy skin tones, could they have turned their bodies into markers of modernity without repositioning themselves as employees rather than workers? As someone born into an economically marginal existence, did my godmother require class mobility and social climbing to scale the heights of New Womanhood? Her class trajectory diverged radically from that of my father's and godfather's people, who in those struggling years bartered clothing for milk to feed the children. At that period my father's family owned no camera, no uncontested claims to whiteness, few photographs. In the broadest class terms, his family lived not so very differently from my godmother's own sisters, who ended their working lives as an unemployed secretary and a clerk.

When the time comes to make a point there always seems to be at least one story held in reserve. In this final anecdote, a set piece, my godmother has mustered the courage to learn how to ride after a stable on the North Side promises to give her a horse that won't "go aflurry." By this time Trudy has vanished from her life; to where, my godmother won't say. She has signed up for riding lessons with a new friend named Mary.

> That was one of the days that we were going for a lesson. So after the lesson, we'd go over to this bar and have some beer. In a booth. And this girl came over and sat down with us and started talking. A very nice girl. All of a sudden, she said she's a lesbian. I felt like saying, "So what!" but I didn't. But I suppose she thought we two together, maybe we are, too. She said, "I'd love to have you over to my house." And I said, "Oh no," I said, "We've got to get on." I said, "We've got dates later on," and so forth. And she spoke a little bit about her lesbian[ism]. It didn't bother me any. I mean, I think she was just as nice a girl as any. But how she came out with it! If it was me, I would have hooked around a little bit about it.

And hook around she did. There followed a series of close women friends, all married; a succession of arguments and broken hearts. The woman who had been to all the joints was no fool. She knew people gossiped about her sexuality: "People thought I was one [a lesbian], but I wasn't." In later years she complained about breasts hanging down past her waist, a failed musculature that resulted, she said, from once binding them tightly to her chest with layer upon layer of muslin. This was not a matter of gender or sexuality, she insisted: It was the fashion. My godmother at a backyard barbecue in the 1990s, watching two women hold hands as they huddled over the grill: "If I had it to do over, I would want to be like them." My godmother in her sitting room in the 1990s, photographs shelved in favor of more mobile portraits: "That Regis Philbin, he's the cutest thing on TV. I wish I had found a fellow like him." All storytelling withheld from memory of the woman who marked her cosmopolitanism, and her hurt.

In modernity gender acquires fixity only as it is taken away, borne through storytelling and bodily imagery into a dreamlike past that later generations mark with their difference and approach from the shelter of nostalgia, or disdain. How to grasp the enticement toward a future that dwells in such a contradictory offering? It's already there, in a sense, in my godmother's album, in the images cornered and pressed onto black construction paper, the landscapes that drew her unrequited into love, the pages tied together with shoelaces, bound in a way my godmother's relationships never would be. Of all the many photographs, Trudy signed just one. The inscription reads:

To Irene:
To whom I never give anything—not even a picture.

Gertrude
10–5–31

## REMEMBERING: DARWIN'S BODIES AT THE BAR

Half a century after Trudy and my godmother parted company, young women on the cusp of what would soon be declared a global economy would, in their turn, use the bodies of preceding generations as a screen. By symbolically converting elders into representatives of a bygone era, they perpetuated the "modern tradition" of treating older people as denizens of the past who scarcely participate in the contemporary world.[17] Stories and throwaway comments depicted women born in earlier decades as the tragically oppressed victims of "gender roles," a phrase come unmoored from the troubling complexities of its emergence in the scholarship of a Robert Merton or Talcott Parsons. "Roles" had become a quasi-sociological shorthand for circumscribed lives that couldn't hold a candle—much less a digital display—to the freedoms enjoyed by "women today."

Of course, in the 1980s many of "yesterday's women" were very much alive. Nor were these women, who had once wrapped themselves in ideologies of progress to confront their own parents and bosses, prepared to go quietly as foolish youth arrogated to themselves the mantle of all things shiny and bright and yet to come. So it was that instead of elaborating time claims in the abstract (things were awful then, things are better now), another generation of women anchored their time claims on the living, breathing bodies encountered in certain age-integrated venues where the women of my godmother's generation occasionally appeared. These venues included households, the venerable site for the production of gender, but also semipublic spaces such as shopping malls, workplaces, and bars.

The judgments about time and change and gender hammered out in these venues *incarnated* historical memory, insofar as younger women understood the older women around them to exemplify the past. In the process, bodies metamorphosed into indices of what Marianne Hirsch has called postmemory, a kind of second-generation memory "mediated not through recollection but through an imaginative investment and creation" consolidated by vigorous narratives that predate someone's birth. While Hirsch developed the concept of postmemory to explain how traumatic experiences, such as the Holocaust, can be conveyed in visceral detail to the children of survivors, the concept could well be extended to globally pervasive narratives such as modernization that encode specific temporalities and relations of power.[18] The move that casts members of an earlier generation as the unwitting prisoners of "gender roles" (which is to say, as prisoners of "their times") requires a huge investment in liberationist narrative before historical memory can turn to self-congratulation, pity, or disdain. But because memories and postmemories alike can be contested, intergenerational venues sometimes became battlegrounds where younger women wished the older women silent (the better to project) and older women endeavored to disrupt the fantastic histories of the young. In the words of Olick and Robbins: "People and groups fight hard for their stories."[19]

In a moment I shall introduce some of the time claims embedded in narratives about one of these venues: the bar. First, however, it is important to point out that, with the historical emergence of imagined communities based at least in part on gender, the embodiment of historical memory became more complicated still. By imagined communities, I have in mind the sort of affiliations described by Benedict Anderson in his classic study of nationalism: affiliations with imaginary entities such as a nation or an ethnic group that have no visible, delimited existence yet evoke a sense of belonging. Rather than being generated by virtue of face-to-face contact, this sense of belonging depends upon properties and/or histories that adherents imagine themselves to share. So it is that Homi Bhabha can speak of the "metaphoricity" of the peoples understood to dwell within these bounds.[20]

Beginning in the 1970s, women across Europe, Australia, and North America began to affiliate themselves with something called "the lesbian community" (also known by the more embracing but, in view of the stigma attached to homosexuality, essentially euphemistic term "the women's community"). Invocations of this collective body bequeathed to many women a sense of membership in (or isolation from) a definable group with a history. That history may or may not have represented a "deep past" that extended back into the mists of time, but it certainly appeared to describe the "near past" of the mid-twentieth century, when lesbians were said to have climbed out of the shadows of secret lives and back-alley bars.[21]

For those who called themselves lesbian, gay, bisexual, or (later) queer, novelty held no virtue when it came to claiming an identity. Like other identity-based "communities" that mobilized constituencies for political action during the late twentieth century, this one laid claim to a history in bids for social validation and access to material resources. Put differently, appeals to history helped credit the very idea of a community as an entity that could bid and comfort, alienate and contest, represent and occasionally win.

It took more than nationalist symbols like the rainbow flag to sustain this sense of attachment. The narration of something called "lesbian and gay history" helped establish species being in the Foucauldian sense, with an emphasis here on the being. Allusions to work by historians such as Elizabeth Kennedy, Madeline Davis, John D'Emilio, and George Chauncey came up quite frequently when I interviewed gay men and lesbians in the 1980s and 1990s. "I haven't really studied it," one San Francisco woman told me. "Now I'm feeling like, oh no! I should go read D'Emilio! I'm supposed to know these things!" Another asked, "Weren't there some people back east who had discovered that most of the butches and femmes back then were working class?" From the documents compiled by local gay history projects to the evidence submitted in child custody cases, assertions of belonging to a group with a past had become integral to the process by which lesbians and gay men began to live their lives as such.[22]

Communities may be imagined, but in time they are also lived, though not nearly so homogenously as people often claim.[23] Narration alone cannot fabricate belonging, because narration takes shape through engagements with powerful practices, industries, and institutions that demand temporal in(ter)ventions. In the United States, for example, the legal system requisitions time by asking gay advocacy groups to construct a history for the relationships they wish to legitimate (the more years together, the better), to construct a chronicle of disparate treatment in order to substantiate allegations of discrimination.[24] Historical continuity commands a premium in Anglo-European courts, as it has for Native Americans pursuing tribal recognition and sovereignty rights, as it has for Australian Aborigines fighting for a land base.[25]

By creating a seamless trajectory for their communities "back" into linear time, lesbians and gay men often found themselves in the ironic position of looking over their shoulders toward "the past" while taking up narratives of modernization.[26] Had the world—well, the United States— ever been a better place for queers? The very act of naming themselves lesbian, gay, queer was a modern acquisition presented as the worthy (albeit improved) successor to the homosexuals, inverts, perverts, fairies, and sexual psychopaths who peopled the imagination of earlier generations.

Yet modernization narratives can be deceptive. Apparently linear, moving from benighted past into a limitless future, they actually offer one of those instances where time curves. Proponents must go back in order to go forward, if only to know what they are so resolutely leaving behind.

Not all this history-making occurred in oral history projects, scholars' studies, and courts of law. Much of it was written across the bodies of older men and women encountered in places like bars. "Those old dykes and fairies" embodied history in the minds of the young. Like my godmother and her friends in the 1930s, women of the late twentieth century used the bodies of their elders to create historical memories. This grassroots contribution to the rise of the imagined community remains unacknowledged, its temporalities unexamined, the gendering of its narratives marked yet curiously untroubled.

A narrative that continually surfaced while I was conducting fieldwork in the San Francisco Bay Area from 1985 to 1990 offers a case in point. I call it "The Old Butch at the Bar." If the lesbian past is another and imagined country, then the Old Butch is its authentic and original native. "The Old Butch at the Bar" reprises the colonial arrival story, only in this case the new "world" awaiting discovery by the young narrator is a gay club or nightspot where queers are known to hang out.

For women who came of age in the 1960s, 1970s, and 1980s, a "women's bar" represented a chance—perhaps the only chance—to meet other gay women. Nevertheless, many initially approached the bars with fear. "I expected to see motorcycles lined up against the bar or something," Liz Andrews explained. In the telling, they were not disappointed. Aspiring young lesbians like Liz expected patrons of the bars to be the incarnation of everything they had ever heard about truck-driving diesel dykes, jaded gym teachers, lecherous alcoholics, and hardened drill sergeants who would order their own mothers to crawl through the mud. In many of the stories these stereotypes come to life, usually in the person of an older woman positioned at the bar, a character depicted as mean, drunk, or despairing, but almost invariably butch.

> I remember the first time [someone] took me to Peg's Place, it was one of the worst experiences I ever had in my life. Then it just compounded [the feeling] that I never wanted to go to bars. . . . There were some people in the front, being really rowdy. We went in and sat at two seats that were at the bar. And this real overweight, heavy-duty, rude woman walked over. She took this dirty coffee cup from in front of [my friend] and she looked at us and said, "That's my seat!" She was the bartender and she was working there! I was so intimidated and so freaked out. I was scared to go in there anyway, and I didn't feel welcome. I wanted to die.

Typically, the woman at the bar who becomes the focus of the story is in her fifties or sixties. She is not older, not an elder, not even middle-aged. She appears to the narrator simply as "old," with all the starkness that term can carry in a society that stigmatizes aging. Whether alone or with friends, the old woman in these stories generally "just sits there," her passivity at odds with her perceived masculinity except when challenged by the young. Occasionally she ventures over to the pool table or more rarely the dance floor, but the bar is her station. For her there are no high scores at the pinball machine, no political debates around a back table, no quick wit in the bathroom line, no parking lot escapades, no bid to escort someone home, no thought of showing up for work the next day. The Old Butch may be described as ugly, isolated, or depressed. She is not just butch but emphatically butch, embodying the legacy of a lesbian past in which "butch/femme roles" are understood to have prevailed.

Gina Pellegrini, who came out into the atmosphere of The Duchess in 1970s New York, remembered the hostilities she and her friends exchanged with the regulars who sat at the bar:

> Some were really nasty. They would be at that bar on the same barstools every time I would go in there. So I named them "fossils," because they never moved. They didn't! So I said, "Oh, the fossils are here again." One was Bernice or something like that. She was the nastiest, most bitter woman I've ever met in my life. She was about fifty-something, kickin' sixty. . . . She'd give us a hard time for being young and causing a ruckus. That was the word she used.

There is much more going on in these narratives than a failure by the uninitiated to understand the codes of working-class bar culture. (Don't sit where someone has left a glass. Have some respect. Never let an insult go unchallenged.) If the Old Butch at the bar represents, in the eyes of the young, calcified remains from another era, then she embodies history as well as time's passage.

Like the older women in my godmother's stories, the Old Butch enters as a living fossil, less dinosaur than one of those mysteriously still extant creatures like the dragonfly or the opossum that have managed to endure since antiquity while others have gone the way of time. Her body joins a panoply of *lieux de mémoire*—museums, monuments, cemeteries, notions of lineage and generation—all sites where "memory crystallizes and secretes itself" in ways that insist upon a history.[27]

In her guise as a living fossil, the Old Butch has profound implications for gender theory. If, as Franco Moretti has convincingly argued, "the forms with which we picture historical moments to ourselves are crucial to the fashioning of our identity," then encounters that anchor historical memory in bodies readily become integral to the production of gender.[28] This contention goes well beyond the now rather commonplace view that gender is, in some sense, a verb, perpetually accomplished in the course of performance or interaction. To say that historical memory engenders bodies is to add a temporal dimension to the *mechanism* of gender's production under conditions of the latest capitalism. Different ways of counting and claiming time, accordingly, affect the specific forms of gendering that ensue. At issue is not so much how gender constructs have changed through time, but rather how perceptions of the way things were in the past shape the construction of gender in the present, and how the bodies of older women serve to sediment younger women's perceptions. Given, that is, an allegiance to modernity.

Consider the difference between my godmother's story of meeting the lesbian in the bar and the bar stories offered by younger narrators. My godmother used bodies, narrative, and photographic images to gender herself by emphasizing the contrasts between her life and the way she imagined life had been for women many years her senior. But her bar story has none of the elements of historical contrast—you are then, we are now—so prominently displayed here. "I'd love to have you over to my house," the woman at the bar says, and in response my godmother attempts a tactful if tactical withdrawal by insisting that she and her friend have to leave; they have dates. (Lesbians apparently have no dates, sex being, as they say, the headliner.) There may or may not have been older women in the bar when my godmother arrived, but the point is that older women do not appear as characters in her bar story. The New Woman, the Modern Woman, was a time claim to an identity that encompassed her willingness to frequent bars such as these. But the women who supplied the bodily contrasts that anchored her claim—silk versus apron, homemade curls versus that boyish bob—my godmother located in other narratives and other venues.

In stories about The Old Butch at the Bar, however, contrasts between the gender practices of different generations are central. The overstated butchness of the main character(s) situates gender at the heart of the story, while the narrator's trembling or scorn in the face of hard-core butchness qualifies her as (at least for the moment) a woman of another sort. Over at the bar, the Old Butch oscillates between standing in as a generic, gendered exemplar of what it means to be lesbian and standing up for what it meant to be queer in ostensibly less liberated times.

Amy Feldman, who began to call herself gay in the 1970s, described her younger self as a person who chose heterosexually identified women for her first lovers because she felt "intimidated" by lesbians. "As a matter of fact, I was afraid to come out as a lesbian because I thought I was gonna turn into this fat, ugly bulldyke if I said I was one of them." "Butch" can mean many things to many people, some extremely positive, but the particular rendition of butch conveyed by these narratives elicits pity or terror.[29] The character of the Old Butch is overbearing and over-weight (a code term for unattractive in a society that glorifies thinness). She socializes with what one woman called "the white shirts, black pants crowd, who were the most deeply into roles and the most violent." For many of the young narrators, as for many in society at large, butches epit-omized the gender-inversion model of homosexuality: girls who always wanted to be boys, women with biceps, tailored pants, and an attitude. Whether these stories fetishize the Old Butch as an icon of pride and resistance or as a victim born into a less liberated era, her character remains frozen in time.

Lourdes Alcantara was talking to a white woman who knew a little Spanish on her first trip to a lesbian bar "when suddenly I saw her dance with a woman. A really tough woman, that looked like a man! That was my first shock, too. How can a woman look like a man?" Jenny Chin depicted a woman with "chains on her ankle, and she weighs 300 pounds, and she's got this scowl on her face, and she's just an angry whatever." There is something primitivized about these images: the contorted fea-tures, the senseless aggression, the butch qua butch portrayed as a throw-back to earlier times.[30] The gendering of the Old Butch's body, like the gendering of her relationships, becomes a marker of premodernity in ways that would have been incomprehensible to my godmother's friends, who flirted with homosexuality even as they styled themselves heralds of a future.

What separates my godmother's bar story of the 1940s from the bar stories of younger women that featured characters of my godmother's age? What accounts for the absence of age and gender markers in the former and their prominence in the latter? Unlike my godmother's stories, tales of The Old Butch at the Bar were spun in the era of imagined lesbian com-munity, itself an outgrowth of the social movements of the mid-twentieth century. By the 1970s and 1980s, the setting for the younger women's sto-ries, many lesbians had already begun to think of themselves as members of (or outcasts from) a group that possessed its own discrete history. Whether they felt that "the women's community" was a place for middle-class white girls or exactly the kind of queer they understood themselves to be, the notion of a community that alternately marginalized and involved individual lesbians had become part of common speech.

A particular "vision" of history, Ana María Alonso notes, is "con-structed in relation to and inflected by the struggles of the moment."[31] In the long shadow cast by the women's and gay movements, narrators cre-ated representations of the gendering of lesbians in the past that they used as foils for their own practices. Echoing my godmother's refrain—"We have it better; those old women didn't know any better"—they, too, used gender to lay claim to modernity.[32] But to effect this distinction, they periodized history in ways that linked gender to notions of an emerging lesbian (sub)culture.

Incorporated into the character of the Old Butch at the Bar is a particular way of chronicling "lesbian history." Lesbian communities, like the wider society, get credited with a legacy of changing gender relations. In this rough-and-ready periodization, the Old Butch immersed in "roles" represents the 1950s. Narrators identified the 1970s as the period of androgyny and lesbian-feminism, then skipped ahead to the mid-1980s, when a "new" butch/femme emerges as an option rather than an expectation. Their accounts were not nearly as nuanced as those developed by historians such as Elizabeth Kennedy and Madeline Davis, who carefully distinguish the butch/femme of the 1950s from that of the 1930s and 1940s. In the later bar stories, the 1960s becomes a lost decade, while the years before 1949 fade from history into the relatively timeless past. As happened in the family values debates, the 1950s come to represent the baseline for "tradition," despite evidence of the decade's aberrant character in the history of the United States.[33] Old Butches appear to dwell in a postcolonial variant of despotic time, the sticky, swampy, uneventful temporality of oriental despotism: time that takes prisoners, time without duration.[34]

Interesting, then, that the women telling these stories consistently and insistently associated their butch characters with the 1950s, despite the fact that most of the described encounters would have occurred between 1965 and 1989. The figure of the Old Butch condenses nostalgia for the simple life portrayed in *Father Knows Best*, the working-class stage set of *The Honeymooners*, the ignorant characters and demeaning scripts written for *Amos 'n' Andy*, and the threat to public order posed by motorcycle gangs in *The Wild One*. Her ability to condense such a range of meanings owes much to another aspect of commodification under the latest capitalism: the packaging of U.S. history into decades, the better to retail all manner of retro styles and nostalgia.[35]

After locating the character of the Old Butch in a decade—the 1950s—that has come to symbolize racial injustice, gender oppression, contested moralities, and (for some Anglos) the fiction of a once-white nation, narrators had to grapple with a highly politicized history. The Old Butch accordingly becomes a reference point for the truncated historical memory called "the way things used to be," a reference point from which the storyteller can attempt to distance or distinguish herself. By exiling the Old Butch from modernity, younger women catapulted themselves in a direction called progress.

How precisely did they exile her and how did they use gendered periodizations of history to claim a different trajectory? With racialized forms of social Darwinism, on the one hand, and biographies cast in terms of decades, on the other.

Gina Pellegrini was not alone in calling the Old Butches "fossils." Others called them "dinosaurs" or "throwbacks" to another era. In a world saturated with social Darwinism, this is the terminology of extinction: a temporal lexicon of creatures who once roamed the earth but rightly should no more. Although the Old Butch might be a living fossil, her survival as such appears to block the road to modernity, if not utopia. This same vocabulary of dinosaurs and throwbacks mobilizes a dangerously classed and racialized rhetoric. It is of a piece with the typecasting of working-class men as unskilled laborers and unreasoning brutes ("Neanderthals," in classist parlance). Applied to the character of the Old Butch, it is of a piece with post-Emancipation depictions of black and brown people as physically threatening, unable to evolve (assimilate), and therefore "left behind."[36] It partakes, as well, of the temporality and judgment implicit in reports that various races, classes, ethnic groups, or once-colonized nations "trail" with respect to wages, computer access, preparedness for governance, or city life. This "signifying time-lag of cultural difference" sustains modernity's "ambivalent temporality," authorizing some to define a present even as it engenders a past.[37]

After placement on an evolutionary time scale, even white working-class butches come out with something deeper than a tan. Many writers have noted the racism incorporated into depictions of evolution as a ladder, a timeline, or a scale. The scale doubles as a racial continuum, with black providing a starting point, followed by various shades of brown, bronze, and beige, with white defining the pole of civilization, modernity, and the now.[38] When Catherine Lutz and Jane Collins analyzed imagery in the *National Geographic,* they found skin tone mapped onto space and time, with Africa garnering the fewest articles. The darker black, the farther back, goes this racist equation, with nudity and other tropes of "the primitive" largely reserved for women with darker skin. The effect of this spatiotemporal ranking, which orders complexity into a progressive scale, is to create what Stephen Jay Gould calls "a single series of worthiness, invariably to find that oppressed and disadvantaged groups—races, classes, or sexes—are innately inferior and deserve their status."[39]

In this sense, the argument that that the Old Butch is a racialized character does not hang on a lexicon. Yet the evolutionary language used by narrators in their bar stories can be revealing. Calling a character a "throwback" to the 1950s does more than yoke women who affect "classic" butch style to a decade in which they might have been children, or heterosexually married, or spending their evenings somewhere else than the bars. Darwin himself used the concept of reversion to illustrate his argument for natural selection, though he assigned reversion no overt moral valence. The child who "reverts in certain characters" to its grandparent, the domesticated fowl born with barred and white-edged tail feathers like "any wild rock-pigeon," might appear to move backward in time, or alternatively, to represent the unexpected eruption of the past into the affairs of today. Yet Darwin greeted with skepticism the view that "domestic varieties, when run wild, gradually but certainly revert in character to their aboriginal stocks."[40] Even if they emerged, ancestral characteristics would persist only under certain conditions, conditions that were very much of the present.

Popular discourse, however, made few distinctions as it set about adapting the work of the naturalists to matters of race. In popular discussions of reversion, "the throwback" was a pejorative term applied to a dark(er)-skinned child born to light(er)-skinned parents. This particular emissary from the ancestors thwarted any attempts by the relatives to "lighten up," much less to pass. Scholarly discourse followed suit. "In characterizing either lesbians' or African American women's bodies as less sexually differentiated than the norm (always posited as white heterosexual women's bodies)," writes Siobhan Somerville, "anatomists and sexologists drew upon notions of natural selection to dismiss these bodies as anomalous 'throwbacks' within a scheme of cultural and anatomical progress."[41]

In the color politics of the day (perhaps this day), the throwback violated modernity by scoffing at linear conceptions of time that had seduced people into believing they could leave the past behind. Her tiny body supplied a touchstone for the historical memory of race-mixing, a trace of the miscegenation, the history of rape under slavery, that Jim Crow laws were supposed to have helped the populace forget. Like the Old Butch, she comes into this world a dark figure, a wild figure, disturbingly temporal yet misplaced, invariably haunting. If Somerville is correct in arguing that the institution of the color line and the invention of "the homosexual" were contemporaneous and inextricable historical developments, then the Old Butch and the baby must be more than analogues.

Of course, there is yet another, related definition of throwback: a setback to progress. If the goal is androgyny or bleached-out skin or some fictive neutrality with respect to color and class and gender, then the unexpectedly ebony infant who grows up into that old-time butch represents a roadblock indeed. Evolutionary theory still informs this conception of the throwback, here in the form of a widespread misunderstanding of natural selection. As Stephen Jay Gould has been at pains to point out, nothing in Darwin's theory of natural selection claims that selection must yield something better, that evolution means progress, or that later-appearing species are any higher or more advanced. "If an amoeba is as well adapted to its environment as we are to ours, who is to say that we are higher creatures?" Such claims represent an unholy alliance of the concept of natural selection with ideologies of modernity and, often, eugenic theories of fitness. As Gould reminds readers, "Natural selection has a place in all anti-Darwinian theories that I know."[42]

In *Inherit the Wind*, the play based upon the Scopes trial, Drummond, the Clarence Darrow character, calls his opponents "clockstoppers" and purveyors of "medieval nonsense."[43] Yet when the trial was originally held in 1925, the fight to ban the teaching of evolution in public schools drew support from the populist perception that Darwinism fostered hate and rationalized corporate greed. Far from seeking to subordinate science to religion or, in linear fashion, turn back the hands of time, opposition to evolutionary narratives emerged from a broad-based social movement that sought to regulate the powerful entities early twentieth-century corporations had become. While merchants in the Tennessee town where the trial was held erected billboards of monkeys hawking patent medicine and added Simian Soda to the drugstore menu, anti-evolutionists edged closer to a key insight: The slide from Darwinism to social Darwinism depends upon the conviction that living things can be arranged into a single progressive sequence.

It is important to understand just what is entailed in this mistake, for it has everything to do with how ideologies of modernity come to find their confirmation in practices of gender. To rank creatures or species in an ascending sequence, a person must have a criterion for ranking.[44] In bar stories, gender is the criterion that assigns the Old Butch and the narrator to their respective places in the series. And a raced, classed sort of gender it is. (Needless to say, the series does not incorporate a zero in the sense developed in the second chapter: There is no potential here to become temporarily unsexed, passing into genderlessness, if only for a moment.) The Old Butch in her wing-tipped shoes was quick to resort to her fists, quick to order her woman around. Narrators, for their part, were quick to claim that they gendered their own bodies and relationships in ways that were superior, more evolved, especially with respect to equality. It could only follow that the Old Butch was destined for extinction, even in the minds of narrators who romanticized the adventures of "those old dykes."

I want to reiterate that the Old Butch is a representation, a one-dimensional portrait, flattened out through a series of contrasts, and therefore in no sense a description of older women in the bars as they "really were" at the time.[45] One could say the same for the relatively flattering portraits younger narrators drew of themselves. Like my godmother, who imagined a life for *her* mother devoid of the pleasures and worldliness she believed her generation enjoyed, these narrators historicized themselves, their newly invented community, and their peers by locating memories of the past in presumably differently gendered bodies.

The gendered historical sequence they established went something like this: Those 1950s dykes had roles. We have either androgyny, or no roles, or roles for some, in which case they are new and improved roles. Having established this chronology, narrators went about inserting themselves into the sequence. Many who characterized themselves as "fluid" or "androgynous" called themselves "children of the 1970s." Those who associated themselves with the 1980s and 1990s tended to make careful distinctions between the "new" butch/femme of their day and "classic," "old-fashioned," or "traditional" butch/femme from years gone by. Sarah Voss, who identified herself as "a 1990s butch," considered butches like Ruby "old school." To quote Ruby, Sarah lowered her voice an octave: "She was the sort of old-fashioned butch who'd say, 'Yep, the way I want to go is I want to be shot in bed by a jealous husband.'" Sarah's playful account of Ruby's antediluvian ways performs many of "tradition's labors": connecting narratives of a past to narratives of identity, after linking that past to a future and a now.[46]

If classic butch/femme was supposed to be compulsory, the new butch/femme was as optional as an accessory. No one had to be "into roles." On the other hand, even middle-class girls with only one respectable shade of nail polish, not a hammer in the house, had been coming out femme and butch, respectively. Thus "roles," portrayed as confining and restrictive in the 1950s, had come to be considered a "choice" by the 1980s.[47] This transformation piggybacked on the historical memories elaborated in venues such as the bars, where the bodies of Old Butches provided the scaffolding for such contrasts.

So it might be said, following Fadi Abou-Rihan, that "one becomes queer not only in opposition to the straight but in opposition to other queers as well."[48] Yet our kind of, your kind of, my kind of queer take shape through processes vastly more complex than establishing a series of observed contrasts or timeless structuralist oppositions, be those differences defined in terms of skin color, birthplace, or trust funds. As women told their stories, they used interpretive frameworks of degeneration, progress, and the like to elaborate difference, yielding contrasts that evoked imagined attributes and historicity as much or more than observation.

In taking up the language of modernity and choice—butch/femme as an option, alternative, or lifestyle—narrators allied notions of freedom and progress with the rhetoric of free trade, consumption, and globalization.[49] Younger narrators described butches of the late twentieth century (mind you, not the older butches still alive at the time) as less "rigid," more touchable, apt to do "their share" of the shopping, and not as protective of femmes. Turn-of-this-century femmes were also supposed to be different: They were as likely to wear a T-shirt as high heels. They had more say in bed. Who knows, they might even be caught taking out the garbage. All in all, the new butch/femme presented itself as more egalitarian, more progressive, and more representative of what relationships in a modern world should be.

Something curious happened in the process of laying out this simple line that pointed toward a better, more equitably gendered tomorrow: The track that led to modernity began to turn cyclical and elliptical in unexpected ways, as the character of the Old Butch doubled back upon a future. Not her future—being immune to change, she has nothing to anticipate—but her narrators'.

The same Old Butches who incarnated the narrator's vision of a collective lesbian history sometimes appeared to offer disturbing clues about what lay in store for the young observer. Gloria Silva, a runaway at seventeen, remembered her first visit to a lesbian bar "like it was yesterday":

> The atmosphere was very dark, very depressing: the drinking,
> the way the women were dressed, the role-playing that was
> going on, the toughness. . . . I would look at these women and
> I'd say, "Oh my god, there are older lesbians! So you mean that
> I'm gonna be a lesbian when I'm that age?" I lived my life from
> day to day. I didn't think of myself as a lesbian as an older per-
> son, so when I saw it, it was too much to face. In some ways I
> was facing my own homophobia.

As Gloria's narrative moves ahead several decades from yesterday with a speed that approaches light, time curves and gender contracts. Suddenly this bell-bottomed child glimpses herself tough, masculinized, depressed . . . an Old Butch! Sarah Voss, generally a careful analyst, also conflated historical changes in gender practices with changes in the gendering of an individual over the course of a life cycle:

> I look at those ancestors that embarrassed me [then], now that
> I'm leading their life. . . . I think as you get older, you look
> butcher, too. Mia Farrow at twenty was real cute in her little
> haircut. Mia Farrow at forty, if she wasn't living with Woody
> Allen, would be perceived in a very different and much more
> hostile way. So I look at those women and I think, "God, you
> are great. Thank you for going on before."

These futures, of course, are no less imagined than the pasts selectively projected onto the bodies of older women in the dim bar light. A glimpse of twilight years spent downing beer after beer mobilized race and class in ways that terrorized younger women, especially those who were middle-class and/or white. It was not just the thought of gaining a hundred pounds that made them flee, but the expectation of downward mobility, the prospect of learning to push other women around, the chilling thought of becoming a predator or a brute.

In her guise as a phantom from the lesbian past, the Old Butch elicited a range of responses toward the history of gendering in the community that women pictured themselves joining. For some of them, she remained a tragic, feared, or despised figure, the very "nightmare on the minds of the living" famously evoked by Karl Marx in *The Eighteenth Brumaire* to account for the influence exerted by "the tradition of all the dead generations." This embodied reading cast the once New Women from earlier in the century as always and already retrograde, always and already old: if not precisely dead, then dead weight, their passing eagerly awaited by younger women who aspired, through regendering, to usher "the community" into a modernity without a history. A perfect illustration of how "the modern not only invented tradition, it depends upon it," the two terms acquiring meaning only in relation to one another.[50]

There were other narrators, telling me their stories after intervening years of experience and reflection, for whom Old Butches conjured up a very different sort of dream. After reporting her initial shock that a woman could "look like a man," Lourdes Alcantara added without hesitation, "But now I understand that, in a way, we are trying to create a new image. If we are taking that from men, who cares? If we are taking that from women, who cares? As long as it's our own." In this case narrators attempted to capture the activities of their elders for their own modernizing project: the creation of social relations they took to be unprecedented, perhaps utopian, most certainly "lesbian." The imagined community as bounded community, moving forward.

In both readings, the figure of the Old Butch crept up on younger women, just like time and age and history. At the very moment that she became embodied in the language of storytelling, representing apprehensions about the narrator's future or locked into the contours of "tradition," she offered a bellwether for perceptions of social change and the refashioning of gender in a queer context. The next section explores why these are not necessarily two layered or competing conceptions of time—linear versus cyclical, modernizing progress versus endless repetition, up out of the bars versus waiting for the butch within to emerge.[51] Memories, historical or otherwise, do not move so much backward (or forward) as in-

and-out, through and around, in a process through which forgetting becomes not just the flip side of remembering, but its price.[52]

How could any historical memory that proceeds toward modernity by way of ahistorical contrasts between now and then, us and them, do otherwise? When the body of the Old Butch recurs in "first bar stories" told by younger women, it is invariably as a practitioner without a partner. Although the Old Butch is widely understood to have participated in something called "roles" or "butch/femme," femmes are conspicuously absent from the narrative.[53] Ki-ki—a midcentury term for women who identified as neither femme nor butch—does not even register. Indeed, entire congeries of practices loosely denominated as "butch/femme" disappear from stories set in the allegedly androgynous 1970s, and with them, any cognizance that butch/femme bars persisted in many black and Latino neighborhoods throughout this period. The decade of the 1960s, with its unisex fashions, its demands for social justice and equality, manages to elude these stories altogether, the better to draw stark temporal contrasts.

There are no Old Freedom Marchers leaning against the bar, though in truth, by the time these stories were set, there may well have been. For that matter, there are no Aging Hippies, no Retired Department Store Clerks, no Veterans of El Movimiento, no one whose presumed biography in any way compares to the lives lived by my godmother or Trudy. These are not random absences, but absences structured by inequalities and by a narrative that bifurcates time into the forward-looking now versus days long gone, then proceeds to claim tomorrow for the teller.

The time claims built upon the edifice of embodiment, accordingly, occupy shaky historical ground: I honor you, replace you, displace you, hope never to replicate your travails. Looking at you, I see so much more clearly the superiority of my experiences, the greater opportunities I enjoy, the freedoms built into my relationships, the (place superlative here). All without hearing you speak. And thus it is with regret that I must hurry to thank you or dispatch you, claim the present for my own, because my gendering trumps your gendering. It is the best of times and the best of times . . . for women.

So are ideologies of modernity reproduced, not necessarily with reference to the wonders of now-suspect technologies or accumulated knowledge, but in the case of gender, on the back of that most "primordial" of disciplinary sites: the human body. So is gender constituted, not just through performance or divisions of labor or socialization, but through processes that route history through memory and memory through flesh. So does modernity shed its own histories, allowing women of subsequent generations to picture themselves moving toward a brighter, more equal, untrammeled future, without hearing the echoes of condescension and conquest in this formulation, without questioning its linearity of vision, without linking their time claims to globalization.

All this is perhaps not so very different from the way that my god-mother forgot her mother, the better to remember the hardships of her mother's life. To picture a mother who had roamed farther from home at thirteen than my godmother did in her first sixty-five years . . . well, that might have complicated, just a bit, the story line of progress. There is a certain poetic justice in the inability of later generations to picture my godmother and Trudy dressed to the nines for an evening out at the roller derby, calling for body slams against the boards, glorying in the flying elbows and shying away from the blood. These were not homebodies. They were bargoers without being bar dykes, working women whose labor gave them some sort of purchase (they thought) on days yet to come. Why should later generations have understood their sense of themselves as modern women laying claim to a future that they believed belonged to them, even if it meant leaving older relatives "behind"? After all, their own sisters and mothers had had little enough to say about the histories projected through vision and photography onto them.

The embodiment of historical memory precludes certain kinds of historical understandings, even as it reinforces the conviction of having a history and experiencing change. In this regard it matters very much that when my godmother recounted stopping with her friend for a drink after riding lessons, she remembered taking a seat in a booth, with nary an Old Butch in sight. Thirty or forty years later, a younger woman recounting the scene would likely have disappeared my godmother's companion and placed my godmother where, iconically, she should have been sitting: not in a booth, but at the bar.

These are significant and telling omissions, transpositions, that serve as a reminder of where the value of this excursion into the history of the imagined community lies: less in the accuracy of particular women's depictions than in the ways that embodiment can foster historical memory, and in so doing, reconfigure allegiances, engender identities, engage struggles over what shall count as betterment or equality, and influence what can convincingly be claimed for "the times." So, again, is gender constituted under conditions of modernity, via memories that are never illusory for all their entanglement in ideology and the construction of a now. Historical memory is materially productive, of gendered solidarities and local communities, of labor practices that invoke capitalisms fast or slow, of the many profits that accrue to fashion, of friendship, of nightlife, of migration under the sign of freedom. Each desire, each development, restyled or banished, in its turn, from a gendered awareness of a past.

The most common models of temporality in North America are either too linear or too cyclical to explain what happens as people forget, remember, forget to remember, remember to forget, remember that they have forgotten, and devise intricately collective ways to traverse time. A different sort of science metaphor is required to understand these temporal movements than pseudo-Darwinian evolution, the graduated ruler known as a timeline, or the Euclidean geometry that maps out life cycles in the two-dimensional space of a perpetually rotating circle. In the links explored here between historical memory, gender, and embodiment lies a clue. The bodies of those Old Butches have opened up a wormhole of sorts, a rent in the fabric of spacetime with the potential to turn analysts of gender into time travelers, depositing us somewhere, somewhen, at another end.

## MEMORY'S CRUCIBLE, TIME'S ARCHER

What does it mean to speak of embodied historical memory as a wormhole? Why should the gloomy character of the Old Butch, the icy warmth of sepia photographs, prove capable of transporting someone through time? And what kind of time is this that condenses memories, works its magic through contrast, freezes gender in order to reproduce it and register its forms of passage?

Exchanged in the telling of stories, these corporeal images do more than add bodies to an already expanding list of objects where memory seeks refuge: landscape, monuments, living history museums, and the like. Ada Louise Huxtable has rightly critiqued the tendency to treat commodities such as photographs as historical talismans, calling this approach "the preoccupation of a materialistic society that values objects too highly and believes that they can ensure memory."[54] In the hands and mouths of the narrators considered here, however, bodies give gendered memories not so much an assurance of their own transmission as a part in the production of social relations. The best friend who searches your eyes in an old photograph, the regulars stationed at the bar, lend their bodies to the making of both historical memories and identities. Yet these memories are not random, these identities far from abstract, called as they are into being through historical circumstance, by storytellers enchanted with a modernity inextricable from capitalism's many promises.

My godmother's rotary lawn mower gives way to the Briggs & Stratton engine, pantyhose replaces silk stockings, mass-produced brands of beer acquire new symbolism when ordered in preference to newly introduced microbrews. In each case, it becomes increasingly difficult to live *as* a woman, whatever rendition of woman, however one genders herself "woman," without access to things bought and sold. In each case, she is hailed as a particular kind of woman by the emergence of niche marketing. She may be a menthol smoker, Marlboro smoker, secondhand-smoke-abjuring air-filter-purchasing nonsmoker, all available choices raced, classed, *and* gendered for the North American market. In each case, too, there has been little enough change in the average relative purchasing power of the jobs that give women the means to buy. Real wages fell for much of the late twentieth century. Cashier remained the fastest-growing occupation—a woman's occupation, a poor woman's occupation, quite often a woman of color's occupation—as the century turned the corner.

Yet women are not just the prisoners of ideology, consumerist or otherwise. Here is where the creativity of their stories and the metaphor of the wormhole come into play. Like the skulls that appear in Renaissance European paintings, bodies that screen historical memories offer up memento mori: a humbling reminder to the viewer that she has to die. This accounts for their apparently cyclical effect on some narrators, who came to see in the Old Butch a portent of aging and a less than salutary future. As mobile screens, the same bodies can also serve as memento of another kind: a reminder to narrators that they have to live and an invitation to reflect upon how or why.[55]

In a very different way than the zero moments discussed in the second chapter, or the repetition embedded in performance, embodied historical memories call attention to the manner in which gender depends upon time for its production. Zero moments involve movements in and out of classification, movements whose occurrence cannot be explained except with reference to specific historical conditions and power. Performativity theories of gender arose in the birthplace of "fast capitalism" as the shift to flexible accumulation rendered the repetitive character of gendered displays evident, as it were, from a distance. Embodied historical memories emphasize that with contemporary capitalism, where ideologies of modernity continue to thrive, to gender is to historicize. To historicize, however oversimplified and even ahistorical the resulting time frames (now, then) may become in their application to families, communities, friends.

But of course modernity and repetition are not the only temporalities on offer. Time claims open possibilities for "locating" market-individuated selves within a wealth of temporalities, the continuous cycle and the past-present-future line of progress being only the most celebrated.[56] To treat the bodies of Old Butches, mothers, and like-mothers as a wormhole is to broach the possibility of other forms of time travel.

In physics a wormhole describes a fleeting passage that opens at sub-microscopic levels in the quantum foam, a seething, frothing particle brew in which space manifests probabilities for different curvatures and shapes but has no definitive structure. Quantum foam is everywhere, in black holes no less than bodies. A much-debated theoretical possibility would allow people to enter a wormhole in order to travel to another region of space-time, an alternate universe, if you like.[57] Although mathematical calculations can describe a traversable wormhole, it would require vast amounts of energy to send a human body through such a minuscule passage. Interestingly enough, the mathematical description of a wormhole brings us back to the concepts of zero and paradox that open this book, because "a wormhole is a paradox caused by a zero in the equations of general relativity."[58] In practice, there may never be a device capable of generating the so-called exotic matter required to enlarge and hold open the hole long enough for a body to move through.

Applied to the less literal forms of time travel described here, however, wormholes open onto alternate universes on a regular basis. Substitute the temporal-visual metaphor of the wormhole for the strictly visual metaphor of the screen and you arrive in another timeplace each time you juxtapose your body with an older body in stories that describe family relations, community relations, in terms of changes in gendered practice. As you tunnel your way into the lived experience attributed (however wrongly) to that older woman, your understanding of your own experience shifts. This is not because the relationship between you and Mom, or your buddies and Ruby, or your baby and Aunt Lucia *is* a wormhole in even a metaphorical sense of the term. Wormholes, like the narration of embodied memories, are not stable enough for that. This temporary, temporal opening connects bodies to memory to time, and in the process, opens up an ephemeral opportunity to glimpse how the workings of time relate to the workings of power.

Should you traverse the wormhole only to find yourself in modern times, you are likely to have made your way by establishing a series of historical contrasts, much like my godmother, her peers, and the "new kids" at the bars. History itself is one sign of the modern, its concomitant the historicization of memory.[59] Within modernity the measure of a life—to be sure, a life regularly evaluated and surveyed—can only be taken with respect to its *difference* from elders who come to figure as predecessors. For modernity, as Homi Bhabha notes, cannot be narrated without "the future anterior," the tensive notions of time lag and supersession that incorporate "a projective past."[60] Not all futures lie ahead.

Historically locating the production of time and memory thus yields a very different account of the relationship between memory and family life than the one described for sociology by Maurice Halbwachs. For Halbwachs, "the" family played a critical part in generating constructions of the past, both because it provided a context in which formative experiences occurred and because it passed down interpretations of those experiences to succeeding generations. Contrary to this model of memory, which Halbwachs dubbed "mnemonic socialization," the evidence examined in this chapter argues that memories are not packaged entities subject to inheritance, possession, loss, or transmission.[61]

Historical memories are not things. They emerge from social practices that take distinctive forms under distinctive historical conditions. The practice of using bodies to draw contrasts between generations, for example, is not a timeless universal process for producing gender. Quite the contrary: Generation-based contrasts supply a framework for the production of gender *when and where ideologies of modernity prevail*. It is not simply that modernity represents a break with some past, as Anthony Giddens contends. It is also that discontinuity (by way of contrast) becomes a technique for establishing time claims that give shape to gender and perpetuate the very ideologies of modernity from which they draw their strength. Like capitalism, the process is expansionary.

Older accounts of modernization, like older accounts of physics, speak of time's arrow, stipulating a time that travels in one direction only. A unidirectional flow of time might seem to be a prerequisite for histories and chronologies of any sort. But embodied historical memories travel more in the manner of a closed timelike curve, the arrow looping through four or more dimensions until you "arrive back" at the place from which you started, your manner of dwelling in this place altered by the journey itself. This is neither linearity nor circularity in the way that Euclid understood it, nor are all their dimensions accessible to vision.

For all the discussion that has focused on time's arrow, very little has converged upon time's archer.[62] When people author time claims, they send those arrows flying in many directions, some imperceptible, some begging the very question of time. There can be no time claim without a time frame: history, infinity, chronology, generation, era, future/past. Implicit in these claims are modes of temporality (regressing, moving ahead, modern traditions, coming back around) and morality (stolen futures, lost generation, better days). In relativizing fashion, time claims tether me, you, and our brother's keeper to our respective timespots (1990s butch, twenty-first-century woman, follower of the old ways, old-fashioned). Time claims can even naturalize or denaturalize the very modes of reckoning embedded within them. My godmother's sister Elsie was partial to that most North American of genres, the jeremiad. "I feel sorry for you kids," she used to say, "growing up in a world where your parents don't have time to make you toys, a world where you have to lock your doors." No borrowing from neighbor ladies, no scissors grinders crying out for sales, no doctors making house calls, no feeding the hungry out that now securely barred back gate. A much bleaker assessment of the times than the one offered by her sister, though equally linear. An entirely different take on the politics and economics of change.

As time's archers, people like my godmother and her sister work creatively to embody memory and the time traveling it entails. Within narrative the most celebrated time travel paradoxes dissolve. Could you go back in time to murder your own grandparents? Of course, and stay to resurrect them, as well. In the process, time claims not only help produce gender (race, nation, class . . .) in the form of identity; they may also weave a political stance into the fabric of memory itself.

Nancy Scheper-Hughes has characterized the recent proliferation of debates about memory as a grand romance "with remorse and with reparation . . . a master narrative of the late twentieth century, as individuals and entire nations struggle to overcome the legacies of suffering ranging from rape and domestic violence to state-sponsored dirty wars and 'ethnic cleansing.'"[63] Renato Rosaldo writes of the "imperialist nostalgia" that afflicts colonists of urban neighborhoods, rural fields, and overseas settlements who mourn the passing of the way of life that their arrival has destroyed. "We speak so much of memory," observes Pierre Nora, "because there is so little of it left." Then there are the elderly Spanish peasants, economically marginalized by government industrialization programs and "prosperity consciousness," whom Ruth Behar found to be "plagued, not by nostalgia, but by a sense of having lived anachronistically for too long." Romance, nostalgia, anachronism: In those stories about what your mother could or couldn't do, did or didn't live to see, lie your own constructed freedoms, but also the work of advertisers, corporations, and the state.[64]

Family histories and community histories, as well as the culture industry, can also foster what the cultural theorist Lauren Berlant terms "paramnesias," in which images "organize consciousness, not by way of explicit propaganda, but by replacing and simplifying memories people actually have with image traces of political experience about which people can have political feelings that link them to other citizens and to patriotism." Such a trend is only exacerbated when global industries design products to elicit identities and then encourage people to signify identities through commodities, the dialectic of niche marketing that can sell you back "your" past.[65] Who can resist the MasterCard designed to celebrate family/ethnic heritage, festooned (as appropriate) with an image of kente cloth or China's Great Wall?

The answer is, of course, that many can and do resist, sometimes in ways that lead to engaging contradictions. "Memoricide" is a word coined to describe actions such as the deliberate shelling of national libraries, the forced relocation (kidnapping) of Romani and Native American children to boarding schools where they had their stories and languages systematically beaten out of them. Memoricide is a rhetorical weapon coined to fight back.[66] Without a rhetoric for political mobilization, language reacquisition programs and library rebuilding programs scramble for funds. Important as these initiatives are, they often address their goals with a vocabulary of possession, theft, and loss, the very metaphors that proved so inadequate to describe my godmother's "confusion" as she aged.[67]

Treating memory as a disembodied possession makes it easier to recognize memoricide in the form of government-sponsored assimilation programs. Treating memory as a disembodied possession makes it harder to recognize memoricide in the kind of paramnesias detailed by Berlant. Killing memory with the making of memory is a less obvious method, but no less effective for it.

Little did my godmother know—despite, or because of, her own time claims—that she was about to assume a backward place in a chronology called women's liberation. Little did middle-aged women in the bars know that they were on their way to living in a timeless past called then. In the impressions my young cousins and I traded at family gatherings, my godmother became "so queer you can see her coming," the complexities of her desire reduced to a case of "denial." The house painting that she understood as an escape from the constricted interiors occupied by her elder sisters led us to pity her for being locked into a "role." We asked why she never cooked, never asked what it meant for a woman in 1931 to have the wherewithal to navigate a car. We managed to forget the histories of our own delight as we worked side by side with her in the tomato patch, water sliding down taut green skins into cupped pairs of hands, back into the sweltering ground.

Far be it from us in our circumscribed wisdom to get trapped into the lives endured by our mothers, godmothers, and their friends. Wars, environmental destruction, race riots, and the gutting of poverty programs aside, weren't we the lucky ones. These days, in America, girls can grow up to be whatever they want to be. At least that's what the ads tell us. These days, in America, the New Butch lives better than ever. At least that's what the ads tell us. Like the younger women Lisa Rofel interviewed in China, however differently positioned with respect to colonial histories, we did not cast off modernity so much as "recast . . . its deferred enchantments." Like the students in Gerald Early's course on the American novel, traveling through a racialized, sexualized museum called the past, we worked hard "to reconstruct ourselves out of the remains of our ancestors, ourselves in another guise."[68]

As we learned to pick up the bow and deliver time claims in our own right, we too used historical memory to gender our way to freedom. Time traveling, unraveling, yoked history to gender to raced and classed bodies with a conviction that kept us from apprehending, quite, the moments when memory (like gender) zeroed out, the privilege of living long enough to narrate. The paths taken by our trajectories, once mapped out by Newton, entirely predictable to the eye, seemed to loop, twist, vanish, move in and out of sight. Our target: a future that was not exactly waiting, nor yet properly past. A rain of arrows falling just short of globalization.

© Kath Weston

# CHAPTER FIVE

# THE GLOBAL ECONOMY NEXT TIME: WHEN GENDERS ARE NOT ENOUGH

Instead of being honest and saying, "Whether you like it or not, there's a new global order and we, the elites and the multinationals, will decide who eats and who doesn't," they say, "There are inexorable laws of the free market we must all adhere to. And don't worry, if the free market is left to perform its miracles, all these nasty social problems will be solved". . . . Today, [the rich nations'] arms of oppression and domination are not [just] guns, but calculators.

—*Benedita da Silva*

He can't look at the moon without calculating the distance.
He can't look at a tree without calculating the firewood.
He can't look at a painting without calculating the price.
He can't look at a menu without calculating the calories.
He can't look at a man without calculating the advantage.
He can't look at a woman without calculating the risk.

—*Eduardo Galeano,*
*"Window on a Successful Man"*

So you thought you could change the world. Or not. Somehow you managed to get on your feet after they released you from prison, the army, an ivy league college. You spent evenings volunteering at a women's health clinic, couldn't volunteer because you had to work three jobs to make it on what they pay a nurse's aide, stayed home in front of the television, worried more about your investments than your health. You organized a neighborhood association, marched for affordable housing, dieted, looked for food in Dumpsters, applied for a credit card, made scathing comments about immigrants and handouts. You had a nightmare in which your trust fund disappeared. You never dreamed of having a trust fund. You decided to skip the march to put in some overtime, because you could use the money and besides, you never know.

Saturday you told your girlfriend you couldn't believe what a bargain you got on your sweater, without ever once thinking about what the price tag meant for the life of the woman who sewed the cloth. No, wait: The very first thing you thought when you saw that sweater marked down to such a ridiculous price was how some poor woman across the border must be getting paid too little to make it. Then you bought the sweater anyway, because after all it's been a cold winter, and what would leaving it lying there do to help its maker. With or without that sweater, you gender (/race/class/ . . . ) yourself each time you dress to meet the light of day.

In time you've grown older, wiser, realized the magnitude of the problems, the futility of trying to change matters so complicated and so vast. Or not. And all the while, ignoring heartbreak and the best of intentions, the world has gone right along. Changing.

## A MEDITATION ON CHANGE

Like contingency, change is a modern concept. Change doesn't amount to much of anything unless you propose to calculate the distance you think you've come. In this sense, change is a perfect vehicle for (space)time travel under conditions of capitalist accumulation. It uses all the tools of inventory, advertising, and accountants. Incomes raised by so much, employment dropping by how much, bodily proportions measured and averaged, acre-feet of water measured and redistributed, plots of land surveyed, plots of land enclosed, coils of barbed wire produced, cans of beverages sold, numbers of women incarcerated, numbers of women freed from debt bondage.

And there's the rub. Activism also traffics in change. For what are social movements if not a social change project? The calculating temporality of change guides those who have taken up grassroots organizing, those who have spent their lives in the service of corporations, those who have sacrificed years of income to study gender relations, and everyone in between. Gender studies, for its part, advertises its accomplishments using thoroughly time-ridden notions such as fresh, new, subversion, today, and a moving something called a cutting edge. Nourished by windswept roots in the women's, GLBT, civil rights, and human rights movements, this emerging discipline remains enamored of originality (primary, earliest, first), if not the absolute and measurable advance.

Change is another of the formative time claims that operate right here, right now to constitute gender. People who have to wend their way through the latest in capitalism often learn to produce gender as a constant that must be constantly reconfigured, usually in that old direction called progress. Like my godmother and her successors in the bars, they exercise a historical imagination to identify presumed contrasts between generations, claiming a past in order to supersede it and gendering themselves in the process. Gender relations can then appear as a given even as they are seduced into new forms by states, corporations, universities, and military establishments that protest their helplessness in the face of a temptress called—you guessed it—Change.

Sometimes social relations change least when they proclaim an interest in change. During the 2001 U.S. incursion into Afghanistan after the bombing of the World Trade Center, terrorism may have been the headliner, but making the world safer for Afghani women ran a close second in attempts to rally support for the cause. It is a story as old as colonialism, this business of pointing to ("brown") women's oppression as reason enough to intervene.[1] Wives burned (*sati*) in parts of India? Who could blame the British for establishing the Raj to show "the natives" how to live and gender properly? (Who, indeed.) Woman as justification for the indefensible, a yardstick for progress: a metaphor of change that invests heavily in measurement and calculation. During the bombing campaign against the Taliban government, major media in the United States portrayed Afghanistan as a Stone Age nation whose fighting forces hid out in caves. U.S. troops were lauded for their futuristic technology, with no mention of the fact that the United States also stations personnel and weapons in cave complexes deep in the mountains of its own country. Quite apart from the open question of whether Afghani women will or will not be better off under a new regime, what is striking is the historical continuity in the way that gender and time figure in these representations.[2] The nation sends its forces into another country in the name of modernization, betterment, and change (especially for women), but the time claims themselves haven't changed much in two hundred years.

When it comes to politics, change runs the gamut. Like other turn-of-this-century time claims, change can be used to seek reform (it's time for a change), to pitch products (go buy the latest), to authorize (we have always been here: no change), and to aggrandize (more! more!). Change is not a process apart from us that happens to or through us. Considered as a particular sort of time claim, rather than an occurrence, change disseminates a way to grasp the times, in the dual sense of apprehension and acquisition.

Of course, change is not the only possible claim that can be made upon time and even change adopts specific guises with specific consequences for the production of gender. The guise of modernity, explored in the last chapter, is only one, though one of no little importance. The promise of some future liberation, explored earlier in the book, is another. As for the present, nothing conjures up visions—yes, visions—of change like the mention of globalization.

Although globalization proceeds for the present, it entails the fantasy of a future. An expanding capitalism sets up infinities of need, making need "the manner in which this future appears, as the organic form of expectation."[3] With something new on offer, all the time, who can ever have enough? With opportunities to earn currency few and far between in so many locations, small wonder that women recruited by transnational corporations into factories that pay less than it costs to live acquiesce because they need a job. If time be an archer, then under conditions of globalization, need takes aim and directs the archer's shot.

## MAKING CAPITALISM FAST: THE OLD TOOLKIT

If this book has a larger purpose, it is to encourage the development of tools of perception designed for apprehending gender in the time of the Now.[4] That time, this Now, is the shifting set of politicoeconomic relationships and power imbalances loosely called globalization. That time, this Now, involves great quantities of material privilege for some, a hard-scrabble fight over minuscule amounts of resources for others. It is a time of great suffering and great wealth. Globalization not only means many things to many people, it can mean very different things for people differently situated with respect to gender(/race/class/nation/ . . . ).

For this Now, and perhaps any now, visually oriented tools for analyzing gender relations have proved inadequate. These well-worn tools capture the restrictions, the allure, and sometimes even the plasticity associated with gendering in the shadow of global capital, but they cannot hope to deal with the histories and movements of capital that lead to rampant commodification. To better grasp the limitations of these tools and the promise of the more time-sensitive concepts developed in the preceding chapters, it helps to have a look at the old gender studies toolkit.

The old gender studies toolkit is filled with instruments for understanding and overturning stasis. Rummage around a bit, brush aside a few wrenches, and you come upon social constructs, roles, norms, scripts, numbered genders, technologies of inventory and accounting. Use these tools to loosen a few of the screws that hold the current social order in place and resistance is supposed to ensue. If you believe that you are trapped in a static something called a role, you can hope to break out. If you think you have learned how to gender from a script, you can live to write an alternative play. If you know that gender takes shape in and through other key social relations (nation, race), it's harder to accept colorless generalities about Women versus Men. If you understand gender as a social construct, heavy lifting no longer seems intrinsically feminine or masculine, just as something besides nature dictates the work reserved for warriors or merchants or slaves. If you grew up assuming there can be but two genders, the idea of three genders, much less intersexuality, should come as a bit of a shock. Why go back to living in the same old way after that? Inequalities that might once have seemed inevitable, perhaps innate, begin to look like nothing of the sort.

One might suspect that such tools for overturning stasis would come in handy for an analysis of commodification, and so they have. Commodification is a particularly lucrative form of reification. As such, commodification yields ground before anything that can demonstrate that all this buying and selling, all this fixing a value upon time and persons and things, is not set in stone. Under other circumstances, the worth of a woman's labor might be calculated very differently, or not subject to calculation at all. No toolkit is complete without a hammer, yet a hammer to shatter the frozen visage of reification does not a toolkit make. And these particular hammers—norms, constructs, roles—have the disadvantage of helping to reify that which they seek to shatter. Efforts to demystify gender represent an important step but a baby step for time travelers en route to the Now.

What else is needed (infinities of need aside)? Conceptual tools that can relate the production of gender to shifts in global capital and the ideologies that sustain them. An ability to "see" that gender relations could be otherwise tells little about what sustains them, much less how to *make* them otherwise through anything other than a leap of imagination. The frozen aspect of gender may yield ground before an analysis that rails at stasis, but it cannot give way, because gender becomes commodified through relations of inequality and economies of power that will not bend to knowledge alone. Quite the contrary: Those very economies are often in the business of producing knowledge.

Worse yet, because tools of overturn such as social constructionism and role theory are directed at stasis, they tend to underestimate—radically—the investment of a globalizing economy in change. Read discussions of gender from the 1970s through 1990s (and sometimes still today), and you will walk away with an image of feminists lining up against some solid, intractable foe: if not constructs or roles, then perhaps something more systematic: patriarchy, hegemony, capitalism, imperialism, colonialism, domination, not to mention globalization itself. In these accounts, change is a promise belonging to a future, not a time claim capable of being incorporated into visions of equality and corporate rule alike.

After decades of anthropological and historical research, few disputed that tremendous variability could exist in the number of recognized genders, conceptions of femininities and masculinities, and the activities considered men's or women's work. What they couldn't understand was why inequalities tied to gender should have persisted after being exposed as rather arbitrary arrangements that were anything but natural. As cultural inventions, they should have been easy enough to change. Or should they?

One culprit implicated in the confusion was the early feminist distinction between sex and gender, which associated sex with nature and gender with whatever culture might make of biology. Sex gave bodies musculature; gender decreed that only certain bodies should develop those muscles. Gender, not sex, opened the possibility for muscles to become a signifier of difference in some times and places but not others.

The sex/gender distinction seemed an excellent tool to pull out when someone invoked biological differences to justify inequality. Given the different cultural possibilities, what right could there be to bar women from construction sites or boardrooms? To deny African-American women fiduciary responsibility? To relegate working-class Latinas to janitorial service or following the harvest?

The sex/gender distinction was less well suited for understanding an age of genetic engineering in which biology could be altered in any laboratory or surgical suite. Sex/gender pictured nature (sex) as something permanent, indelible, a past-present-future bedrock atop which gender (culture) could construct its palaces. (Of course, were biology nearly so constant, there would be no hormone therapy, no cloning, no cancer.[5]) Gender, for its part, looked easily mutable because the sex/gender distinction formulated gender primarily in terms of culturally prescribed arrangements. But as we have seen, much more than "culture" is at work in the production of gender relations. For one thing, there is the global economy. For another, there is power.

As it turns out, the taken-for-granted in life is not always the province of fixed beliefs that it is the privilege of critique to dislodge. Gendered inequalities remain intractable not because they are immovable or solid—if that were the case, gender theorists could stop looking for different tools and simply hammer away with renewed vigor. Rather, the impression of solidity in this particular Now is achieved through movement, or at least the illusion of constant motion. In the global economy, corporations trumpet the newest, latest, most time-efficient products, anything to keep consumers moving, which is to say, buying. Employees hardly have time to think, much less organize, in jobs where one now does the work of two. Ready for a change? Corporations can handle that as well. Most companies will be more than happy to sell you the pleasures of resistance along with your next "think different" computer or running shoes that promise to distance you from the pack. There is a reason they call it fast capitalism.[6]

All this motion, however illusory, implies the passage of time. By the late twentieth century, feminists had begun to sense that tools for overturning stasis must prove inadequate, and not only because liberation had never occurred. They attempted to incorporate time into their analyses, primarily through appeals to process and change. Almost overnight, references to gender roles transmuted into "changing gender roles." Fixed norms could no longer compete with normativity, the new emphasis on the context for their enforcement and reproduction. Gender began to operate as a verb, with countless millions now busy "gendering" and "doing gender." (Significantly, this action-oriented emphasis cropped up in other realms of identity politics, where people were found to be "doing race" and "doing class" as well.[7]) By the time the century turned, as we have seen, gender had dissolved for many into performativity, repeated, repeated, repeated, until it sure *looked* like gender extended all the way down.

Treating gender as a process and a verb—something performed, figured, normalized, accomplished, done—represented an important corrective to the earlier emphasis on fixed norms and static constructs. Although performativity and the change-driven variant of role theory were hardly compatible, they were united by the importance they granted to vision and movement. They were united, as well, by the limitations associated with any documentary approach to time.

Never use a hammer to unscrew a cabinet; never use a screwdriver for the job a reciprocating saw can pull off. These are all fine tools, but it makes no sense to select them without reference to the task at hand. In order to understand how the time of this global economy, today's Now, travels through gender relations, it is not enough to put gender back into time and time back into gender. Tools that emphasize process, theories that acknowledge (but do not explain) how performances or roles "change," can only document change, or assume it.

Tools directed at stasis, such as constructs, and tools that emphasize motion, such as performativity, might seem to be opposed, yet with respect to power they can have very similar effects. (Depending, of course, on how these tools are used.) To understand why, consider one final scientific analogy. In the seventeenth century, Christiaan Huygens performed a series of experiments with timepieces. He discovered that two pendulum clocks placed side by side could be coordinated so that one timepiece ticked when the other tocked. The phenomenon is called synchronized oscillation. Both clocks move, to be sure, but in such a way that the tick falls atop the tock, reinforcing the basic rhythm. Even though a tock is not a tick, even though each pendulum occupies a different and opposite point on the trajectory at the moment of the beat, the effect is to accentuate regularity.

Tools of stasis and tools of movement in gender theory oscillate in synchrony when they make capitalism fast, both by battening down capitalism's productive relations and accelerating its effects. In the fixing and in the subversion, these tools are capable of perpetuating assumptions that entrench rather than dislodge gendered inequalities. Attempts by late-twentieth-century theorists to embrace "queer," for example, in hopes of denaturalizing older terms such as "gay" and "homosexual," led to some unanticipated outcomes. Queer, defined as difference-from, still gravitated toward the old stomping grounds of gender and sexuality, despite arguments to be made for race, class, and citizenship as equally meaningful loci of difference.[8] One could argue that "queer" has had the unintended effect of granting an illusory coherence and stability to that which people imagine themselves to differ from, whether it be norms, roles, that mythical beast called the mainstream, or their mothers.

We have already seen how the celebration of ambiguously gendered bodies took issue with a body count of numbered genders, how performativity theory enlisted commodities to illustrate its points, how ideologies of modernity and consumption encouraged women to gender themselves by way of contrast with their elders. Even or perhaps especially at the moment of defiance, each anchors in place (but does not place in time) fixed concepts such as genders and norms.

## GENDER IN REAL TIME

Analyzing gender in the "real time" of the Now requires something more. It means recognizing that standardization has a history and political economy of its own. Norm, script, construct, role: These are all standardized measures as well as analytic tools. The same might be said of the concept of fixed and enumerated genders. They are rulers of a sort that people use to judge whether someone measures up, but also whether an act of transgression has found its target. They are calibrated to police borders and to mark off border crossings. Realizing this, it makes no sense to say that gender norms have differed from time to time and place to place. In order to understand gender in the context of a global economy, one has to understand the norm as a social invention and a standardization device carried across the world by cargo ships, radio waves, planes.

The regularizing technologies of biopower described by Michel Foucault—census, height and weight tables, handwriting drills—ushered in an era of perpetual comparison and calculation. Neat penmanship, the weight gain expected of a healthy baby: Such judgments have computation and regulation embedded within them. Interesting, then, that the introduction of standardization devices in social theory such as "customs" and "mores" coincided with the fight to establish national manufacturing standards in an effort to expand markets and inaugurate mass production. Uniform screw threads and time zones for railroads in the nineteenth century, standardized electrical current in the twentieth, telecommunications protocols for the twenty-first: Are these not of a piece with the uniformity attributed to a norm?

By emphasizing the political economy of time travel, this book has submitted the propensity for counting (genders) and calculating (gendered difference) to new scrutiny. The result is a very different approach to time than the one that backgrounds history in order to focus on the practice and process of doing gender. Why limit time travel to the circles of performance, when attention to the global relocation of manufacturing helps explain the popularity of performativity itself, with its industrial rhythms of repetition? Why appeal to history as though it were something that just occurs, when a wormhole offers access to the jumps that memory makes as bodies become a touchstone for the production of gender? Why not travel "back" through histories of trade to find a zero that can be used to understand the violence recently directed at ambiguous bodies? Why not explore how commodities and standardization have come to figure in gender theory, rather than appealing to norms and nail polish by way of explanation? Think tempus quo rather than status quo.

Along the way, I have forged conceptual tools for working with temporal aspects of gender in the time of the Now. These are not tools that can elucidate change per se. As it happens, they are tools better suited to the investigation of change as a time claim that relies upon practices of counting and accounting. Like the zero, like the scientific metaphors of wormholes and evolution and synchronized oscillation, the time claim is a tool. There are many other instruments that might be right for the job of bringing a political economy of time to gender studies. And what would any respectable toolkit be without a few borrowed tools, such as historical memory? The point is to study gender as a social, material relation in time, not some already commodified thing.

Since the days of the Silk Route, since the even earlier period of Buddhist maritime trade, the earth has witnessed many rounds of what could be called globalization. In the latest episode, capital flows and speculation cast a long shadow over trade.[9] Women lost their eyesight making computer chips in special export zones, Japanese salarymen with lifetime employment suddenly found themselves on the streets, young people sought hope in imported music, Brazilian charcoal workers despaired of paying off their debts, male-to-female transsexuals found it impossible to survive on a "woman's wage." Their lives will never be what they would have been without globalization.

Likewise for Colombian women who succumbed to pesticides growing flowers for Northern tables, Canadian men with declining sperm counts, Bedouin daughters who bought lingerie to scandalize their elders, babies resuscitated by doctors working with transnational organizations, Filipinas who surrendered their passports to work in Hong Kong as maids. Not to mention the multitudes who lost their life savings in currency devaluations, families of modest means that could unexpectedly travel the world, mothers who risked prison to buy groceries with bad checks, children medically assigned a sex, women who banged cooking pots in the street to demand water or onions.

"People's experience of time has changed in the new global economy," writes Ida Susser. Poor women, who shuttle back and forth from household to jobs to service providers, must arrive punctually for appointments, then hurry up and wait. Middle-class women, pressured to reconcile the long hours of professional jobs with more than their share of household chores, approach the day as a time-management project. Time becomes another marker of difference and inequality.[10]

Whether or not experiences of time have changed (how exactly would one measure?), it's clear that different claims are being made about time. In the process, time in turn becomes a rationale for making different claims upon bodies, for treating some bodies much better than others. These time claims are more than a bid for individual authority, seized upon by you or me, my godmother or Trudy, to establish ourselves as denizens of the best era (for women) ever. All time claims carry traces of institutional power.

One advantage of the time claim as an analytic tool is the way it situates power relations at the heart of any analysis. Consider the gendered implications of the time claims that permeate descriptions of globalization. For Anthony Giddens, global capitalism binds time and space: Every international investment represents a hope for the future, every bank account a promise.[11] More popularly, the global economy is said to produce time/space compression, a metaphor for living that integrates the best features of the garbage compactor into the global village. What can the identification of these time claims, as such, add to an understanding of gender relations? Spacetime may seem to compress for the woman sitting down to watch satellite TV, but certainly not for nonelite women in areas where corporations have commandeered the water supply and logged the forests. If anything, when those women rise at four A.M. to walk in search of firewood, the hours and kilometers have expanded. Likewise, when a "tribal" (indigenous) woman chains herself to her home in protest as the waters rise in the Narmada Valley behind India's Sardar Sarovar dam project, international investment binds the future to her doorstep with a deadly threat, not a promise.[12] She is up to her neck in historical materialism, not the cultural materialism of performativity theory or the faux-evolutionary materialism of your auntie's socialist feminism.

In the time claims associated with progress, the commodification of gender, time, and culture are often of a piece. Attention, busy women: If you buy this brand of deodorant, that brand of frozen tamales, you can save time, even make time! The pitch is all too familiar. Once commodified, time can be stolen, owned, and hoarded. Marx was not the only one who understood the implications of selling labor power by the hour, the week, the day. In Michael Ende's novel *Momo,* time thieves appear as men in gray suits who entice people to deposit spare minutes in the Timesaving Bank: "People never seemed to notice that, by saving time, they were losing something else. . . . And the more people saved, the less they had."[13]

For the global economy next time, genders will not be enough, nor their subversion. Not when toothpaste manufacturers retail gender in a variety of raced and classed forms, right alongside ambiguity. Not when activists join investors in claiming all the world for change.

## THE SMIRK OF THE NOW

Welcome to twenty-first-century North America, where even time has an attitude. For over a hundred pages, we have traveled through time in an attempt to come to terms with gendering in the time of the Now. Stretching our cramped limbs and stepping down from the starship, we emerge into a time that not only *is* now: It *glorifies* the now. Live for the present, self-help books advise. One day at a time, alcohol recovery programs exhort. *Carpe diem* and all that. Where's the best place in the world to be? Here. What's the best time in the world to be born? Now. This now does not appear to be neutral. It wears a smirk.

It would be a grave mistake to equate Walter Benjamin's time of the Now with the now that wears a smirk. The time of the Now grants political economy a tempo. The smirk of the now falls right into line with ideologies of modernity, perpetuating them rather than reflecting upon them. Exaltation of the now can be just as problematic as any genderless utopia or remembered past. For whose profit, at what expense, does the now curry such favor?

The now, so construed, finds sustenance in the marketing of a certain hip cynicism. The wink of the advertiser to the viewing audience goes along with the wink that says we know it's performance all the way down, but this just confirms that we're already in the know.[14] Our gender essentialisms (if we have them) are better than your essentialisms because they are at best strategic. No matter that this elitism sets up inequities of the very sort we disparage. And so smirkers fall into the illusion that with an understanding of gender constructs—or for that matter, zero moments—comes the capacity to constitute myself, as a bounded self, in any way I like. With a wink and a pat on the head, or a wink and a sneer, many North Americans despair of doing very much at all about gendered inequalities, when they can perceive them. They are not alone, of course. Across what used to be called the Third World, people are asking how to create a future in the absence of a narrative of liberation, without some "epic emancipatory story of total overcoming."[15]

It is never enough to know. Speaking of the daily indignities inflicted on African Americans by white people who ought to know better, James Baldwin observed in *The Fire Next Time*: "Many of them, indeed, know better, but, as you will discover, people find it very difficult to act on what they know. To act is to be committed, and to be committed is to be in danger."[16]

But it can help to know. It can help to know that a genderless world is now and here, not in some far-off revolutionary utopia or down some corporate-paved road. It can help to know that people have been looking in the wrong place for an exit. That's precisely it: looking, instead of also attending to less visual, less durable transits. In the nations that direct this global economy, gender zeros out on a regular basis as bodies are called in and out of classification. "Unsexed" becomes the occasional absence in anyone's life. During that flash of an instant when a person becomes unsexed, gender temporarily passes away, rather than bringing the curtain down on some world-historical stage. Zero, *sunya*, *sifr*—neither existence nor nonexistence—characterizes the briefest of intervals when the ability to "place" someone comes undone. Gender relations in the era of global capitalism: constantly vanishing, never quite gone.

So if "social change" is your business and you want to "get there," it's worth your while to attend to what's already here. The zero that is unsexed holds open a place for regrouping in the wake of those moments when things come undone. Even the historical conditions under which gender disappears are fleeting. The timing of this fascination with ambiguity, the reasons that one body rather than another becomes subject to interrogation, can be explained only with reference to power relations in the time of the Now. And the possibilities that emerge from the flux have everything to do with conditions that are in our power to organize or transform. No reason, then, to indulge in what Bruce Robbins calls "a radical refusal of all imperfection and, with it, of all action."[17] No reason to sacrifice the many shades of skin to a color-blind sense of justice. No reason to pit solidarity against difference.

Zero is not a concept for all time. It is a concept for *this* time, along with, perhaps, some few others. Like the time claim, it opens up a time-space for a politics, but not without its own historical debts. There is sweet irony in taking up one of the signs that has been central to capital's expansion and turning it to other ends.

Like other tools and technologies, the zero is not intrinsically liberatory and carries no inherent politics. The same might be said for counting. Counting is a technique that can be wielded in different historical circumstances by different hands to different ends. We have seen how the practice of counting multiple genders revived the troubling rhetoric of the European voyages of "discovery" and conquest. We have also seen how counting genders can reinforce certain habits of calculation and hierarchical ordering that are very much in accord with commodification. Commodities have their pleasures, but treating gender relations as though they played out at some point-of-sale can have untoward consequences.

In this growth economy, writes Jonathan Rowe, "The real economy—the one that sustains us—has diminished. All that has grown is the need to buy commoditized substitutes for things we used to have for free."[18] Cooking and romance come in packages. Repairs appear with a bill attached, rather than in the form of your cousin. Corporations sell our most intimate identities back to us as trademarks at a fixed price. When an accountant adds up the profits, she will employ a very different use of counting than, say, counting the breath(s) in meditation. Then again, in these times, the counting of the breath, too, might be marketed in the form of a meditation retreat for a tidy sum.

Meanwhile counting is deeply embedded in understandings of how to achieve equality, gendered and otherwise. Abolitionists railed against the constitutional calculus that judged a slave three-fifths of a man.[19] Fractions continue to be used, along with the concept of blood quantum, to qualify citizens as Native American. (Debates within and among indigenous nations persist as to the merits of this Euro-American practice.) Women earn less for every dollar paid to a man, but who's counting? What David Scott has called "political principle of number" partitions electorates into majorities and minorities.[20] Governments that wage war refuse to report the numbers of enemy casualties; groups working for social justice attempt to hold the state accountable by demanding a body count. A headline in a Zimbabwean newspaper after the World Trade Center bombing reads, "1 African = 1 American: New Order Requires New Math," in protest against a political order that the author believes deems "one Anglo-Saxon life . . . worth a million Arabs or Africans."[21] Trade balances, shots fired, political offices held, noncombatants raped, hours spent on household chores, land redistribution, pay equity, wells drilled, synagogue attendance, babies that survive birth: All elicit careful tabulation.

This is a global economy that has yet to come to terms with Brian Rotman's recent work on non-Euclidean approaches to counting, where enumeration is a materialist practice that does not resolve into the contemplation of forms or the computation of things. This is the global economy Randy Martin has in mind when he writes, "By drawing general social creativity into the calculus of profitability, finance joins political economy and culture, albeit at a price."[22] What does it mean to "do gender" in a world where everything has its tally? To study gender in a world dominated by fast capitalism where nothing stays pure?

In effect, there is no arriving for time travelers. Every tool put to use or critiqued in these pages—zero, repetition, utopia, time claims, counting, constructs, roles, evolution, wormholes, time's archer, norms, historical memory, the notion of time travel itself—will eventually have its day. Nor are these tools immune from being wielded by those who would privatize the water supply in order to save women the hours it takes to fetch it, then try to sell that water back to them for money they do not have.

Rather than lamenting the remarkable ability of global capitalism to tailor signs to profits, to gobble up opposition by incorporating the opposition's slogans into ads, why not take a page out of the fast capitalist book? That's what we've done here. The zero that is unsexed, fresh from the spreadsheets and ledgers, also has the capability, if only for an instant, to wipe that smirk off the face of hegemony.

If groups working on gender issues are to have much success in shaping globalization from below, it's clear that they will have to bring more than transnational feminisms to bear on whatever passes for change. Joining hands across borders is an important move, but it's a much stronger move for those who recognize a time claim when they see one. When neoliberalism chants that the future is yours now that everyone can be an entrepreneur, they remember the single mothers in Flora M'mbugu-Schelling's 1992 film *These Hands*. Out in the Tanzanian sun for hour upon hour, half an eye on their children, the women pound boulders into rocks into gravel. Somewhere down the line, the gravel will be ground and mixed into concrete to make the cityscapes that symbolize advance. These mothers are entrepreneurs, to be sure. They are also ragged, spirited, exhausted, and unlikely to see the age of sixty.

To integrate time into "social change" tactics is also to understand that the future may not belong to globalization, at least in its current form.[23] The women in that quarry don't have to live that life. When the U.S. Supreme Court acknowledges injustices, such as the seizure of the Black Hills from Native people, but finds that those injustices brook no remedy because too much time has passed, it helps to think like Rebecca Adamson. Writing in *Indian Country Today*, Adamson cautions readers against placing too much faith in the courts. They may need to devise alternatives to judicial challenges, given that "our nation's foremost repository of justice has served as little more than a clock."[24] The best of these tactics are mobile. They stay humble.

Want to get the jump on gender? Keep your hands up. Move those feet. You can't just trade punches with a fixed and recognizable opponent. You'll have to attend to everything that calls itself time and everything that refuses to call out. You'll have to circle, bend, step up, feint, give a hand, improvise, yield. Go with synchrony, asynchrony. Count, stop counting. Forget space plus time. Try spacetime. Think relations, not things. Think connection, not profits. Gotta dance.

Then, just when you think you've figured it out, along comes the physicist Julian Barbour with his contention that time does not exist. For Barbour, the world is "a timeless book full of different stories that tell of time." Time, like motion, is an illusion inferred from change.[25] In other words, time itself might turn out to be the ultimate time claim. And wouldn't *that* be paradoxical?

# NOTES

## NOW BOARDING: THE STARSHIP GENDER

1. Here and throughout, I use "gender studies" as a more encompassing term to refer to scholarship in the fields of women's studies, queer theory, LGBT (lesbian/gay/bisexual/transgender) studies, and men's studies. Since this book seeks to trouble received conceptions of enumerable genders (Woman plus Man), as well as to investigate the late-twentieth-century fascination with gendered ambiguity, I could do no less. I remain cognizant of and sympathetic to the critique that umbrella terms such as "gender" and "queer" have a tendency to draw attention away from the lives of those with less power who fall under these rubrics. It is no accident that women—especially working-class women, often women of color—figure prominently in the ethnographic and interview material incorporated into the chapters that follow.

2. On fossils as a sort of time machine, along with sea level, magnetometers, ion beam microprobes, the principle of uniformitarianism, and the scientific method, see Ward (1998). Although political economy is peripheral to Ward's project, he notes its bearing on the development of temporally oriented technologies and methodologies, as well as the designation of fossils as markers of time: "With the onset of the Industrial Revolution, knowing the *age* of rocks became a necessary prerequisite to finding industrial minerals, such as coal, iron, and the other materials that fueled and sustained the great Western industrialization of the eighteenth and nineteenth centuries" (5).

## WHAT THE CAT DRAGGED IN: GENDER STUDIES TODAY

1. These observations, while anecdotal, gain credence when viewed against any number of registers of the decline of a socially engaged gender studies in the United States, including the decreasing attendance at conference sessions on topics related to gender, the diminishing contact between university-based gender studies programs and community groups, and the title adopted for a recent essay collection, *Is Academic Feminism Dead?* (Social Justice Group, 2000). All this during a period (the final decade of the twentieth century) when international funding for women's organizations and women's studies programs significantly increased (Basu [2000:74]).

2. Here I throw in my lot with those who approach globalization as a process with a history rather than an unprecedented phenomenon characteristic of the current economic era. Unlike Vásquez (2000), however, I do not locate the first wave of globalization in the late eighteenth and nineteenth centuries. The chapters that follow reach back as far as the medieval period known as the golden age of Islamic science and further still to early Buddhist maritime trade. Unlike critics who point to global trade relations in earlier historical periods primarily as a way to dismiss the inflated claims made for globalization at present, I remain interested in the specifics of global relations in each case, especially with respect to their bearing on gender. For more on the expansive and traveling meaning of the term globalization, see Jameson (1998) and Martin (1999).

3. See Bamberger (1974).

4. Rosaldo and Lamphere (1974) long served as a key text for those convinced of the futility of searching for egalitarian relations between women and men in the past (or across the borders supposed to delineate cultures and nations). In effect, this collection uncoupled the promise of gender equality in an imagined future from evidence of its one-time existence.

5. Buck-Morss (2000). Dreamworlds inevitably succumb to what James Holston (1996:56) has called the utopian paradox, in which "the necessity of having to use what exists to achieve what is imagined destroys the utopian difference between the two that is the project's premise." Although mass dreamworlds, like the state-sponsored modernist planning projects discussed in James Scott (1998), might never be realizable, the dreaming, the planning, and the disillusion are all eminently historical phenomena.

6. Compare Thomas Frank, writing about the elision of class consciousness at a time of widening income disparities (which coincided with the starry-eyed claims made on behalf of postfeminism): "The Cultural Miracle . . . is complacency in years of economic privation . . . .The Cultural Miracle is the Great Disconnection of the American intellect, the virtual extinction of popular thinking in terms of social class at the exact moment when social class has made a most prodigious return" (in Frank and Weiland [1997:258]).

7. Compare, for example, the egalitarian hopes Nancy Chodorow (1978) pinned on shifts in workaday practice (for example, shared parenting) with the road to betterment through collective action mapped out by the Quest Collective, or the technofuturist predictions of a Shulamith Firestone (1971).

8. Rofel (1999). The romantic portrait of Chinese women under the socialism that Rofel describes could be considered a modern variant of orientalism. In this case, the secrets of the Orient allegedly lie less in "ancient wisdom" and more in a hidden understanding of how to achieve "real existing" relations of equality between men and women through mechanisms still veiled from the West.

9. Terminology employed by the United Kingdom–based magazine *New Internationalist*. "Minority world" corresponds roughly to the older usage "First World" and "majority world" to the equally problematic "Third World." The new terms use population figures to highlight inequity by playing with neocolonial assumptions about democracy, who comes first, and who deserves the most of what.

10. Rofel (1999:52) suggests learning to "replace liberation's ontology with its his-

toricity." Debate then shifts away from the question of whether women are or are not liberated (and with respect to what?) to the historical circumstances that encourage women to claim that they have long since achieved liberation.

11. Mani (1998), Spivak (1988, 1999).

12. Kapur and Cossman (1996), Parashar (1992). While Gayatri Spivak's work on postcolonial relations is important both for its scholarly contribution and for the relationships marked out by its circulation, it is noteworthy that a substantial body of related research coming out of South Asia has received scant attention from North American analysts of gender. See, for instance, Chakravarti (1998) and Sangari and Vaid (1989). Par for the course when minority world feminist movements attempt to "respect difference" without delving too deeply? I am grateful to Geeta Patel for introducing me to these texts.

13. On the creative resignification of gender as resource in the United States from the 1980s through 1990s, see Hartsock (1983). In *Render Me, Gender Me* (1996), I discuss the rich and varied forms taken by gendered (/raced/classed/. . .) differences in same-sex relationships. To the degree that earlier feminist calls for a genderless world incorporated the assumption that gender differences emanate from heterosexual, oppressive relations, they grasped neither these possibilities nor the entanglement of gender with other aspects of identity such as race, religion, or nation.

14. Like all generalizations, this one brooks exceptions. Joan Cocks's 1989 book *The Oppositional Imagination*, for example, attempts to hew a path to a genderless world through the thickets of feminist, Marxist, and poststructuralist theory. Nor was a sense of disillusionment confined to stakeholders in gender politics. Wendy Brown (1999) and Norman Birnbaum (2001) argue, in very different ways, that by the late twentieth century a sense of melancholia had come to pervade leftist politics and North American reform politics more generally. Brown (1999:4–5) urges the left to recognize the limited value of freedoms and entitlements (as historically conceived) for the present era, as well as to recognize melancholy for the fetishistic attachment it is.

15. On the move to coalitions, see Reagon (1983). The manifesto written by the Combahee River Collective (1979) ushered in an extensive literature on "intersections" of gender with race, class, and sexuality. Among the most influential early texts were Cherríe Moraga's and Gloria Anzaldúa's (1983) classic collection, *This Bridge Called My Back*, Anzaldúa's (1987) *Borderlands*/La Frontera: *The New Mestiza*, and Bonnie Thornton Dill's (1983) essay "Race, Class, and Gender: Prospects for an All-Inclusive Sisterhood." On women's leadership and feminist contributions to the Hawai'ian sovereignty movement, see Kauanui (1998). Stephanie Woodard (2001) reports on the revival of a Sicangu Lakota and Ihanktonwan Dakota coming-of-age ceremony for girls. For more on the accomplishments of low-income youth in Sisters in Action for Power, see Perez (2001).

16. On women's organizing in Brazilian favelas, see Benjamin and Mendonça (1997). On women's activism under successive regimes in Afghanistan, see Coop (2001), Mishra (2002), and the website of the Revolutionary Association of the Women of Afghanistan (RAWA), www.rawa.org. "Sara: The Special Gift," the first issue in the comic-book series discussed here, was published by UNICEF-ESARO for distribution in Eritrea, Ethiopia, Kenya, Uganda, Tanzania, Malawi, Zimbabwe,

Zambia, Namibia, and South Africa (Mabala et al. 1996). Amrita Basu (2000) examines the relationship between the rhetoric of the global in 1960s/1970s and 1990s feminisms, as well as the role of NGOs and North-South tensions in women's movements.

17. Such complacency was not limited to "women's issues." By the 1990s, in North America at least, congratulation for apocryphal accomplishments had become characteristic of what Anthony Grafton (2000:6) has called "an age whose besetting errors include self-satisfaction, when some students ask why they should read about utopias at all when they live in a perfect society."

18. To take just one example, a 1999 poll commissioned for the *Columbus Dispatch* asked, "Compared with the 1960s, do you think race relations in this country are better, the same or worse?" Thirty-two percent of blacks responded "the same," compared to just 16 percent of whites; only 55 percent of blacks responded "better," compared to 72 percent of whites. When asked a question that gestured toward utopia, the gap narrowed considerably. "Do you think that relations between blacks and whites will always be a problem in the U.S., or do you think that eventually race relations won't be much of a problem?" Sixty percent of white and 66 percent of black respondents replied that race relations would "always be a problem." The poll itself recapitulated a black-white model of race relations by failing to survey respondents from other groups. See "One Problem, Two Views" (1999).

19. For more information on these developments (and lack of developments), see, respectively, the U.S. Census Bureau (1999), Jorde (2000), Gombrich (1988:2, 16), "In the News" (2000:24–25), and Third World Institute (1999/2000). On the concept of renditions in gender theory, see Weston (1996:125–127).

20. Fogarty (1999:12) explains, "There's an old joke you hear from people in Indian Country when they talk about the lack of banking services on their homelands—'They can send a man to the moon, but they can't put a bank on the Pine Ridge reservation.'" He cites a General Accounting Office survey of mortgage lending that found just ninety-one conventional mortgages approved on tribal trust land since 1994. In 1997, the number of mortgages awarded to American Indians on or off reservation land effectively declined. If the credit situation for housing on Native land improves, and there are some indications that it may, it will be due to the determined efforts of activists and lenders, not some inexorable march of progress. On the histories of genocide, conquest, forced assimilation, legislation, and fraud that provide a context for these conditions, see Churchill (1996).

21. Foucault (1978), Hacking (1991).

22. Mohanty (1988).

23. Grewal and Kaplan (1994:19).

24. Abu-Lughod (1990).

25. Frank (1997).

26. The phrase is Tatyana Tolstaya's (2000), commenting upon the stories of Andrei Platanov.

27. The wait for justice in the course of social struggle sometimes receives a Christian inflection, as reflected in the title of Belinda Robnett's (1997) *How Long? How Long?: African-American Women and the Struggle for Civil Rights*. In this case, the title echoes generations of black preachers who used the biblical journey of the Jews

out of slavery in Egypt as an allegory for abolition (and, later, racial justice) in North America.

28. Hennessy (1995:31).

29. This evocative phrase ("visibility is currency") is Peggy Phelan's (1993:19).

30. Victor Burgin (1990) offers a provocative discussion of the Euclidean debts of theories of representation in the 1980s, including the derivation of the cone of vision from Euclid's *Optics*. Late-twentieth-century texts that integrate these visually oriented theories into gender studies include Probyn (1993); for geography, Rose (1993); for psychoanalytics and film theory, Doane (1987), Gamman and Marshment (1989), and Silverman (1992); and for technoscience, Hartouni (1991) and Kirkup et al. (1999). The phrase "global visibility" occurs repeatedly in Ong (1999). Val Daniel (1997:43), writing on violence in Sri Lanka, provides an analysis of the visual imagery entailed in "consciousness": "Even if consciousness need not necessarily employ one's actual eyes, it invokes the notion of the 'mind's eye' and by extension brings us to the threshhold of an 'optic' understanding of whatever we claim to be conscious of."

31. Gee et al. (1996:32).

32. See Barrett (1987), Chanter (1990), Kristeva (1981), and Marks and de Courtivron (1981). Not all studies of "women's time" ground the differences they seek in biology, the semiotic (à la Kristeva), or phallic discourse. Some look to the material effects generated by divisions of labor that set up different bodily regimens for differently gendered bodies (for example, Glucksmann [1998]).

33. Grosz (1995). For a nonfeminist example of an additive approach to the study of space and time, see Szamosi (1986). The issues involved are more complex than they might appear, since they implicitly reference the philosophical debates that Earman (1989) characterizes as absolute versus relational theories of spacetime, which he traces back to Newton and Leibniz through Einstein, Maxwell, Poincaré, Huygens, Kant, and others.

34. Giddens (1991:16).

35. Ollman (1976:52).

36. See Einstein (1961) and Gray (1989).

37. Berggren (1986), Huff (1993), Park (1997).

38. Foucault (1977), Weston (1996).

39. Sen (2000). See also Aggarwal (1995).

40. GLBT: gay, lesbian, bisexual, and transgender.

41. Hammonds (1994:141).

42. Hennessy (1995:31, 36).

43. For a sophisticated discussion of fixity and motion in gender theory, especially with regard to nationalism, see Patel (2001).

44. A tension long recognized in social theory, though not always for its paradoxical effects (see Comaroff and Comaroff 1992 *passim*).

45. See, for example, Mikell (1997). Amrita Basu (2000:70) contends that tensions between material issues and identity-related issues characterized international feminism from 1975 to 1985, giving way to an emphasis on networking and linking local to global activism in the following decade. Despite the shift in emphasis, such tensions have by no means disappeared. "Even today," writes Basu, "the organizations that sponsor campaigns

to extend women's civil and political rights are Northern-based while Southern-based groups are more apt to address poverty, inequality, and basic needs."

46. McVeigh (1997), Polanyi (1944). Amy Dru Stanley (1998) examines the historical circumstances that made the figure of the beggar a threat to a market economy that opposed slavery to contract and equated contractual relations with freedom. In the wake of abolition, new laws sentenced people who refused to enter into wage contracts "voluntarily" to forced labor. In many locations, legislation against beggars and nomads targeted Roma ("Gypsies") (Hancock et al. [1998]). For an example of late-nineteenth-century missionary accounts of poverty that sounded these themes, see Helen Campbell's *Darkness and Daylight; or, Lights and Shadows of New York Life: A Woman's Story of Gospel, Temperance, Mission, and Rescue Work* (1892). Works of social critique vérité from the same period, such as Jacob Riis's *How the Other Half Lives*, adopted a moral tone steeped in romantic assumptions about gender, class, and ethnicity, even as they urged reform.

47. Marx and Engels (1970:49).

48. Davis (1992), Warner (1962).

49. Here I draw on some of the ironies of contemporary North American life observed by Jim Hightower (1998), including his critique of the abstraction known as "the economy."

50. King (1994), Vance (1989).

51. For a sense of the contours of shifting intellectual engagements with gender within anthropology, see Abu-Lughod (1990), Lancaster and di Leonardo (1997), Lugo and Maurer (2000), Moore (1988, 1994), Ortner (1996), Ortner and Whitehead (1981), Reiter (1975), Rosaldo and Lamphere (1974), Yanagisako and Delaney (1995).

52. The description of alienation comes from Marx (1963:134).

53. Hacking (1991).


## UNSEXED: A ZERO CONCEPT FOR GENDER STUDIES

1. Earlier drafts of sections of this chapter were presented at the annual meetings of the American Anthropological Association, the Center for Literary and Cultural Studies (now Humanities Center) at Harvard University, and the Queer Theory on Location Conference at New York University.

2. For more on Community United Against Violence, see Vázquez (1992). On violence, representation, and the politicization of identity, see Halberstam (1993) and Sedgwick (1990:18–21).

3. For shattering explorations of the relationship of violence to representation in ethnography and historiography, respectively, see Malkki (1995) and Pandey (1992, 1993).

4. Weston (1982:144), Linder and Nygaard (1998).

5. Gender, race, nation, and culture are not necessarily the only factors at play in this scenario. Border guards in countries that restrict immigration based on sexuality often employ a gender inversion model as they search for visible markers of homosexuality in what they judge to be an "unfeminine" or "emasculated" appearance (see Luibhéid [1998]).

6. Here the discussion picks up on Rosalind Morris's (1995:585) call for a closer examination of ambiguity and indeterminacy in different sociohistorical contexts.

7. Kelley (1994:23). On the cross-class erotics of British women's entry into occupations such coal mining, see McClintock (1995:101).

8. Walker (1993:886).

9. For an imagined (but not imaginary) illustration of the power-laden "misreadings" that ensue when looking across lines of race/gender/sexuality, see the bathroom story that opens David Eng's and Alice Hom's collection *Q & A: Queer in Asian America* (1998:1). For accounts of hypersexualization in representations of women of color, see, for example, Collins (1991) and Marchetti (1993). On the practices, scholarly and otherwise, that have effectively whitened the term "queer" over the brief course of its reclamation as a designation of pride and resistance, see Hammonds (1994). For a nuanced discussion of conflict and interpretion in the gendering of Asian and Asian-American representations, see Lee (1996).

10. Thus to call her "unsexed" becomes an artifact of the focal point of this book, which engages first and foremost with an intellectual history dubbed "gender theory" that, in turn, has privileged gender, especially in whitened, middle-class forms. One could very well use the same vignette to open an essay called "Unraced," then go on to point out the concurrence of race in this instance with gender, sexuality, and class relations. Both accounts would highlight, with shifting emphases, questions about temporality, power, violence and its narration, moves to classification, and the tortuous routes taken to produce the surreptitious clarity of a sign.

11. See Douglas (1966).

12. The phrase is Lauren Berlant's (2000:44), from her fine analysis of the "national sentimentality" that perpetrates its own forms of violence by eliciting the narration of trauma. Berlant builds upon Wendy Brown's (1995) critique of the emphasis on the wound (the injuries inflicted in situations of inequality) in identity politics. It is no coincidence that the stories of zero moments recounted here take the form of stories of suffering in this time, in this place, although it would be equally possible for gender to zero out in a moment of, say, romantic flirtation.

13. See Feinberg (1996).

14. With this reading I traverse very different literatures that have little enough in common except for their engagement with ambiguity and their appearance in print within little more than a decade. A short, if fairly arbitrary, list might include Gregory Williams's *Life on the Color Line* (1995), Kate Bornstein's *Gender Outlaw* (1994), Cheryl Chase's "Hermaphrodites with Attitude" (1998), Katherine Newman's *Falling from Grace* (1988), James McBride's *The Color of Water* (1996), Katya Gibel Azoulay's *Black, Jewish, and Interracial* (1997), Leslie Feinberg's *Stone Butch Blues* (1993), Barbara Ehrenreich's *Fear of Falling* (1990), and Adrian Piper's "Passing for White, Passing for Black" (1992), as well as a host of novels with similar preoccupations. With a few exceptions, such as Reddy (1994), J. Nelson (1993), and Terry and Urla (1995), these works tend to focus on one strand of identity at a time. Epstein and Straub (1991), Feinberg (1996), and Nataf (1996) highlight gender. Race, culture, and ethnicity occupy a central position in Lazarre (1997), Minerbrook (1996), O'Hearn (1998), Scales-Trent (1995), and Vizenor (1990). The blurring of national identity, with its

implications for other identities, organizes the growing literature on borderlands, transnationalism, and *mestizaje* (see, for example, Anzaldúa [1987], Chong [1994], Heyck [1994], and Urrea [1993]). Likewise for the explosion of work in postcolonial studies on diaspora and hybridity (for example, Bhabha [1994], Lavie and Swedenburg [1996], and Young [1995]). Another group of texts, equally worth reading in this context, considers the relationship of technology to the production of socially ambiguous bodies (see Gray with Figueroa-Sarriera and Mentor [1995], Haraway [1991], and Stone [1995]).

15. Appadurai (1996).

16. For those desiring a taste of (if not a comprehensive introduction to) the vast literature referenced here, see Connell (1987), di Leonardo (1991), King (1994), Modleski (1991), Moore (1988, 1994), Scott (1988), and Zinn et al. (1997).

17. Laqueur (1990:25).

18. Rotman occupies himself primarily with questions of visibility (for example, how the vanishing point as a zero point renders the viewing subject visible). In what follows, I use his work, along with Ifrah's (1985) and Kaplan's (1999), to explore instead the temporal dimensions of gender, especially in relation to the link between visuality and commodification. For an introduction to the literature on medieval Islamic finance and trade routes, see Boone and Benco (1999).

19. Van Egmond (1988). On the historically much later, but no less variable, relation of numeracy to commerce, religion, and recreation in the United States and England following the Industrial Revolution, see P. Cohen (1982).

20. Berggren (1986), Closs (1996), Crosby (1997), Van Egmond (1988).

21. Of course, the questions posed by Arabic/Islamic science did not limit themselves to mundane affairs. Turner (1995:46) links medieval Arabic/Islamic scholars' interest in "number theory, consideration of numbers as real things, exploration of magic squares, and relationships between numbers and letters" to the legacy of Pythagorean thought. This search for mystical connections went hand-in-hand with the use of mathematics to establish times for daily prayer and tools for the administration of empire. On the calculations and machinery employed to establish the Christian calendar of movable feasts, see Gimpel (1988:164–165) and Berggren (1986:30). Berggren traces Christian European interest in astronomy and the "exact sciences" during the Middle Ages to the need to determine afresh each year the date for the celebration of Christ's resurrection.

22. See Al-Daffá (1977:37), Crosby (1997:151), Rotman (1987), and Seife (2000).

23. Crosby (1997:62–63).

24. Berggren (1986:31). See also Eaton (1993:8) on the conquest, in 711 CE, of the "Hindu-Buddhist society of Sind" by "Muslim navies."

25. Compare the account given by Datta and Singh (1962) with those of Joseph (2000), Ifrah (1985), Swetz and Kao (1977), and Yan and Shírán (1987).

26. Kaplan (1999:28, 1).

27. Ifrah (1985:421).

28. Seidenberg (1986:384).

29. Although, in keeping with the complexity of early scientific exchange, Ifrah (1985:382–383, 457) speculates that aspects of Babylonian astronomy may have trav-

eled to South Asia sometime between the third century BCE and the first century of the Common Era.

30. Montgomery (2000:81).

31. See Al-Daffá (1977), Berggren (1986), Haq (1996), Huff (1993), and Turner (1995).

32. Montgomery (2000) underscores the point that matters of translation are themselves constitutive, not just indicative, of scientific research and global exchange.

33. Berggren (1986:30), Gimpel (1988:175), Ifrah (1985), Rotman (1987), Turner (1995).

34. Seidenberg (1986), Al-Daffá (1977:37), Berggren (1986:240). Al-Daffá (1977) here compares an inscription from 876 CE discovered at Gwalior to the earliest known zero found in an Arabic text, which he dates to 873 CE.

35. Barrow (1992), Stewart (1995).

36. Hybrid numeration refers to a system in which "numbers composed of several orders of units are traditionally expressed by placing the sign for 10 between the sign for units of the first order, the sign for 100 between the sign for units of the second order and the sign for units of the third order, and so on" (Ifrah 1985:421). On the uses of finger reckoning for creating a system of place value, see Menninger (1969) and Crosby (1997).

37. Ifrah (1985:431).

38. Rotman (1987:2).

39. For examples of ethnographic research that casts gender in multiples in excess of two, see Herdt (1994), Nanda (1990), Roscoe (1991), and Wikan (1982). For a critique of the conceptualization of third gender in ethnographic writing on *hijras*, see Patel (1997).

40. Epple (1998).

41. For examples of such claims, see Herdt (1997) and Jacobs and Cromwell (1992).

42. Processes from which the academy is not immune: see Cary Nelson (1997), Shulevitz (1995), and Soley (1995).

43. A point argued eloquently by Lawrence Cohen (1995).

44. Herdt (1994). On sexology's historical romance with the Third Sex, see Terry (1995).

45. See Fausto-Sterling (1993, 1997) for a sensitive discussion of the politicized fate that awaits intersexed persons when their just-born bodies emerge into the light of the medical establishment.

46. Melmer (1995).

47. The critique of biopower in Foucault's *History of Sexuality* (1978), which develops an analysis of disciplinary technologies such as the census that configure bodies and populations as objects of knowledge, can also be read as an examination of the disciplinary effects of counting and tabulation under particular regimes.

48. It is noteworthy that The Butch and The Third Gender are related not only through the processes of reification and commodification that have produced them as particular sorts of figures, but also through periodic attempts to qualify The Butch as a Third Gender for the United States.

49. Publications that have, wittingly or unwittingly, heightened the utopian expectations placed upon The Butch include Burana et al. (1994), Butler (1990), Feinberg (1993), Halberstam (1998), Kennedy and Davis (1993), Munt (1997), Nestle (1992), Pratt (1995), and Volcano and Halberstam (1999).

50. Harris and Crocker (1997), Nestle (1987), Newman (1995).

51. In a retrospective look at her work with Madeline Davis in *Boots of Leather, Slippers of Gold*, Liz Kennedy (1995) provides a valuable discussion of the misleading effects of constructing historical accounts that privilege fixity in the sense of a fixed and stable lesbian identity.

52. Weston (1996).

53. Bornstein (1994), Devor (1997), Feinberg (1996), Rubin (1984).

54. For a different cultural take on androgyny, see Strathern's (1993) "Making Incomplete." Strathern characterizes Melanesian conceptions of androgyny as a kind of gender-completeness, the farthest thing from a gender-free state, albeit something that people in later life ideally leave behind.

55. The symbolic equivalents of finger-counting would include counting the spaces between fingers and working in combinations of elbows, shoulders, hips, et cetera (Barrow [1992:45–49, 81–101]).

56. Rotman (1987:13).

57. Ifrah (1985:433). Contrast, too, the version of the medieval European counting board devised by Gerbert of Aurillac in the tenth century upon his return from the study of Arabic/Islamic science in Spain. Gerbert's board arranged round markers with numerals in rows of boxes, but used no counter for zero. Users indicated absence by leaving the corresponding box empty (Crosby [1997]).

58. For an introduction to the canonical texts of this critique, see Anzaldúa [1987], hooks [1981], Hull et al. [1982], Lorde [1984], Moraga and Anzaldúa [1981], and Spivak [1987].

59. Weston (1996).

60. Many thanks to Lauren Berlant for suggesting the use of "undone" as a way to get at the ways in which zero moments inevitably exceed the concerns of sex/gender.

61. Berggren (1986:31). Not to be confused with the notion of a cipherized number system, which refers to using digits (ciphers) "instead of accumulating strokes as the Egyptians and Babylonians did" (29). The term "cipher," like "naught," continued to be used for zero as late as the mid-eighteenth century (Al-Daffá [1977:37]).

62. Rotman (1987:4).

63. Rotman (1987:12). On the tension between interpretations of zero as void versus absence, see Streng (1967).

64. Ifrah (1985:382).

65. Berggren (1986:31).

66. Ifrah (1985:469).

67. For a discussion of Bhaskara's commentary on Aryabhatta's *Aryabhatiya*, thought to contain the first treatment of zero written on the subcontinent, see Abdi (1999).

68. Ifrah (1985:447).

69. See Hinz (1997).

70. Rotman (1987:4).

71. The description of traversing in the act of counting comes from Rotman (1987:13).

72. Al-Daffá (1977:7).

73. Van Egmond (1988), Rotman (1987:4).

74. Field (1997), Rotman (1987).

75. For a related discussion that brings physics to bear on the effective whitening of "queer," see Hammonds (1994). This line of inquiry suggests a host of questions about the part played by mathematical models and metaphors in the naturalization of gender, questions that, in turn, cannot be separated from the historical developments that "mathematized" what later came to be called nature. On the latter, see Dear (1995) and Yoder (1988).

76. See Hacking (1995). This is a line of inquiry that writers such as Rosemary Hennessy (1995) and Susan Willis (1991) have also begun to explore with respect to gender and sexuality, albeit with a different set of questions in mind.

77. Rotman (1987:4). Mary Poovey (1996) considers the gendered introduction of double-entry bookkeeping, which shifted accounting from narrative to numbers, a pivotal development in the establishment of a "representational commensuration" between otherwise disparate phenomena. Representational commensuration prepared the ground for the historical constitution of natural law, lending arguments for women's inferiority a certain plausibility.

78. Unless, as in this case, the Man in the Stetson is selling a gendered product of the second order, such as Stetson brand men's cologne. Ad copy characterizes the Woman Welder as an "urban metalsmith" whose work, like the low-riding Chevy S-10 Xtreme, is "a creation from the other side of the tracks." Her image hovers over both a photograph of the truck and a caption with a suitably gender-bending name (Rocky McIntosh). Both examples of advertising appeared in "Looking Back: A 20th Century Celebration," a special issue of *Sports Illustrated* (29 Nov. 1999, pp. 123 and 93, respectively).

## DO CLOTHES MAKE THE WOMAN?:
## PERFORMING IN AND OUT OF INDUSTRIAL TIME

1. This, despite the extremely perceptive commentary on competing conceptions of temporality in Derrida and Foucault that Judith Butler (1993:245–246) consigns to the footnotes in *Bodies That Matter*.

2. Indeed, the work discipline associated with industrial production has been noted (and critiqued) as much for its linearity—learning to adhere to clock time, the linear sequencing built into assembly "lines"—as its repetitive qualities (see Gupta 1994, Thompson 1993). In social theory (as opposed to labor history), repetition is associated less with industrial capitalism than with "tradition": not the invented sort of tradition described by Hobsbawm and Ranger (1983), but the mystically reified sort that lives on in the pages of Giddens and Pierson (1998). Rituals do indeed involve repetition, but "living traditions" live to be revised, and they have nothing over the production of fast-food meals or "sticky" websites when it comes to reiteration.

3. An earlier version of the middle sections of this chapter appeared in volume 17

of the journal *Genders* under the title "Do Clothes Make the Woman?: Gender, Performance Theory, and Lesbian Eroticism" (1993:1–21).

4. For a sense of anthropological literature on gender and culture that proved particularly influential in the United States during the 1980s and into the 1990s, see Caplan (1987), Herdt (1991), MacCormack and Strathern (1980), and Ortner and Whitehead (1981).

5. On the racialization of allegedly universal Woman, see, for example, Anzaldúa (1990); hooks (1981); Hull, Scott, and Smith (1982); Kerr and Quintanales (1982); and Moraga and Anzaldúa (1983). Monique Wittig (1992) famously questioned whether the rendition of gender/sexuality denominated "lesbian" disallowed claims to womanhood. Key works that linked this earlier discussion of difference to so-called international and postmodernist feminisms include hooks (1990), Mohanty (1995), and Sandoval (1991). On some of the issues at stake in developing an epistemology or epistemologies for gender studies in a "postmodern" era, see Alcoff (1988), Hartsock (1987), and Mascia-Lees, Sharpe, and Cohen (1989).

6. de Lauretis (1987:18).

7. I conducted the major portion of this fieldwork project on gendering, which incorporated both participant observation and fifty-one in-depth interviews, from 1985–1986, with a follow-up visit to the Bay Area in 1987. In 1990 I returned to San Francisco to conduct twelve additional interviews specifically focused on the topic of butch/femme. All the interviews quoted in the pages that follow belong to these interview sets. Extended analysis of the interviews, along with interview excerpts, can be found in Weston (1996).

8. For a recapitulation of early feminist critiques of butch/femme, see Jeffreys (1987). Important texts associated with the second wave of butch/femme include Nestle (1987, 1992) and Newman (1995).

9. Here and throughout, I have followed the ethnographic convention of using pseudonyms to protect the identities of people encountered and interviewed in the field.

10. Over the last two decades of the twentieth century, a growing interest in localized forms of resistance prompted many scholars to draw upon studies of carnival, masquerade, camp, drag, and indeterminacy in their attempts to retheorize gender. See Dolan (1985), Russo (1986), Epstein and Straub (1991), Graham (1995), Halberstam (1998), and Zeig (1985). Holly Devor's (1989) study of women who have been (mis)taken for men offers an example of an approach to gendered "anomalies" that never quite extricates itself from nature/nurture controversies. On the debate over essentialism versus social constructionism, see Epstein (1987), Fuss (1990), and Stein (1990).

11. In this important respect, performativity is conceptually distinct from performance, although the gap between the two has narrowed somewhat as scholars of theater, film, and video have reinvented their endeavors under the rubric of performance studies. Performance begins to exceed the study of acting, directing, spectatorship, and the like to encompass "'being' as such," leaving in its wake the outmoded view of performance as "a second-hand version of some more primary reality" (George 1989:71). For the philosophicolinguistic roots of the concept of performativity, see Austin (1962) and Searle (1969).

12. See also Kessler and McKenna (1978), who argue that asymmetries of power associated with gender differentiation make people in North America likely to attribute male gender identity when they encounter gendered signals that seem contradictory or incoherent.

13. Butler (1990c:334). See also Benamou (1977).

14. Pfohl (1990).

15. Compare de Lauretis (1987:20), who speaks of "a mode of apprehension of all social reality that derives from the consciousness of gender. And from that apprehension, from that personal, intimate, analytical, and political knowledge of the pervasiveness of gender, there is no going back to the innocence of 'biology.'"

16. Case (1988/89:60).

17. Butler (1990a:137).

18. Frye (1983:29).

19. See Jameson (1991), Ewen (1988).

20. See, for example, Friedman (1991), Hanna (1988), Rosaldo (1984), and Weston (1990).

21. Butler (1993:125). Here I have modified Butler's theoretical apparatus somewhat, casting power as an effect of social relations rather than as a force that seems to permeate, if not float above, sociality, the better to oppress or be possessed. The language of hegemonies is also mine; Butler tends to employ a more static, spatial vocabulary of structure, idealization, and norm, occasionally mixing metaphors of space and time ("temporal structure") or joining terminology from disparate, even incompatible, schools of thought ("hegemonic norms"; "dominant" used interchangeably with "hegemonic").

22. Stein (1989:38).

23. As with any generalization for the purpose of comparison, there is a danger in overdrawing this contrast. That lesbians during the first wave of butch/femme had a concept of superficial posturing and recognized the existence of discontinuities among these domains is evident from the midcentury witticism, "Butch on the streets, femme in the sheets."

24. See Kennedy and Davis (1989, 1993).

25. Ponse (1978:115–117).

26. The phrasing comes from Case (1988/89:65).

27. Weston (1991).

28. Dollimore (1991:45).

29. Butler (1993:2–5).

30. The term "spin doctor" comes from North American politics, where it describes public relations staff who attempt to manipulate the media by placing a "spin" on a policy or news story in order to benefit a political candidate or officeholder (see Gitlin [1990]). Butler (1990d), in particular, has been careful to recognize (without necessarily theorizing) social constraints on individual performances of gender.

31. On the commercialization of sexuality during the twentieth century, see D'Emilio and Freedman (1988), Ehrenreich, Hess, and Jacobs (1986), and Seidman (1991).

32. Jagose (1996:89). See also Butler (1993:231).

33. For Case (1988/89:56–57), butch and femme "are not split subjects, suffering the torments of dominant ideology. They are coupled ones who do not impale themselves on the poles of sexual difference or metaphysical values, but constantly seduce the sign system through flirtation and inconstancy into the light fondle of artifice, replacing the Lacanian slash with a lesbian bar." Unlike Case, who tends to depict butch/femme as a self-determining subject position, Butler (1991:3) recognizes some of the problems with a critique that attributes an inherent reflexiveness to a film or (by extension) to a practice such as butch/femme. On the temptation to ascribe categorically an inordinate amount of efficacy to strategies of microresistance, see Abu-Lughod (1990).

34. "Butch/Femme Soirée" (1990). I am grateful to Marie O'Connor for bringing this announcement to my attention. On different types of drag, and the relationship between drag and camp, see Bergman (1993) and Newton (1979, 1993).

35. Moretti (1988:343). For critiques of the utopian aspects of some variants of feminist and postmodernist theory, see Leitch (1989) and Montag (1988).

36. Voluntaristic interpretations of identity formation and gender practice merely append the question "how free?" to the thoroughly Anglo-European conception of free will, without inspecting the cultural and historical context that underpins "free will" in turn. See, for example, Jagose (1996), who has difficulty moving beyond this agency-under-constraint model in her understanding of queer theory.

37. Brydon (1998:11). See also Appadurai (1986) and Handler (1990).

38. On the links between the first wave of butch/femme and community-building, see Kennedy and Davis (1989, 1993) and Faderman (1991). For a critical look at the concept of community in relation to sexual identity formation, see Weston (1997).

39. On the association of androgyny with particular modes of dress and with conformity, see Echols (1989), Krieger (1983), Stein (1989), and Wilson (1990).

40. Bright (1990), Loulan (1984), Samois (1982).

41. Grant (1990), Vance (1984).

42. Roseberry (1989:10). On the eroticization of the first wave of butch/femme earlier in the century, see Kennedy and Davis (1993), Nestle (1992), Newton (1985), and Penn (1991). Although Faderman (1992) correctly notes the centrality of eroticism to the so-called butch/femme revival of the 1980s, she is too quick to reduce the significance of nouveau butch/femme to the creation of erotic contrasts.

43. For the classic exposition of the uncertainty principle, see Heisenberg (1930, 1989).

44. The particular way in which one becomes implicated depends, of course, on one's positioning within fields of race and class relations. The reference to Radclyffe Hall appears in Blackman and Perry (1990:78). The commentary on *The Mikado* derives from Jeff Nunokawa's observations on parallels between the vision of a totally malleable sexuality and orientalist romanticizing of ethnicity (in Solomon [1992]). See also Torgovnick (1990).

45. The phrase is Butler's (1991:2).

46. Dreyfus and Rabinow (1983) make effective use of the onion analogy to explain aspects of poststructuralist, specifically Foucauldian, thought.

47. Butler (1993:123).

48. Thomas (1996:12).

49. Butler (1993:124).

50. And more: According to Butler, injury can become what Gayatri Spivak (1993: 122) calls an "enabling violation" when "interpellation . . . loses its status as a simple performative, an act of discourse with the power to create that to which it refers, and creates more than it ever meant to, signifying in excess of any intended referent."

51. Foucault (1978), Hacking (1991).

52. See Phelan (1993:146).

53. Deleuze (1994:76, 70).

54. Butler (1993:140).

55. See Frank (1997).

56. Rosalind Morris (1995:571–572) insightfully connects the operations of repetition in performance theory to the uses of reiteration in practice theory, specifically in Bourdieu's *Outline of a Theory of Practice* (1972).

57. Martin (1994). The classic discussion of Fordism appears in Harvey (1989).

58. Hacking (1991:191).

59. Thus Butler (1993:125), in her reading of the film *Paris Is Burning* addresses "the kind of reiteration of norms which cannot be called subversive, but which lead to the death of Venus Xtravaganza," as well as the question of "whether parodying the dominant norms is enough to displace them." (In this passage "dominant norms" and "hegemonic norms" are used interchangeably.)

60. Benjamin (1968:224).

61. Illouz (1997).

62. Frege (1980:87).

63. Debord (1983:25).

64. Compare Anthony Giddens (1998:128), who assigns repetition to a primitivized notion of "tradition," as though recurrent purchases of Happy Meals at McDonald's and websites that entice the visitor to return do not partake, intimately, of reiteration.

65. This would include what Morris (1995:585) suggestively terms "the extraordinary resonance between the notions of ambiguity in performance theory and the principle of general equivalence that defines the commodity economy in which that theory has emerged," as well as Hennessy's (2000:109) contention that "more flexible gender codes and performative sexual identities . . . are quite compatible with the mobility, adaptability, and ambivalence required of service workers today and with the new more fluid forms of the commodity." In *Perform or Else*, Jon McKenzie (2001) intriguingly identifies performance as the ruthless successor to the eighteenth- and nineteenth-century elaboration of "discipline."

## THE GHOSTS OF GENDER PAST:
## TIME CLAIMS, MEMORY, AND MODERNITY

1. Abridged versions of sections of this chapter have been presented at Harvard University, Trinity College, Western Michigan University, and Wellesley College.

2. The literature on ethnotemporality, which concerns cultural variations in the perception and construction of time, is vast. Classic accounts appear in Geertz (1973) and

Ortiz (1969). More recently scholars such as Geeta Patel (2000) have sought to displace the study of cultural difference and temporality from an ethnographic frame, the better to examine how temporalities develop in and through nationalist movements, colonialist legacies, and transnational economies.

3. On self-styled (and community-styled) contrasts between the *cholos* and *cheros* of today and the *pachucos* of yesteryear, see Cintron (1997) and Vigil (1998). Historical memory of *pachucos* owes something, as well, to the dissemination of the movie based on Luis Valdez's (1992) play *Zoot Suit*.

4. The literature on historical memory is, if anything, even more extensive than the research on ethnotemporality. Following early attempts to draw out the social or "collective" aspects of memory (Halbwachs [1992], Le Goff [1992]), scholars have gone on to elaborate the related but distinctive concepts of historical memory, social memory, historical consciousness (Comaroff and Comaroff [1987]), collective memory (Thelan [1989]), counter-memory (Foucault [1977b], Lipsitz [1990]), communal memory (Ebron [1998]), and postmemory (Hirsch [1996]). They have also begun to examine the history of mnemonics (see Hutton [1993], Olick and Robbins [1998], Spence [1984], Yates [1999]). Many authors find mnemonic devices in ritual practice (for example, Ruth Behar [1996:64], who characterizes the Spanish Catholic mass as "a memory tool for restoring the connection to one's own ancestors"). Others consider practices as varied as torture, genre painting, and circumcision to offer forms of mnemonic marking (Boyarin [1994:22], Fabian [1996]). Among the most perceptive commentators on the political implications of media-generated mnemonic imagery is Angela Davis (1994:37), who notes the ease with which "a politics of liberation" can be reduced to "a politics of fashion" ("'Angela Davis—the Afro'"), yielding historical memories that are at once ahistorical and apolitical. The demise of social movements complicates this process by placing certain historical meanings out of memory's reach (see, for example Ritter's [1997] discussion of the effects of the waning of Populism on historical memory in North America). Marita Sturken (1997b:690) explores how media images produce an "iconic history" capable of screening out alternative images that document historical events; thus the mushroom cloud displaces images of neighborhoods devastated by nuclear weapons. A significant portion of the literature on historical memory concerns remembrance of war, displacement, and genocide (Fujitani et al. [2000], Fussell [1975], Hammond [1997]; Hirsch [1992, 1996], Linenthal [1995], Said [2000], Sherman [1999], Soyinka [1999], Sturken [1997a, 1997b], Swedenburg [1995], Winter [1995], Yoneyama [1999]). An overlapping literature links historical memory to nation-building (Barthel [1996], Fabian [1996], King [1998], Osagie [1997], Slyomovics [1998], Zerubavel [1995]) and ethnic/racial/cultural identities (Comaroff and Comaroff [1992], Ebron [1998], Fabre and O'Meally [1994]). Yet another overlapping body of scholarship examines the meaning of landscape (Darby [2000], Santos-Granero [1998], Schama [1995]) and place in the narration of history, sometimes by the displaced (Diner [2000], Lewis [1995], Slymovics [1998], Swedenburg [1995]). Overall, studies have shifted from treating historical memory as a possession or a thing to an examination of mnemonics as a form of practice linked to particular social sites (Olick and Robbins [1998:112]).

5. Despite increasing attention to material objects (textiles, jewelry, monuments,

sunken ships) as sites for the production of historical memory (for example, Forty and Kuchler [1999], Kwint et al. [1999]), bodies have scarcely figured as mnemonic sites in this sense. (Stephen Bann [1989:113] comes close with his thesis that suits of armor once served as metonyms for the human body that rendered bodies "representative of the otherness of history." Marita Sturken [1997b:688] comes closer in exploring how survivors "place their bodies within the discourse of remembering" when they return to visit the sites of their internment.) Nor have most accounts of the operations of historical memory explored the relationship between how people use materials to make memories and how certain conceptions of the past come to be widely shared (Frisch [1989]). When bodies incarnate historical memories in the manner discussed in this chapter, then, the process is not to be confused with Jonathan Boyarin's (1994:25) insightful discussion of the relationship between memory and organicism. Boyarin uses "embodied memories" to refer to "the hidden ways in which state ideologies appeal to organic experience and commonsense dimensionality to legitimize themselves." While the time claims considered in this chapter do enlist nationalist ideologies, especially as entailed in conceptions of community-building and modernity, these claims are informed by corporate practice and commodity flows, as well as historical conditions and nation-states. In contrast to Boyarin, for whom gender hardly figures, I am interested in how social relations become gendered relations, in part through the usage of bodies as a scaffolding for historical memory.

6. For a wealth of unexpected insights into the institutional production of "confusion," see Diamond's (1992) analysis of narrative in the political economy of the nursing home industry.

7. On the context for the emergence of theories of memory that "see memory traces as evidence of loss," see Olick and Robbins (1998:107). Contrast the memory project outlined by John Frow in *Time and Commodity Culture* (1997:224): "The question of an alternative conception of memory that I want to formulate is this: how can memory be thought as *tekhnè*, as mediation, as writing?"

8. The same might be said for collective memory "loss." See Jennifer Cole's (2001) powerful account of the unexpected return of traumatic memories of living under French colonial rule in Madagascar, after an extended period of forgetting in which those memories appeared to be lost. In this case, the trigger for memory was not a photograph but elections.

9. Here and throughout, I base my characterizations on extended conversations with my godmother over a period of many years, supplemented by a formal taped interview.

10. For treatments of these themes specifically in relation to the changing political economy (and skyline) of Chicago, where all the women in this family history came of age, see Fine (1990) and d'Eramo (1996). On the relationship of newly commodified entertainments to changes in labor relations, sexuality, and family life, see Peiss (1986, 1989). To understand how the metaphorical rise of amusements and the vertical rise of the city implicated race relations (including shifts in who counts as what "race"), these sources are most usefully read in dialogue with Carby (1992) and Nasaw (1999).

11. Karl Mannheim (1952:281) long ago noted that, despite the philosophical diffi-

culties entailed in demarcating a generation, a liberal positivist conception of generations had bolstered unilinear conceptions of progress. At issue here is how this alliance becomes implicated in the production of other identity practices, including gender.

12. For an extended treatment of the gendered differences in same-sex relationships that are glossed by terms such as "butch" and "femme, including a consideration of the problems inherent in any attempt to assimilate these categories to the abstractions of "masculine" and "feminine," see Weston (1996).

13. Fine (1990).

14. On the great migration to the Chicago area specifically, see Grossman (1989).

15. Ruiz (1998:50–55).

16. On the part played by public amusements in the consolidation of whiteness, see Nasaw (1993). Hazel Carby (1992) has written the definitive work on the policing of African-American women's bodies in the cities. For an introduction to the activism, migration patterns, cultural riches, and restrictive socioeconomic policies that gave life to the neighborhood that was Bronzeville, see Mullen (1999), along with Bolden (1999) and, of course, Gwendolyn Brooks's (1945) *A Street in Bronzeville*. On some of the ways that residential segregation has shaped historical memory for African Americans, see Lewis (1995).

17. Copper (1988), Macdonald with Rich (1983).

18. Hirsch (1992, 1996:659). For Hirsch, photography becomes the (not a) medium connecting memory to postmemory, what you have lived to what you imagine others to have lived. See also Bann (1989:111), who cites Walter Benjamin to argue that photography supplies "a kind of paradigm for historical concreteness."

19. Olick and Robbins (1998:126).

20. Bhabha (1994:141).

21. Alonso (1988), Weston (1997). Or, as in the title of Neil Miller's (1995) survey of gay and lesbian history, "out of the past." Bravmann (1991, 1994) takes up the question of how some predominantly white gay men and lesbians have gone to the Greek classics to racialize a deep past for themselves. Along with Gutiérrez (1989), he makes a similar point regarding the use of historical sources on Native American/First Nations Two-Spirits (so-called berdache).

22. See Bravmann (1997). In a sense, history has provided the sort of authentication apparatus for queer identity that David Scott (1991:278) saw anthropology once proposing to supply for people of African descent in the Americas by linking (ex-)slave communities to Africa. Scott found "this sustained preoccupation with the corroboration or verification of authentic pasts" problematic at best, both because it presumes that anthropology's task is to establish verifiable continuities between present and past and because it ignores the rich discursive field of "tradition." Beginning in the 1980s, scholars (many of them queer) produced works of "gay history" that found their way into the hands of lawyers, nonspecialists, and a host of individuals raised to ask the questions "Who am I?" and "What does this mean for who I am?" The more widely circulated texts include Bérubé (1990), Chauncey (1994), D'Emilio (1983), Faderman (1981, 1991), Kennedy and Davis (1993), and Newton (1993). Dipesh Chakrabarty (1996:61) argues that such subaltern histories will inevitably have "a split running through them," since they are "constructed within a particular kind of historicized

memory, one that remembers History itself as a violation, an imperious code that accompanied the civilizing process that the European Enlightenment inaugurated in the eighteenth century as a world-historical task." In this manner, the discipline of history becomes implicated in the generation of what Akhil Gupta (1992:76) has called "structures of feeling that bind space, time, and memory in the production of location" within a global political economy.

23. For an astute critique of the homogeneity that informs Benedict Anderson's account of imagined communities, as well as the obliviousness to power that modernity commands when treated as something more substantive than a time claim, see Kelly and Kaplan (2001). In applying Anderson's concept of imagined community to lesbian/gay communities, it is worth bearing in mind Heather Love's (2001:491) observation about queer studies: "One of the central paradoxes of queer studies is that its dreams for a better future are founded on a history of suffering, stigma, and violence. Like any transformative criticism, queer historiography always has a somewhat hostile relationship to the past it takes as its object." The same could be said of much scholarship grounded in human rights discourse. As Joshua Dienstag (1997:3) eloquently remarks, political theory, "rather than relying on concepts of abstract right and duty, often attempts to guide by giving its readers a particular sense of time. . . . To put it another way: the project of political theory is often not so much to reform our morals as it is to reform our memories."

24. Weston (1998:57–82).

25. See Blu (1980), Deloria and Wilkins (1999), and Povinelli (1993).

26. It should be emphasized that some historians, such as D'Emilio and Freedman (1988), explicitly rejected narratives of progress and liberation from sexual repression. Yet they, along with colleagues such as Chauncey (1994), would continue to wrestle with the problem of how to write a history in which assumptions about historical continuity (for example, between the invert and the gay) might prove anachronistic, just as references to a community, subculture, or "world" might be disavowed by the very people the terms were intended to encompass. In any case, the circulation of books on gay history, broadly conceived, served to reinforce the linear conception of time that underpins modernization narratives.

27. Nora (1989:7).

28. Moretti (1988:344)

29. On the multiple, shifting (but not free-floating) meanings carried by "butch," "femme," and other gendered descriptors, see Weston (1996).

30. Degeneracy theories of homosexuality were already well elaborated by the 1880s in the writings of sexologists such as Krafft-Ebing, who portrayed lesbians as gender inverts whose "masculine" characteristics marked them as (in Smith-Rosenberg's [1989:270] words) "atavistic throwbacks." Such primitivized imagery tends to be racialized and classed in deprecating ways (Lutz and Collins [1993], Torgovnick [1990]), of which more below. Of course, the theme of degeneration has a much longer, pre-Darwinian genealogy in North American writing. One case in point is Thomas Jefferson's 1781 *Notes on the State of Virginia*, penned as a rebuttal to the theory advanced by European naturalists that "New World" flora and fauna were peculiarly susceptible to deterioration (see Delbanco 2000:56).

31. Alonso (1992:412).

32. See Dirks (1990:28): "Whereas the modern has celebrated the history of freedom, the modernized has been dependent on both the history of unfreedom and the sociology of inexorable process."

33. Coontz (1992), Stacey (1996).

34. See Bhabha (1994:246).

35. So it is, half a century after Adorno, that Huyssen (1995:7) can observe, "Memory is no longer primarily a vital and energizing antidote to capitalist reification via the commodity form, a rejection of the iron cage homogeneity of an earlier culture industry and its consumer markets." Quite the contrary: when the Holocaust can be retailed through tourist packages and film productions (see Cole [2000]), there can be no uncorrupted "outside" to commodification.

36. See also Boyarin (1994:25): "Other ethnic groups that fail to fit schemata of universal progress can be seen as actually dead, walking *fossils,* such as the Jews for Hegel or Toynbee" (my emphasis). In the case of the United States, Turner (1994) and Marlon Riggs's early film *Ethnic Notions* discuss how historical circumstances and political conflict have shaped this imagery. Even the color-coding has shifted over the years. During the anti-Chinese agitation of the nineteenth century, California newspapers described Chinese and Japanese immigrants as sexual predators with skin shaded brown or occasionally black. In the aftermath of the Chinese Exclusion Act, internment camps, and the U.S. entry into World War II, the media colored people of East Asian descent "yellow," stirring up fears of a Yellow Peril while capitalizing on the implications of cowardice carried by term (Marchetti [1993], Takaki [1993]).

37. Bhabha (1994:237 *passim*). He goes on: "The *new or the contemporary* appear through the splitting of modernity as event and enunciation, the epochal and the everyday. Modernity as a *sign* of the present emerges in that process of splitting, that *lag,* that gives the practice of everyday life its consistency as *being contemporary*" (242). This is a process implicated in what Fabian (1983) calls "allochronism," the practice of treating certain contemporaries as denizens of a past when "what is usually being denied is not just the concurrence of their existence but responsibility for their continuing oppression" (Gupta [1994:168]). See also Harootunian (2000).

38. Gould (1989), Rydell (1984), Stocking (1993).

39. Lutz and Collins (1993), Gould (1996:56–57). See also Asad (1993).

40. Darwin (1964:13, 25, 14).

41. Somerville (2000:29). On color politics within families, see Martinez-Alier (1989) and Russell et al. (1992).

42. Gould (1977:36, 44, respectively). See also Beer (1983:13), who notes that the theory of evolution "has persistently been recast to make it seem that all the past has been yearning towards the present moment and is satisfied now." Likewise, "descent" and "ascent" describe the same temporal route, but convey very different judgments about the passage (9).

43. In Larson (1997:241).

44. Gould (1977).

45. For the classic account of classic butch/femme that stakes its claims in the terrain of history rather than historical memory, see Kennedy and Davis (1993).

46. See Scott (1991:278–79).

47. Faderman 1992, Weston 1996.

48. Abou-Rihan (1994:258).

49. Weston (1998:83–94), Jameson and Miyoshi (1998).

50. Marx (1963), Dirks (1990:27).

51. Akhil Gupta (1994:171) makes a carefully argued case for the persistence of cyclical metaphors in (post)industrial "Western" societies, and thus, for the analytic bankruptcy of reified oppositions such as linear versus cyclical: "Ever since Quesnay, the central metaphors employed to understand the capitalist economy have been ones of circularity. For example, Marx's analysis of capitalism rests on the circular process whereby money is turned into more money through the extraction of surplus value in the production and circulation of commodities." Following Gupta's argument, although such oppositions may be analytically bankrupt, they can prove profitable indeed to the degree that they rationalize inequalities and underpin commodity production.

52. To take just one well-known though still not well-realized example: Nationalist "memory" of common origins often depends upon "the shared forgetting of a common violence" (Boyarin [1994:25]). Exposing this relationship between nationalist memory and collective forgetting is a key objective of Native American struggles to rewrite historical markers and secure historic landmark status for sites of genocidal conflict such as the Sand Creek Massacre in contemporary Colorado (Stockes [2000]). For Sturken (1997a) the Vietnam Veterans Memorial is an instance of a monument that serves as a screen memory, encouraging viewers to project memories onto the American names inscribed in the wall even as it conceals (through omission) Vietnamese who died in the same war.

53. On the relative (and related) absence of femme-identified women from writing on lesbian communities, see Munt (1997) and Newman (1995).

54. Huxtable (1999:15).

55. Contrary to common perceptions, memories are as likely to mortal-ize as immortalize, creating embodied understandings that fall short of "forever." If photography constitutes, as Barthes (1993) contended, a carnal medium, how much more so for the bodies that labor in households or offices, the bodies "killing time" at the bar.

56. Just as the metaphor of time travel opens an analytically dangerous temptation to spatialize time "by seeing it as a line along which one can travel" (Penley [1991:76]). This turn to vision leads to paradoxes in which the line loops back upon itself as the traveler, say, kills her grandmother and so eliminates a self who nevertheless survives to execute the deed. Note that many of the classic time-travel paradoxes presume a Euclidean universe in which parallel lines do not meet.

57. Gott (2001), Kaku (1997). Of course, wormholes are not the only model in physics that might permit time travel. For an example of how time travel might work without resorting to a wormhole, see Alcubierre's (1994) discussion of possibilities for a distortion of spacetime in which spacetime is induced to expand behind a spaceship and contract in front of it, allowing the ship to travel faster than the speed of light. See also Davies (2002).

58. Seife (2000:184).

59. See Dirks (1990).

60. Bhabha (1994:252).

61. Halbwachs (1992).

62. For further discussion of time's arrow and time-travel paradoxes in relation to contemporary physics, see Price (1996), Pickover (1998), and Nahin (1993). Boyarin (1994:8) does a masterful job of calling attention to "the politics of dimensionality," which include drafting certain (generally Newtonian) conceptions of space and time into the service of the state.

63. Scheper-Hughes (1999:14). Not to mention some of the very historical conditions that historical memory attempts to ignore, interpret, or explain. Barry Schwartz (1991:226) puts the matter succinctly: "A society remembering an apparently alien past is constituted by the very past it is remembering." In another sense, memory might be said to be acquiring its own histories (Hoffman [2000]), allowing scholars to ask not only why and when people remember or forget, but also why what was once forgotten can later be memorialized, albeit in forms shaped by intervening historical developments. See, for example, Iyunolu Osagie's (1997) essay on the resurgence of historical consciousness about the Amistad slave revolt in Sierra Leone, the site of both capture and return, after over a century in which the event had slipped from popular awareness. On the late twentieth-century "memory boom," see also Amadiume and An-Na'im (2000) and Huyssen (1995). Interestingly, that master narrative obtains even at the cellular level, where bodies are said to be guarded by immune cells that "retain a memory of disease-causing agents," making memory the body's first line of defense when it comes time to "fend off a later onslaught" ("Malaria Disrupts . . ." [1999]). On memory metaphors applied to HIV/AIDS, see Sturken (1997a).

64. Rosaldo (1989), Nora (1989:7), Behar (1996:42). For a compelling discussion of "new capitalism" as the purveyor of identities, see Gee, Hull, and Lankshear (1996). On heritage retailing and retelling, see Arnold, Davies, and Ditchfield (1998), Barthel (1996), and Lowenthal (1985). For a perspective on the media's part in "solidify[ing] popular memory," see Mohan and Maley (1997).

65. Berlant (1997:57), Verlichak (2000).

66. Likewise for "memory wars," a concept elaborated by Geoffrey White (cited in Knight [1997]) to characterize the conflict between different, generally nationalist, tellings of the Asia-Pacific war. "Memory wars" has the advantage of allowing consideration of the different politicized interpretations that frame memories, rather than simply marking their presence, absence, nurturing, and obliteration. Invoking the rhetoric of war, however deliberately, can also have drawbacks, including a tendency to treat alternate constructions of memory as oppositionally aligned into coherent and warring factions, as occurred during the controversy over the Smithsonian Institution's Enola Gay exhibit (Harwit [1996], Linenthal and Engelhardt [1996]). Joseph Rhea (1997) raises the intriguing idea that political struggles over particular *lieux de mémoire* can themselves exert a powerful shaping influence on historical memory.

67. The lexicon of loss also downplays the part played by institutions, states, and corporations in fashioning life as a great game, lodging responsibility instead with the individual who has lost. Imagine being so careless as to lose one's figure or, worse yet, misplace one's job!

68. Rofel (1999:95), Early (1998:711).

1. See Spivak (1988). On change as a concept that emerges at a certain point in historiography, see Koselleck (1979).

2. For a sense of the skepticism with which many women and women's organizations greeted the return of the mujahideen Northern Alliance forces to power in Afghanistan, given the abysmal human rights record of the Northern Alliance, see Pazira (2002), Pegu (2001), and the Declaration of the Revolutionary Association of the Women of Afghanistan (RAWA) on the Occasion of International Human Rights Day (2001).

3. Deleuze (1994:73).

4. The time of the Now is Walter Benjamin's term for a historical, dialectical understanding of temporality and what English speakers colloquially call "the times." For a creative application of his concept to left politics, including identity politics, see Wendy Brown (1999).

5. On the limits of social constructionism, see Vance (1989). For a discussion of biology as a symbol of permanence in North American identity politics, see Weston (1996).

6. On the retailing of resistance, see Nicholson (1998). For more on fast capitalism, see Gee, Hull, and Lankshear (1996) and Frank and Weiland (1997). Authors who have investigated and elaborated ideologies of capitalist acceleration range from Paul Virilio in *Speed and Politics* (*Vitesse et politique*) (1986) to Richard DeGrandpre in his popular and controversial book, *Ritalin Nation* (1999). Whether or not today's globalizing economy is indeed as quick to move as it is to market, its administrators are certainly highly skilled at depicting the globe in a frenzy of motion.

7. As in, for example, Jackson (2001). For an essay that exemplifies the shift in emphasis to gender as practice ("doing gender"), see West and Zimmerman (1987).

8. For a critique of the whiteness encoded into "queer," in practice if not in prescription, see Hammonds (1994).

9. Greider (1997). For a look at a much earlier period of globalization dominated by trade, see Ray's (1994:67) discussion of the expanding trade routes that linked India to Egypt as early as the first century CE.

10. Susser (1996:418).

11. Giddens (1998: 100).

12. On the dam project, see the special issue of *New Internationalist*, "Do or Die: The People Versus Development in the Narmada Valley" (2001).

13. Ende (1984:68). On the proliferation of metaphors of saving, banking, and investing in contemporary social relations, see Wills (1989) and Weston (2002).

14. Frank (1997), Nicholson (1998).

15. Scott (1999:215).

16. Baldwin (1963:23).

17. Robbins (1999:4).

18. Rowe (1999:33).

19. Leon Higginbotham (1996:69 *passim*) offers a scathing analysis of the circumlocutions that established "three-fifths of all other Persons" as the standard under

which slaves were to be counted for purposes of taxation and representation in the U.S. Constitution of 1787, a document that purposefully omitted any mention of slavery.

20. Scott (1999).

21. Mahoso (2001:14). See also Bearak (2002) and Fairness and Accuracy In Reporting (2001).

22. Rotman (2000), Martin (1999:4).

23. For a critique of the "must prevail" sentiment that pervades many discussions of the current global economy, see Harold James's (2001) discussion of how the Great Depression put the brakes on globalization for a good long while. For an activist manual that develops the concept of globalization from below, see Brecher et al. (2000).

24. Adamson (2000:A5).

25. Barbour (2000:305). To be more specific: "All the solutions of a Newtonian system correspond to unique paths, but they very seldom resemble the one history we do experience, in which records of earlier instants are contained in the present instant. This simply does not happen in general in Newtonian physics, which has no inbuilt mechanism to ensure that records are created. It is a story of innumerable histories but virtually no records of them," whereas "quantum mechanics could create a powerful impression of history by direct selection of special configurations that happen to be time capsules and therefore appear to be records of history. There will be a sense in which history is there, but the time capsule, which appears to be its record, will be the more fundamental concept" (283).

# REFERENCES

Abdi, Wazir Hasan. "Ideas of Time and Space." *History of Indian Science, Technology, and Culture: AD 1000–1800*. Vol. 3. Ed. A. Rahman. New Delhi: Oxford, 1999. 94–128.

Abou-Rihan, Fadi. "Queer Marks/Nomadic Difference: Sexuality and the Politics of Race and Ethnicity." *Canadian Review of Comparative Literature/Revue Canadienne de Littérature Comparée* 21.1–2 (1994): 255–263.

Abu-Lughod, Lila. "The Romance of Resistance: Tracing Transformations of Power Through Bedouin Women." *American Ethnologist* 17. 1 (1990): 41–55.

Adamson, Rebecca. "Election Time is Correction Time." *Indian Country Today* (27 Dec. 2000): A5.

Aggarwal, S. N. *The Heroes of Cellular Jail*. New Delhi: Publication Bureau, Punjabi University, Patiala, 1995.

Alcoff, Linda. "Cultural Feminism Versus Post-Structuralism: The Identity Crisis in Feminist Theory." *Signs* 13.3 (1988): 405–436.

Alcubierre, Miguel. "The Warp Drive: Hyper-Fast Travel within General Relativity." *Class. Quantum Grav.* 11 (1994): L73–L77.

Al-Daffá, Ali Abdullah. *The Muslim Contribution to Mathematics*. Atlantic Highlands, N.J.: Humanities, 1977.

Alonso, Ana María. "The Effects of Truth: Re-presentations of the Past and the Imagining of Community." *Journal of Historical Sociology* 1.1 (1988): 33–57.

———. "Gender, Power, and Historical Memory: Discourses of *Serrano* Resistance." *Feminists Theorize the Political*. Ed. Judith Butler and Joan W. Scott. New York: Routledge, 1992. 404–425.

Amadiume, Ifi, and Abdullahi A. An-Na'im. *The Politics of Memory: Truth, Healing, and Social Justice*. New York: St. Martin's, 2000.

Anzaldúa, Gloria. *Borderlands/La Frontera: The New Mestiza*. San Francisco: Aunt Lute, 1987.

———, ed. *Making Face, Making Soul:* Haciendo Caras. San Francisco: Aunt Lute, 1990.

Appadurai, Arjun. *The Social Life of Things*. Cambridge: Cambridge, 1986.

———. *Modernity at Large: Cultural Dimensions of Globalization*. Minneapolis: U of Minnesota P, 1996.

Arnold, John, Kate Davies, and Simon Ditchfield. *History and Heritage: Consuming the Past in Contemporary Culture*. Shaftesbury, Dorset: Donhead Publishing, 1998.

Asad, Talal. *Genealogies of Religion: Discipline and Reasons of Power in Christianity and Islam*. Baltimore: Johns Hopkins U, 1993.

Atkins, Dawn. *Looking Queer: Body Image and Identity in Lesbian, Bisexual, Gay, and Transgender Communities*. New York: Haworth, 1998.

Austin, John L. *How to Do Things With Words*. Cambridge, Mass.: Harvard UP, 1962.

Azoulay, Katya Gibel. *Black, Jewish, and Interracial: It's Not the Color of Your Skin, but the Race of Your Kin, and Other Myths of Identity*. Durham, N.C.: Duke UP, 1997.

Baldwin, James. *The Fire Next Time*. New York: Dial, 1963.

Bamberger, Joan. "The Myth of Matriarchy: Why Men Rule in Primitive Society." *Woman, Culture, and Society*. Ed. Michelle Zimbalist Rosaldo and Louise Lamphere. Stanford, Calif.: Stanford UP, 1974. 263–280.

Bann, Stephen. "The Sense of the Past: Image, Text, and Object in the Formation of Historical Consciousness in Nineteenth-Century Britain." *The New Historicism*. Ed. H. Aram Veeser. New York: Routledge, 1989. 102–115.

Barbour, Julian. *The End of Time: The Next Revolution in Physics*. New York: Oxford UP, 2000.

Barrett, Michèle. "The Concept of 'Difference.'" *Feminist Review* 26 (1987): 29–41.

Barrow, John D. *Pi in the Sky: Counting, Thinking, and Being*. Oxford: Clarendon, 1992.

Barthel, Diane. *Historic Preservation: Collective Memory and Historical Identity*. New Brunswick, N.J.: Rutgers UP, 1996.

Barthes, Roland. *Camera Lucida: Reflections on Photography*. Trans. Richard Howard. London: Vintage, 1993.

Basu, Amrita. "Globalization of the Local/Localization of the Global: Mapping Transnational Women's Movements." *Meridians: Feminism, Race, Transnationalism* 1.1 (2000): 68–84.

Bearak, Barry. "Uncertain Toll in the Fog of War: Civilian Deaths in Afghanistan." *New York Times on the Web*. 10 Feb. 2002. www.nytimes.com.

Beauvoir, Simone de. *The Second Sex*. New York: Knopf, 1993.

Beer, Gillian. *Darwin's Plots: Evolutionary Narrative in Darwin, George Eliot, and Nineteenth-Century Fiction*. London: Routledge, 1983.

Behar, Ruth. *The Vulnerable Observer: Anthropology That Breaks Your Heart*. Boston: Beacon, 1996.

Bellamy, Edward. *Looking Backward, 2000–1887*. New York: Penguin, 1982.

Benamou, Michel. "Presence and Play." In *Performance in Postmodern Culture*. Ed. Michel Benamou and Charles Caramello. Madison, Wis.: Coda Press. 3–7.

Benjamin, Medea and Maisa Mendonça. *Benedita da Silva: An Afro-Brazilian Woman's Story of Politics and Love*. Oakland, Calif.: Institute for Food and Development Policy, 1997.

Benjamin, Walter. *Illuminations*. Trans. Harry Zohn. New York: Schocken, 1968.

———. *The Arcades Project*. Trans. Howard Eiland and Kevin McLaughlin. Cambridge, Mass.: Harvard UP, 1999.

Berggren, J. L. *Episodes in the Mathematics of Medieval Islam*. New York: Springer-Verlag, 1986.

Bergman, David, ed. *Camp Grounds: Style and Homosexuality*. Amherst: U of Massachusetts P, 1993.

Berlant, Lauren. *The Queen of America Goes to Washington City: Essays on Sex and Citizenship*. Durham, N.C.: Duke UP, 1997.

———. "The Subject of True Feeling: Pain, Privacy, and Politics." *Cultural Studies and Political Theory*. Ed. Jodi Dean. Ithaca, N.Y.: Cornell UP, 2000. 42–62.

Bérubé, Allan. *Coming Out Under Fire: The History of Gay Men and Women in World War Two*. New York: Free Press, 1990.

Bhabha, Homi K. *The Location of Culture*. New York: Routledge, 1994.

Birnbaum, Norman. *After Progress: American Social Reform and European Socialism in the Twentieth Century*. New York: Oxford UP, 2001.

Blackman, Inge, and Kathryn Perry. "Skirting the Issue: Lesbian Fashion for the 1990s." *Feminist Review* 34 (1990): 78.

Blu, Karen I. *The Lumbee Problem: The Making of an American Indian People*. New York: Cambridge UP, 1980.

Bolden, B. J. *Urban Rage in Bronzeville: Social Commentary in the Poetry of Gwendolyn Brooks, 1945–1960*. Chicago: Third World, 1999.

Boone, James L., and Nancy L. Benco. "Islamic Settlement in North Africa and the Iberian Peninsula." *Annual Review of Anthropology* 28 (1999): 51–71.

Bornstein, Kate. *Gender Outlaw: On Men, Women, and the Rest of Us*. New York: Routledge, 1994.

Bourdieu, Pierre. *Outline of a Theory of Practice*. Trans. Richard Nice. New York: Cambridge UP, 1972.

Boyarin, Jonathan. "Space, Time, and the Politics of Memory." *Remapping Memory: The Politics of TimeSpace*. Ed. Jonathan Boyarin. Minneapolis: U of Minnesota P, 1994. 1–37.

Bravmann, Scott. "Invented Traditions: Take One on the Lesbian and Gay Past." *NWSA Journal* 3.1 (1991): 81–92.

———. "The Lesbian and Gay Past: It's Greek to Whom?" *Gender, Place and Culture* 1.2 (1994): 149–167.

———. *Queer Fictions of the Past: History, Culture, and Difference*. New York: Cambridge UP, 1997.

Brecher, Jeremy, Tim Costello, and Brendan Smith. *Globalization from Below: The Power of Solidarity*. Cambridge, Mass.: South End, 2000.

Bright, Susie. *Susie Sexpert's Lesbian Sex World*. Pittsburgh: Cleis, 1990.

Brooks, Gwendolyn. *A Street in Bronzeville*. New York: Harper, 1945.

Brown, Wendy. *States of Injury*. Princeton, N.J.: Princeton UP, 1995.

———. "Resisting Left Melancholy." *boundary 2* 26.3 (1999): 19–27.

Brydon, Anne. "Sensible Shoes." *Consuming Fashion: Adorning the Transnational Body*. Ed. Anne Brydon. New York: Berg, 1998. 1–22.

Buck-Morss, Susan. *Dreamworld and Catastrophe: The Passing of Mass Utopia in East and West*. Cambridge, Mass: MIT, 2000.

Burana, Lily, Roxxie, and Linnea Due, eds. *Dagger: On Butch Women*. San Francisco: Cleis, 1994.

"Butch/Femme Soirée: A Night of Gender Confusion." *San Francisco Bay Times* 11.6 (1990): 64.

Butler, Judith. *Gender Trouble: Feminism and the Subversion of Identity*. New York: Routledge, 1990. (a).

————. "Imitation and Gender Insubordination." *Inside/Out: Lesbian Theories, Gay Theories*. Ed. Diana Fuss. New York: Routledge, 1990. 13–31. (b).

————. "Gender Trouble, Feminist Theory and Psychoanalytic Discourse." *Feminism/Postmodernism*. Ed. Linda J. Nicholson. New York: Routledge, 1990. 324–340. (c).

————. "Performative Acts and Gender Constitution: An Essay in Phenomenology and Feminist Theory." *Performing Feminisms: Feminist Critical Theory and Theatre*. Ed. Sue-Ellen Case. Baltimore: Johns Hopkins UP, 1990. 270–282. (d).

————. "Lana's 'Imitation': Melodramatic Repetition and the Gender Performative." *Genders* 9: (1991): 1–18.

————. *Bodies That Matter: On the Discursive Limits of "Sex"*. New York: Routledge, 1993.

Campbell, Helen. *Darkness and Daylight; or, Lights and Shadows of New York Life: A Woman's Story of Gospel, Temperence, Mission, and Rescue Work*. Hartford, Conn.: A. D. Worthington & Co., 1892.

Caplan, Pat, ed. *The Cultural Construction of Sexuality*. London: Tavistock, 1987.

Carby, Hazel. "Policing the Black Woman's Body in an Urban Context." *Critical Inquiry* 18 (1992): 738–755.

Case, Sue-Ellen. "Towards a Butch-Femme Aesthetic." *Discourse* 11.1 (1988–1989): 55–73.

Chakrabarty, Dipesh. "Marx After Marxism: History, Subalternity, and Difference." *Marx Beyond Marxism*. Ed. Saree Makdisi, Cesare Casarino, and Rebecca E. Karl. New York: Routledge, 1996. 55–70.

Chakravarti, Uma. *Rewriting History: The Life and Times of Pandita Ramabai*. New Delhi: Kali for Women, 1998.

Chanter, Tina. "Female Temporality and the Future of Feminism." *Abjection, Melancholia, and Love: The Work of Julia Kristeva*. Ed. John Fletcher and Andrew Benjamin. New York: Routledge, 1990. 63–79.

Chase, Cheryl. "Hermaphrodites with Attitude: Mapping the Emergence of Intersex Political Activism." *GLQ* 4.2 (1998): 189–211.

Chauncey, George. *Gay New York: Gender, Urban Culture, and the Making of the Gay Male World, 1890–1940*. New York: Basic, 1994.

Chodorow, Nancy. *The Reproduction of Mothering: Psychoanalysis and the Sociology of Gender*. Berkeley: U of California P, 1978.

Chong, Denise. *The Concubine's Children: The Story of a Chinese Family Living on Two Sides of the Globe*. New York: Penguin, 1994.

Churchill, Ward. *From a Native Son: Selected Essays in Indigenism, 1985–1995*. Boston: South End, 1996.

Cintron, Ralph. *Angels' Town:* Chero *Ways, Gang Life, and Rhetorics of the Everyday.* Boston: Beacon, 1997.

Closs, Michael P., ed. *Native American Mathematics.* Austin: U of Texas P, 1996.

Cocks, Joan. *The Oppositional Imagination: Feminism, Critique, and Political Theory.* New York: Routledge, 1989.

Cohen, Lawrence. "The Pleasures of Castration: The Postoperative Status of Hijras, Jankhas and Academics." *Sexual Nature, Sexual Culture.* Ed. Paul R. Abramson and Steven D. Pinkerton. Chicago: U of Chicago P, 1995. 276–304.

Cohen, Patricia Cline. *A Calculating People: The Spread of Numeracy in Early America.* Chicago: U of Chicago P, 1982.

Cole, Jennifer. *Forget Colonialism? Sacrifice and the Art of Memory in Madagascar.* Berkeley: U of California P, 2001.

Cole, Tim. *Selling the Holocaust: From Auschwitz to Schindler; How History is Bought, Packaged, and Sold.* New York: Routledge, 2000.

Collins, Patricia Hill. *Black Feminist Thought: Knowledge, Consciousness, and the Politics of Empowerment.* New York: Routledge, 1991.

Comaroff, John, and Jean Comaroff. *Ethnography and the Historical Imagination.* Boulder: Westview, 1992.

Combahee River Collective. "A Black Feminist Statement." *Capitalist Patriarchy and the Case for Socialist Feminism.* Ed. Zillah R. Eisenstein. New York: Monthly Review, 1979. 362–372.

Connell, R. W. *Gender and Power.* Stanford, Calif.: Stanford UP, 1987.

Coontz, Stephanie. *The Way We Never Were: American Families and the Nostalgia Trap.* New York: Basic, 1992.

Coop, Stephanie. "Sowing the Seeds of Revolution." *The Japan Times* 18 Dec. 2001.

Copper, Baba. *Over the Hill: Reflections on Ageism Between Women.* Freedom, Calif.: Crossing, 1988.

Crosby, Alfred W. *The Measure of Reality: Quantification and Western Society, 1250–1600.* New York: Cambridge UP, 1997.

Daniel, E. Valentine. *Chapters in an Anthropography of Violence: Sri Lankans, Sinhalas, and Tamils.* Delhi: Oxford UP, 1997.

Darby, Wendy Joy. *Landscape and Identity: Geographies of Nation and Class in England.* Oxford: Berg, 2000.

Darwin, Charles. *On the Origin of Species.* Cambridge, Mass.: Harvard UP, 1964.

Datta, B., and A. N. Singh. *History of Hindu Mathematics.* Bombay: Asia Publishing House, 1962.

Davies, Paul. *How to Build a Time Machine.* New York: Penguin, 2002.

Davis, Angela. "Afro Images: Politics, Fashion, and Nostalgia." *Critical Inquiry* 21 (1994): 37–45.

Davis, Mike. *City of Quartz: Excavating the Future in Los Angeles.* New York: Vintage, 1992.

Dear, Peter. *Discipline and Experience: The Mathematical Way in the Scientific Revolution.* Chicago: U of Chicago P, 1995.

Debord, Guy. *Society of the Spectacle.* Detroit: Black & Red, 1983.

DeGrandpre, Richard. *Ritalin Nation: Rapid-Fire Culture and the Transformation of Human Consciousness.* New York: Norton, 1999.

de Lauretis, Teresa. *Technologies of Gender: Essays on Theory, Film, and Fiction.* Bloomington: Indiana UP, 1987.

———. "Eccentric Subjects: Feminist Theory and Historical Consciousness." *Feminist Studies* 16.1 (1990): 115–150. (a).

———. "Sexual Indifference and Lesbian Representation." *Performing Feminisms: Feminist Critical Theory and Theatre.* Ed. Sue-Ellen Case. Baltimore: Johns Hopkins UP, 1990. 17–39. (b).

Delbanco, Andrew. "Sunday in the Park with Fred." *New York Review of Books* 20 Jan. 2000: 55–57.

Deleuze, Gilles. *Difference and Repetition.* Trans. Paul Patton. New York: Columbia UP, 1994.

Deloria, Vine, Jr., and David E. Wilkins. *Tribes, Treaties, and Constitutional Tribulations.* Austin: U of Texas P, 1999.

D'Emilio, John, and Estelle B. Freedman. *Intimate Matters: A History of Sexuality in America.* New York: Harper, 1988.

d'Eramo, Marco. *Das Schwein und der Wolkenkratzer: Eine Geschichte unserer Zukunft.* Munich: Rowohlt, 1996.

Devor, Holly. *Gender Blending: Confronting the Limits of Duality.* Bloomington: Indiana UP, 1989.

———. *FTM: Female-to-Male Transsexuals in Society.* Bloomington: Indiana UP, 1997.

Diamond, Timothy. *Making Gray Gold: Narratives of Nursing Home Care.* Chicago: U of Chicago P, 1992.

Dienstag, Joshua Foa. *"Dancing in Chains": Narrative and Memory in Political Theory.* Stanford, Calif.: Stanford UP, 1997.

di Leonardo, Micaela. Ed. *Gender at the Crossroads of Knowledge: Feminist Anthropology in the Postmodern Era.* Berkeley: U of California P, 1991.

Dill, Bonnie Thornton. "Race, Class, and Gender: Prospects for an All-Inclusive Sisterhood." *Feminist Studies* 9.1 (1983): 131–150.

Diner, Hasia R. *Lower East Side Memories: A Jewish Place in America.* Princeton, N.J.: Princeton UP, 2000.

Dirks, Nicholas B. "History as a Sign of the Modern." *Public Culture* 2.2 (1990): 25–32.

"Do or Die: The People Versus Development in the Narmada Valley." Special issue of *New Internationalist* July 2001.

Doane, Mary Ann. *The Desire to Desire: The Woman's Film of the 1940s.* Bloomington: Indiana UP, 1987.

Dolan, Jill. "Gender Impersonation Onstage: Destroying or Maintaining the Mirror of Gender Roles?" *Women and Performance* 2.2 (1985): 5–11.

Dollimore, Jonathan. *Sexual Dissidence: Augustine to Wilde, Freud to Foucault.* Oxford: Clarendon, 1991.

Douglas, Mary. *Purity and Danger: An Analysis of Concepts of Pollution and Taboo.* New York: Praeger, 1966.

Dreyfus, Hubert L., and Paul Rabinow. *Michel Foucault: Beyond Structuralism and Hermeneutics*. Chicago: U of Chicago P, 1983.

Early, Gerald. "Adventures in the Colored Museum: Afrocentrism, Memory, and the Construction of Race." *American Anthropologist* 100.3 (1998): 703–711.

Earman, John. *World Enough and Space-Time: Absolute versus Relational Theories of Space and Time*. Cambridge, Mass.: MIT P, 1989.

Eaton, Richard M. "Islamic History as Global History." *Islamic and European Expansion: The Forging of a Global Order*. Ed. Michael Adas. Philadelphia: Temple UP, 1993. 1–36.

Ebron, Paulla A. "Enchanted Memories of Regional Difference in African American Culture." *American Anthropologist* 100.1 (1998): 94–105.

Echols, Alice. *Daring to Be Bad: Radical Feminism in America, 1967–1975*. Minneapolis: U of Minnesota P, 1989.

Ehrenreich, Barbara. *Fear of Falling: The Inner Life of the Middle Class*. New York: Perennial, 1990.

Ehrenreich, Barbara, Elizabeth Hess, and Gloria Jacobs. *Re-Making Love: The Feminization of Sex*. Garden City, N.Y.: Doubleday, 1986.

Einstein, Albert. *Relativity: The Special and the General Theory*. New York: Crown, 1961.

Ende, Michael. *Momo*. London: Penguin, 1984.

Eng, David L., and Alice Y. Hom, eds. *Q & A: Queer in Asian America*. Philadelphia: Temple UP, 1998.

Epple, Carolyn. "Coming to Terms with Navajo *Nádleehí*: A Critique of *Berdache*, "Gay," "Alternate Gender," and "Two-Spirit." *American Ethnologist* 25.2 (1998): 267–290.

Epstein, Julia, and Kristina Straub, eds. *Body Guards: The Cultural Politics of Gender Ambiguity*. New York: Routledge, 1991.

Epstein, Steve. "Gay Politics, Ethnic Identity: The Limits of Social Constructionism." *Socialist Review* 93/94 (1987): 9–56.

Ewen, Stuart. *All Consuming Images: The Politics of Style in Contemporary Culture*. New York: Basic, 1988.

Fabian, Johannes. *Remembering the Present: Painting and Popular History in Zaire*. Berkeley: U of California P, 1996.

Fabre, Geneviève, and Robert O'Meally, eds. *History and Memory in African-American Culture*. New York: Oxford UP, 1994.

Faderman, Lillian. *Surpassing the Love of Men: Romantic Friendship and Love Between Women from the Renaissance to the Present*. New York: Morrow, 1981.

———. *Odd Girls and Twilight Lovers: A History of Lesbian Life in Twentieth-Century America*. New York: Columbia UP, 1991.

———. "The Return of Butch and Femme: A Phenomenon in Lesbian Sexuality of the 1980s and 1990s." *Journal of the History of Sexuality* 2.4 (1992): 578–596.

Fairness and Accuracy In Reporting (FAIR). "Action Alert: How Many Dead? Major Networks Aren't Counting." 12 Dec. 2001. http://www.fair.org/activism/afghanistan-casualties.html.

Fausto-Sterling, Anne. "The Five Sexes." *The Sciences* Mar./Apr. 1993.

———. "How to Build a Man." *The Gender/Sexuality Reader*. Ed. Roger N. Lancaster and Micaela di Leonardo. New York: Routledge, 1997. 244–248.

Feinberg, Leslie. 1993. *Stone Butch Blues*. Ithaca, N.Y.: Firebrand, 1993.

———. *Transgender Warriors: Making History from Joan of Arc to RuPaul*. Boston: Beacon P, 1996.

Field, J. V. *The Invention of Infinity: Mathematics and Art in the Renaissance*. New York: Oxford UP, 1997.

Fine, Lisa M. *The Souls of the Skyscraper: Female Clerical Workers in Chicago, 1870–1930*. Philadelphia: Temple UP, 1990.

Firestone, Shulamith. *The Dialectic of Sex: The Case for Feminist Revolution*. New York: Bantam, 1971.

Fogarty, Mark. "Bankers Who Dare: Taking Extraordinary Steps to Lend in Indian Country." *American Indian Report* Feb. 1999: 12–15.

Forty, Adrian, and Susanne Kuchler, eds. *The Art of Forgetting*. Oxford: Berg, 1999.

Foucault, Michel. *Discipline and Punish: The Birth of the Prison*. Trans. Alan Sheridan. New York: Vintage, 1977. (a).

———. *Language, Counter-Memory, Practice: Selected Essays and Interviews*. Ed. Donald F. Bouchard. Ithaca, N.Y.: Cornell UP, 1977. (b).

———. *The History of Sexuality, Volume 1: An Introduction*. New York: Vintage, 1978.

Frank, Thomas. *The Conquest of Cool: Business Culture, Counterculture, and the Rise of Hip Consumerism*. Chicago: U of Chicago P, 1997.

Frank, Thomas, and Matt Weiland, eds. *Commodify Your Dissent: Salvos from The Baffler*. New York: Norton, 1997.

Frege, Gottlob. *The Foundations of Arithmetic: A Logico-Mathematical Enquiry into the Concept of Number*. 2nd ed. Trans. J. L. Austin. Evanston, Ill.: Northwestern UP, 1980.

Friedman, Jonathan. "Consuming Desires: Strategies of Selfhood and Appropriation." *Cultural Anthropology* 6.2 (1991): 154–163.

Frisch, Michael. "American History and the Structures of Collective Memory: A Modest Exercise in Empirical Iconography." *Journal of American History* 75.4 (1989): 1130–1155.

Frow, John. *Time and Commodity Culture: Essays in Cultural Theory and Postmodernity*. New York: Clarendon, 1997.

Frye, Marilyn. *The Politics of Reality: Essays in Feminist Theory*. Trumansburg, NY: Crossing, 1983.

Fujitani, T., Geoffrey M. White, and Lisa Yoneyama, eds. *Perilous Memories: The Asia-Pacific War(s)*. Durham, N.C.: Duke UP, 2000.

Fuss, Diana. *Essentially Speaking: Feminism, Nature, and Difference*. New York: Routledge, 1990.

Fussell, Paul. *The Great War and Modern Memory*. New York: Oxford UP, 1975.

Galeano, Eduardo. *Walking Words*. Trans. Mark Fried. New York: Norton, 1995.

Gamman, Lorraine, and Margaret Marshment, eds. *The Female Gaze: Women as Viewers of Popular Culture*. Seattle: Real Comet, 1989.

Gee, James Paul, Glynda Hull, and Colin Lankshear. *The New Work Order: Behind the Language of the New Capitalism*. St. Leonards, Australia: Unwin, 1996.

Geertz, Clifford. *The Interpretation of Cultures*. New York: Basic, 1973.

George, David. "On Ambiguity: Towards a Post-Modern Performance Theory." *Theatre Research International* 14.1 (1989): 71–85.

Giddens, Anthony. *Modernity and Self-Identity: Self and Society in the Late Modern Age*. Stanford, Calif.: Stanford UP, 1991.

Giddens, Anthony, and Christopher Pierson. *Conversations with Anthony Giddens: Making Sense of Modernity*. Stanford, Calif.: Stanford UP, 1998.

Gimpel, Jean. *The Medieval Machine: The Industrial Revolution of the Middle Ages*. 2nd ed. Cambridge, U.K.: Wildwood, 1988.

Girshick, Lori B. *No Safe Haven: Stories of Women in Prison*. Boston: Northeastern UP, 1999.

Gitlin, Todd. "Blips, Bites and Savvy Talk: Television's Impact on American Politics." *Dissent* 37.1 (1990): 18–26.

Glucksmann, Miriam A. "'What a Difference a Day Makes': A Theoretical and Historical Exploration of Temporality and Gender." *Sociology* 32.2 (1998): 239–258.

Gombrich, Richard F. *Theravada Buddhism: A Social History from Ancient Benares to Modern Colombo*. London: Routledge, 1988.

Gott, J. Richard. *Time Travel in Einstein's Universe: The Physical Possibilities of Travel Through Time*. New York: Houghton, 2001.

Gould, Stephen Jay. *Ever Since Darwin: Reflections in Natural History*. New York: Norton, 1977.

———. *Wonderful Life: The Burgess Shale and the Nature of History*. New York: Norton, 1989.

———. *The Mismeasure of Man*. 2nd ed. New York: Norton, 1996.

Grafton, Anthony. "Over the Rainbow." *New York Review of Books* 47.19 (2000): 4–6.

Graham, Paula. "Girls' Camp? The Politics of Parody." *Immortal, Invisible: Lesbians and the Moving Image*. Ed. Tasmin Wilton. New York: Routledge, 1995. 163–181.

Grant, Judith. "Rethinking Desire." *Women's Review of Books* 7.4 (1990).

Gray, Chris Hables, with Heidi J. Figueroa-Sarriera and Steven Mentor, eds. *The Cyborg Handbook*. New York: Routledge, 1995.

Gray, Jeremy. *Ideas of Space: Euclidean, Non-Euclidean, and Relativistic*. 2nd ed. Oxford: Clarendon, 1989.

Greenhouse, Carol J. *A Moment's Notice: Time Politics Across Cultures*. Ithaca, N.Y.: Cornell UP, 1996.

Greider, William. *One World, Ready or Not: The Manic Logic of Global Capitalism*. New York: Simon, 1997.

Grewal, Inderpal, and Caren Kaplan, eds. *Scattered Hegemonies: Postmodernity and Transnational Feminist Practices*. Minneapolis: U of Minnesota P, 1994.

Grossman, James R. *Land of Hope: Chicago, Black Southerners, and the Great Migration*. Chicago: U of Chicago P, 1989.

Grosz, Elizabeth. *Space, Time, and Perversion: Essays on the Politics of Bodies*. New York: Routledge, 1995.

Gullberg, Jan. *Mathematics: From the Birth of Numbers*. New York: Norton, 1997.

Gupta, Akhil. "The Song of the Nonaligned World: Transnational Identities and the Reinscription of Space in Late Capitalism." *Cultural Anthropology* 7.1 (1992): 63–79.

———. "The Reincarnation of Souls and the Rebirth of Commodities: Representations of Time in 'East' and 'West.'" In *Remapping Memory: The Politics of TimeSpace*. Ed. Jonathan Boyarin. Minneapolis: U of Minnesota P, 1994. 161–183.

Gutiérrez, Ramon A. "Must We Deracinate Indians to Find Gay Roots?" *Out/Look* 1.4 (1989): 61–67.

Hacking, Ian. "How Should We Do the History of Statistics?" *The Foucault Effect: Studies in Governmentality*. Ed. Graham Burchell, Colin Gordon, and Peter Miller. Chicago: U of Chicago P, 1991. 181–195.

———. *Rewriting the Soul: Multiple Personality and the Sciences of Memory*. Princeton, N.J.: Princeton UP, 1995.

Halberstam, Judith. 1993. "Imagined Violence/Queer Violence: Representation, Rage, and Resistance." *Social Text* 37 (1993): 187–199.

———. *Female Masculinity*. Durham, N.C.: Duke UP, 1998.

Halbwachs, Maurice. *On Collective Memory*. Trans. L. A. Coser. Chicago: U of Chicago P, 1992.

Hammond, Phil, ed. *Cultural Difference, Media Memories: Anglo-American Images of Japan*. London: Cassell, 1997.

Hammonds, Evelynn. "Black (W)holes and the Geometry of Black Female Sexuality." *differences* 6.2–3 (1994): 126–145.

Hancock, Ian, Siobhan Dowd, and Rajko Djuric, eds. *The Roads of the Roma: A PEN Anthology of Gypsy Writers*. Hertfordshire: U of Hertfordshire P, 1998.

Handler, Richard. 1990. "Consuming Culture (Genuine and Spurious) as Style." *Cultural Anthropology* 5.3 (1990): 346–357.

Hanna, Judith Lynne. *Dance, Sex, and Gender: Signs of Identity, Dominance, Defiance, and Desire*. Chicago: U of Chicago P, 1988.

Haq, S. N. "The Indian and Persian Background." *History of Islamic Philosophy*. Ed. S. H. Nasr and O. Leaman. London: Routledge, 1996. 152–170.

Haraway, Donna. *Simians, Cyborgs, and Women: The Reinvention of Nature*. London: Free Association, 1991.

Harootunian, Harry. *Overcome by Modernity: History, Culture, and Community in Interwar Japan*. Princeton, N.J.: Princeton UP, 2000.

Harris, Laura, and Elizabeth Crocker, eds. *Femme: Feminists, Lesbians, and Bad Girls*. New York: Routledge, 1997.

Hartouni, Valerie. "Containing Women: Reproductive Discourse in the 1980's." *Technoculture*. Ed. Constance Penley and Andrew Ross. Minneapolis: U of Minnesota P, 1991. 27–56.

Hartsock, Nancy C. M. *Money, Sex, and Power: Toward a Feminist Historical Materialism*. New York: Longman, 1983.

———. "Rethinking Modernism." *Cultural Critique* 7 (1987): 187–206.

Harvey, David. *The Condition of Postmodernity: An Enquiry into the Origins of Cultural Change*. Cambridge, Mass.: Blackwell, 1989.

Harwit, Martin. *An Exhibit Denied: Lobbying the History of Enola Gay*. New York: Copernicus, 1996.

Haug, Wolfgang Fritz. *Critique of Commodity Aesthetics: Appearance, Sexuality, and Advertising in Capitalist Society*. Minneapolis: U of Minnesota P, 1986.

Heisenberg, Werner. *The Physical Principles of the Quantum Theory*. Trans. Carl Eckart and Frank C. Hoyt. Chicago: U of Chicago P, 1930.

———. *Physics and Philosophy: The Revolution in Modern Science*. New York: Penguin, 1989.

Heller, Agnes. *The Theory of Need in Marx*. London: Allison & Busby, 1976.

Hennessy, Rosemary. "Queer Visibility in Commodity Culture." *Cultural Critique* 29 (1995): 31–76.

———. *Profit and Pleasure: Sexual Identities in Late Capitalism*. New York: Routledge, 2000.

Herdt, Gilbert. "Representations of Homosexuality: An Essay in Cultural Ontology and Historical Comparison, Parts I and II." *Journal of the History of Sexuality* 1.3/4 (1991): 481–504, 603–632.

———., ed. *Third Sex, Third Gender: Beyond Sexual Dimorphism in Culture and History*. New York: Zone, 1994.

———. *Same Sex, Different Cultures: Exploring Gay and Lesbian Lives*. Boulder, Colo.: Westview, 1997.

Heyck, Denis Lynn Daly. *Barrios and Borderlands: Cultures of Latinos and Latinas in the United States*. New York: Routledge, 1994.

Higginbotham, A. Leon, Jr. *Race and the American Legal Process*. Vol. II. *Shades of Freedom: Racial Politics and Presumptions of the American Legal Process*. New York: Oxford UP, 1996.

Hightower, Jim. *There's Nothing in the Middle of the Road but Yellow Stripes and Dead Armadillos*. New York: Harper, 1998.

Hinz, Evelyn J., ed. "The Lure of the Androgyne." Special issue of *Mosaic* 30.3 (1997).

Hirsch, Marianne. "Family Pictures: *Maus*, Mourning, and Post-Memory." *Discourse* 15.2 (1992): 3–29.

———. "Past Lives: Postmemories in Exile." *Poetics Today* 17.4 (1996): 659–686.

Hobsbawm, Eric, and Terence Ranger, eds. 1983. *The Invention of Tradition*. New York: Cambridge UP, 1983.

Hoffman, Eva. "The Uses of Hell." *New York Review of Books* 9 Mar. 2000: 19–23.

Holston, James. "Spaces of Insurgent Citizenship." *Architectural Design* 66.11–12 (1996): 54–59.

hooks, bell. *Ain't I a Woman: Black Women and Feminism*. Boston: South End, 1981.

———. *Yearning: Race, Gender, and Cultural Politics*. Boston: South End, 1990.

Huff, Toby E. *The Rise of Early Modern Science: Islam, China, and the West*. New York: Cambridge UP, 1993.

Hull, Gloria, Patricia Bell Scott, and Barbara Smith. *All the Women Are White, All the*

*Blacks Are Men, But Some of Us Are Brave: Black Women's Studies*. New York: Feminist P, 1982.

Hutton, Patrick H. *History as an Art of Memory*. Hanover: U of Vermont P, 1993.

Huxtable, Ada Louise. "Museums: Making It New." *New York Review of Books* 22 Apr. 1999: 10–15.

Huyssen, Andreas. *Twilight Memories: Marking Time in a Culture of Amnesia*. New York: Routledge, 1995.

Ifrah, Georges. *From One to Zero: A Universal History of Numbers*. Trans. Lowell Bair. New York: Viking, 1985.

Illouz, Eva. *Consuming the Romantic Utopia: Love and the Cultural Contradictions of Capitalism*. Berkeley: U of California P, 1997.

"In the News." *Tricycle: The Buddhist Review* Fall 2000: 24–25.

Jackson, John L. *Harlemworld: Doing Race and Class in Contemporary Black America*. Chicago: U of Chicago P, 2001.

Jacobs, Sue-Ellen, and Jason Cromwell. "Visions and Revisions of Reality: Reflections on Sex, Sexuality, Gender, and Gender Variance." *Journal of Homosexuality* 23.4 (1992): 43–69.

Jagose, Annamarie. *Queer Theory*. Victoria: Melbourne UP, 1996.

James, Harold. *The End of Globalization: Lessons from the Great Depression*. Cambridge, Mass.: Harvard UP, 2001.

Jameson, Fredric. *Postmodernism, Or, the Cultural Logic of Late Capitalism*. Durham, N.C.: Duke UP, 1991.

———. "Notes on Globalization as a Philosophical Issue." *The Cultures of Globalization*. Ed. Fredric Jameson and Masao Miyoshi. Durham, N.C.: Duke UP, 1998. 54–77.

Jameson, Fredric, and Masao Miyoshi, eds. *The Cultures of Globalization*. Durham, N.C.: Duke UP, 1998.

Jay, Martin. *Downcast Eyes: The Denigration of Vision in Twentieth-Century French Thought*. Berkeley: U of California P, 1994.

Jeffreys, Sheila. "Butch and Femme: Now and Then." *Gossip* 5 (1987): 65–95.

Jorde, Sigurd. "South Africa: One Rape Every 30 Seconds." *World Press Review* July 2000: 45–46.

Joseph, George Gheverghese. *The Crest of the Peacock: The Non-European Roots of Mathematics*. Princeton, N.J.: Princeton UP, 2000.

Kaku, Michio. *Visions: How Science Will Revolutionize the 21st Century*. New York: Doubleday, 1997.

Kaplan, Robert. *The Nothing That Is: A Natural History of Zero*. Oxford: Oxford UP, 1999.

Kapur, Ratna, and Brenda Cossman. *Subversive Sites: Feminist Engagements with Law in India*. New Delhi: Sage, 1996.

Kauanui, J. Kēhaulani. "Off-Island Hawaiians 'Making' Ourselves at 'Home': A [Gendered] Contradiction in Terms?" *Women's Studies International Forum* 21.6 (1998): 681–693.

Kelley, Robin D. G. *Race Rebels: Culture, Politics, and the Black Working Class*. New York: Free, 1994.

Kelly, John D., and Martha Kaplan. *Represented Communities: Fiji and World Decolonization*. Chicago: U of Chicago P, 2001.

Kennedy, Elizabeth Lapovsky. "Telling Tales: Oral History and the Construction of Pre-Stonewall Lesbian History." *Radical History Review* 62 (1995): 58–79.

Kennedy, Elizabeth Lapovsky, and Madeline D. Davis. "The Reproduction of Butch-Fem Roles: A Social Constructionist Approach." *Passion and Power: Sexuality in History*. Ed. Kathy Peiss and Christina Simmons with Robert A. Padgug. Philadelphia: Temple UP, 1989. 241–256.

———. *Boots of Leather, Slippers of Gold: The History of a Lesbian Community*. New York: Routledge, 1993.

Kenny, Anthony. *Frege: An Introduction to the Founder of Modern Analytic Philosophy*. New York: Penguin, 1995.

Kerr, Barbara T., and Mirtha N. Quintanales. "The Complexity of Desire: Conversations on Sexuality and Difference." *Conditions 8* 3.2 (1982): 52–71.

Kessler, Suzanne J., and Wendy McKenna. *Gender: An Ethnomethodological Approach*. Chicago: U of Chicago P, 1978.

King, Alex. *Memorials of the Great War in Britain*. Oxford: Berg, 1998.

King, Katie. *Theory in Its Feminist Travels: Conversations in U.S. Women's Movements*. Bloomington: Indiana UP, 1994.

Kirkup, Gill, Linda Janes, and Kathryn Woodward, eds. *The Gendered Cyborg: A Reader*. New York: Routledge, 1999.

Knight, John. "Japanese War Memories." *Cultural Difference, Media Memories: Anglo-American Images of Japan*. London: Cassell, 1997. 201–215.

Koselleck, Reinhart. *Vergangene Zukunft: Zur Semantik Geschichtlicher Zeiten*. Frankfurt am Main: Suhrkamp, 1979.

Krieger, Susan. *The Mirror Dance: Identity in a Women's Community*. Philadelphia: Temple UP, 1983.

Kristeva, Julia. "Women's Time." *Signs* 7.1 (1981): 13–35.

Kwint, Marius, Christopher Breward, and Jeremy Aynsley, eds. *Material Memories: Design and Evocation*. Oxford: Berg, 1999.

Lancaster, Roger N., and Micaela di Leonardo. *The Gender/Sexuality Reader*. New York: Routledge, 1997.

Landes, David S. *Revolution in Time: Clocks and the Making of the Modern World*. Cambridge, Mass.: Harvard UP, 1983.

Laqueur, Thomas. *Making Sex: Body and Gender from the Greeks to Freud*. Cambridge, Mass.: Harvard UP, 1990.

Larson, Edward J. *Summer for the Gods: The Scopes Trial and America's Continuing Debate Over Science and Religion*. New York: Basic, 1997.

Lavie, Smadar, and Ted Swedenburg, eds. *Displacement, Diaspora, and Geographies of Identity*. Durham, N.C.: Duke UP, 1996.

Lazarre, Jane. *Beyond the Whiteness of Whiteness: Memoir of a Black Mother of White Sons*. Durham, N.C.: Duke UP, 1997.

Lee, Jee Yuen. "Why Suzie Wong Is Not a Lesbian: Asian and Asian-American Lesbian and Bisexual Women and Femme/Butch/Gender Identities." *Queer*

*Studies: A Multicultural Reader*. Ed. Brett Beemyn and Mickey Eliason. New York: New York UP, 1996. 115–132.

Le Goff, Jacques. *History and Memory.* Trans. Steven Rendall and Elizabeth Claman. New York: Columbia UP, 1992.

Leitch, Vincent B. "Writing Cultural History: The Case of Postmodernism." *Feminism and Institutions: Dialogues on Feminist Theory*. Ed. Linda Kauffman. Cambridge, Mass.: Blackwell, 1989. 166–173.

Lewis, Earl. "Connecting Memory, Self, and the Power of Place in African American Urban History." *Journal of Urban History* 21.3 (1995): 347–371.

Lewontin, R. C. *It Ain't Necessarily So: The Dream of the Human Genome and Other Illusions*. New York: New York Review of Books, 2000.

Linder, Marc, and Ingrid Nygaard. *Void Where Prohibited: Rest Breaks and the Right to Urinate on Company Time*. Ithaca, N.Y.: ILR Press, 1998.

Linenthal, Edward T. *Preserving Memory: The Struggle to Create America's Holocaust Museum*. New York: Viking, 1995.

Linenthal, Edward T., and Tom Engelhardt, eds. *Memory Wars: The Enola Gay and Other Battles for the American Past*. New York: Holt, 1996.

Lipsitz, George. *Time Passages: Collective Memory and American Popular Culture*. Minneapolis: U of Minnesota P, 1990.

Lorde, Audre. *Sister Outsider*. Trumansburg, N.Y.: Crossing, 1984.

Loulan, JoAnn. *Lesbian Sex*. San Francisco: Spinsters, 1984.

Love, Heather. "'Spoiled Identity': Stephen Gordon's Loneliness and the Difficulties of Queer History." *GLQ* 7.4 (2001): 487–519.

Lowenthal, David. *The Past Is a Foreign Country*. New York: Cambridge UP, 1985.

Lugo, Alejandro, and Bill Maurer, eds. *Gender Matters: Rereading Michelle Z. Rosaldo*. Ann Arbor: U of Michigan P, 2000.

Luibheid, Eithne. "'Looking Like a Lesbian': The Organization of Sexual Monitoring at the United States-Mexican Border." *Journal of the History of Sexuality* 8.3 (1998): 477–506.

Lutz, Catherine A., and Jane L. Collins. *Reading National Geographic*. Chicago: U of Chicago P, 1993.

Mabala, Richard, et al. *Sara: The Special Gift*. Nairobi: UNICEF-ESARO, 1996.

MacCormack, Carol, and Marilyn Strathern, eds. 1980. *Nature, Culture, and Gender*. Cambridge: Cambridge UP, 1980.

Macdonald, Barbara, with Cynthia Rich. *Look Me in the Eye: Old Women, Aging and Ageism*. San Francisco: Aunt Lute, 1983.

Mahoso, Tafataona. "1 African = 1 American: New Order Requires New Math." *World Press Review* Dec. 2001: 14–15. Reprinted from *The Sunday Mail*, Harare, Zimbabwe, 21 Sept. 2001.

"Malaria Disrupts the Immune System." *Science News* 156 3 July 1999: 4.

Malkki, Liisa. *Purity and Exile: Violence, Memory, and National Cosmology Among Hutu Refugees in Tanzania*. Chicago: U of Chicago P, 1995.

Mani, Lata. *Contentious Traditions: The Debate on Sati in Colonial India*. Berkeley: U of California P, 1998.

Mannheim, Karl. "The Problem of Generations." *Essays on the Sociology of Knowledge.* New York: Oxford UP, 1952.

Marchetti, Gina. *Romance and the "Yellow Peril": Race, Sex, and Discursive Strategies in Hollywood Fiction.* Berkeley: U of California P, 1993.

Marks, Elaine, and Isabelle de Courtivron, eds. *New French Feminisms.* New York: Schocken, 1981.

Martin, Biddy. *Femininity Played Straight: The Significance of Being Lesbian.* New York: Routledge, 1996.

Martin, Emily. *Flexible Bodies: Tracking Immunity in American Culture from the Days of Polio to the Age of AIDS.* Boston: Beacon, 1994.

Martin, Randy. "Globalization? The Dependencies of a Question." *Social Text 60* 17. 3 (1999): 1–14.

Martinez-Alier, Verena. *Marriage, Class, and Colour in Nineteenth-Century Cuba: A Study of Racial Attitudes and Sexual Values in a Slave Society.* Ann Arbor: U of Michigan P, 1989.

Marx, Karl. *The Eighteenth Brumaire of Louis Bonaparte.* New York: International, 1963.

———. "Economic and Philosophical Manuscripts." *Karl Marx: Early Writings.* Trans. T. B. Bottomore. New York: McGraw-Hill, 1964.

Marx, Karl, and Frederick Engels. *The German Ideology.* Ed. C. J. Arthur. New York: International, 1970.

Mascia-Lees, Frances E., Patricia Sharpe, and Colleen Ballerino Cohen. "The Postmodernist Turn in Anthropology: Cautions from a Feminist Perspective." *Signs* 15.1 (1989): 7–33.

McBride, James. *The Color of Water: A Black Man's Tribute to His White Mother.* New York: Riverhead, 1996.

McClintock, Anne. *Imperial Leather: Race, Gender, and Sexuality in the Colonial Context.* New York: Routledge, 1995.

McKenzie, Jon. *Perform or Else: From Discipline to Performance.* New York: Routledge, 2001.

McVeigh, Robbie. "Theorizing Sedentarism: The Roots of Anti-Nomadism." *Gypsy Politics and Traveller Identity.* Ed. Thomas Acton. Hertfordshire: U of Hertfordshire P, 1997. 7–25

Meijer, Irene Contera, and Baukje Prins. "How Bodies Come to Matter: An Interview with Judith Butler." *Signs* 23.2 (1998): 275–286.

Melmer, David. "Girls' Team Put Through Gender Check: Parent Says Racism Root of the Problem." *Indian Country Today* 18 Dec. 1995: A1–A2.

Menninger, Karl. *Number Words and Number Symbols: A Cultural History of Numbers.* Cambridge, Mass.: MIT P, 1969.

Mikell, Gwendolyn, ed. *African Feminism: The Politics of Survival in Sub-Saharan Africa.* New York: Routledge, 1997.

Miller, Neil. *Out of the Past: Gay and Lesbian History from 1869 to the Present.* New York: Vintage, 1995.

Minerbrook, Scott. *Divided to the Vein: A Journey into Race and Family.* New York: Harcourt, 1996.

Mishra, Pankaj. "The Afghan Tragedy." *New York Review of Books* 17 Jan. 2002: 43–49.

Modleski, Tania. *Feminism Without Women*. New York: Routledge, 1991.

Mohan, Uday, and Leo Maley III. "Orthodoxy and Dissent: The American News Media and the Decision to Use the Atomic Bomb Against Japan, 1945–1995." *Cultural Difference, Media Memories: Anglo-American Images of Japan*. Ed. Phil Hammond. London: Cassell, 1997. 139–174.

Mohanty, Chandra. "Under Western Eyes: Feminist Scholarship and Colonial Discourses." *Feminist Review* 30 (1988): 61–88.

Montag, Warren. "What Is at Stake in the Debate on Postmodernism?" In *Postmodernism and Its Discontents*. Ed. E. Ann Kaplan. New York: Verso, 1988. 88–103.

Montgomery, Scott L. *Science in Translation: Movements of Knowledge Through Cultures and Time*. Chicago: U of Chicago P, 2000.

Moore, Henrietta L. *Feminism and Anthropology*. Minneapolis: U of Minnesota P, 1988.

———. *A Passion for Difference: Essays in Anthropology and Gender*. Bloomington: Indiana UP, 1994.

Moraga, Cherríe, and Gloria Anzaldúa, eds. *This Bridge Called My Back: Writings by Radical Women of Color*. New York: Kitchen Table Women of Color, 1983.

Moretti, Franco. "The Spell of Indecision." *Marxism and the Interpretation of Culture*. Ed. Cary Nelson and Lawrence Grossberg. Urbana: U of Illinois P, 1988. 339–346.

Morris, Rosalind C. "All Made Up: Performance Theory and the New Anthropology of Sex and Gender." *Annual Review of Anthropology* 24 (1995): 567–592.

Mullen, Bill. *Popular Fronts: Chicago and African-American Cultural Politics, 1935–1946*. Urbana: U of Illinois P, 1999.

Munt, Sally. *Butch-Femme: Theorizing Lesbian Genders*. London: Cassell, 1997.

Nahin, Paul. *Time Machines: Time Travel in Physics, Metaphysics, and Science Fiction*. New York: American Institute of Physics, 1993.

Nanda, Serena. *Neither Man Nor Woman: The Hijras of India*. Belmont, Calif.: Wadsworth, 1990.

Nasaw, David. *Going Out: The Rise and Fall of Public Amusements*. New York: Basic, 1993.

Nataf, Zachary I. *Lesbians Talk Transgender*. London: Scarlet, 1996.

Nelson, Cary. *Manifesto of a Tenured Radical*. New York: New York UP, 1997.

Nelson, Jill. *Volunteer Slavery: My Authentic Negro Experience*. Chicago: Noble, 1993.

Nestle, Joan. *A Restricted Country*. Ithaca, N.Y.: Firebrand, 1987.

———, ed. *The Persistent Desire: A Femme-Butch Reader*. Boston: Alyson, 1992.

Newman, Katherine S. *Falling from Grace: The Experience of Downward Mobility in the American Middle Class*. New York: Vintage, 1988.

Newman, Leslea. *The Femme Mystique*. Boston: Alyson, 1995.

Newton, Esther. *Mother Camp: Female Impersonators in America*. Chicago: U of Chicago P, 1979.

———. "The Mythic Mannish Lesbian: Radclyffe Hall and the New Woman." *The

*Lesbian Issue: Essays from SIGNS*. Ed. Estelle B. Freedman, et al. Chicago: U of Chicago P, 1985. 7–26.

———. *Cherry Grove, Fire Island: Sixty Years in America's First Gay and Lesbian Town*. Boston: Beacon P, 1993.

Nicholson, Daniel R. "Selling Identity to Generation X." *Undressing the Ad: Reading Culture in Advertising*. Ed. Katherine Toland Frith. New York: Peter Lang, 1998. 175–196.

Nora, Pierre. "Between Memory and History: *Les Lieux de Mémoire*." *Representations* 26 (1989): 7–25.

O'Hearn, Claudine C., ed. *Half and Half: Writers on Growing Up Biracial and Bicultural*. New York: Pantheon, 1998.

Olick, Jeffrey K., and Joyce Robbins. "Social Memory Studies: From 'Collective Memory' to the Historical Sociology of Mnemonic Practices." *Annual Review of Sociology* 24 (1998): 105–140.

Ollman, Bertell. *Alienation: Marx's Conception of Man in Capitalist Society*. 2nd ed. Cambridge, Mass.: Cambridge UP, 1976.

"One Problem, Two Views: The Color Chasm, Day Eight: Reconciliation." *The Columbus Dispatch* 18 April 1999.

Ong, Aihwa. *Flexible Citizenship: The Cultural Logics of Transnationality*. Durham, N.C.: Duke UP, 1999.

Ortiz, Alfonso. *The Tewa World: Space, Time, Being, and Becoming in a Pueblo Society*. Chicago: U of Chicago P, 1969.

Ortner, Sherry B. *Making Gender: The Politics and Erotics of Culture*. Boston: Beacon P, 1996.

Ortner, Sherry B., and Harriet Whitehead, eds. *Sexual Meanings: The Cultural Construction of Gender and Sexuality*. New York: Cambridge UP, 1981.

Osagie, Iyunolu. "Historical Memory and a New National Consciousness: The Amistad Revolt Revisited in Sierra Leone." *The Massachusetts Review* 38.1 (1997): 63–83.

Pandey, Gyanendra. "In Defense of the Fragment: Writing About Hindu-Muslim Riots in India Today." *Representations* 37 (1992): 27–55.

———, ed. *Hindus and Others: The Question of Identity in India Today*. New York: Viking, 1993.

Panourgiá, Neni. *Fragments of Death, Fables of Identity: An Athenian Anthropography*. Madison: U of Wisconsin P, 1995.

Parashar, Archana. *Women and Family Law Reform in India*. New Delhi: Sage, 1992.

Park, David. *The Fire Within the Eye: A Historical Essay on the Nature and Meaning of Light*. Princeton, N.J.: Princeton UP, 1997.

Patel, Geeta. "Homely Housewives Run Amok: Lesbians in Marital Fixes." *Public Culture*, forthcoming.

———. "Home, Homo, Hybrid: Translating Gender." *College Literature* 24.1 (1997): 133–150.

Pazira, Nelofer. "Caught in the Middle, Again." *World Press Review* (Jan. 2000): 22.

Pegu, Rinku. "Afghan Women Don't Trust the NA Either." *Tehelka.com* 16 Nov. 2001.

Peiss, Kathy. *Cheap Amusements: Working Women and Leisure in Turn-of-the-Century New York*. Philadelphia: Temple UP, 1986.

———. "'Charity Girls' and City Pleasures: Historical Notes on Working-Class Sexuality." *Passion and Power: Sexuality in History*. Ed. Kathy Peiss and Christina Simmons with Robert A. Padgug. Philadelphia: Temple UP, 1989. 57–69.

Penley, Constance. "Time Travel, Primal Scene, and the Critical Dystopia." *Close Encounters: Film, Feminism, and Science Fiction*. Ed. Constance Penley et al. Minneapolis: U of Minnesota P, 1991. 63–80.

Penn, Donna. "The Meanings of Lesbianism in Post-War America." *Gender & History* 3.2 (1991): 190–203.

Perez, Amara. "Sisters in Action for Power Raise Roof: Girls and Young Women Learn to Lead the Struggle for Social Change." *RESIST Newsletter* 10.5 (2001): 1–3.

Pfohl, Stephen. "Welcome to the PARASITE CAFE: Postmodernity as a Social Problem." *Social Problems* 37.4 (1990): 421–442.

Phelan, Peggy. *Unmarked: The Politics of Performance*. New York: Routledge, 1993.

Pickover, Clifford A. *Time: A Traveler's Guide*. New York: Oxford UP, 1998.

Piper, Adrian. "Passing for White, Passing for Black." *Transition* 58 (1992): 4–32.

Polanyi, Karl. *The Great Transformation: The Political and Economic Origins of Our Time*. Boston: Beacon, 1944.

Ponse, Barbara. *Identities in the Lesbian World: The Social Construction of Self*. Westport, Conn.: Greenwood, 1978.

Poovey, Mary. "Accommodating Merchants: Accounting, Civility, and the Natural Laws of Gender." *differences* 8.3 (1996): 1–20.

Povinelli, Elizabeth A. *Labor's Lot: The Power, History, and Culture of Aboriginal Action*. Chicago: U of Chicago P, 1993.

Pratt, Minnie Bruce. *S/he*. Ithaca, N.Y.: Firebrand, 1995.

Price, Huw. *Time's Arrow and Archimedes' Point: New Directions for the Physics of Time*. New York: Oxford UP, 1996.

Probyn, Elspeth. *Sexing the Self: Gendered Positions in Cultural Studies*. New York: Routledge, 1993.

Revolutionary Association of the Women of Afghanistan. "Declaration of the Revolutionary Association of the Women of Afghanistan (RAWA) on the Occasion of International Human Rights Day." 10 Dec. 2001. www.rawa.org.

Ray, Himanushi P. *The Winds of Change: Buddhism and the Maritime Links of Early South Asia*. Delhi: Oxford UP, 1994.

Reagon, Bernice Johnson. "Coalition Politics: Turning the Century." *Home Girls: A Black Feminist Anthology*. Ed. Barbara Smith. New York: Kitchen Table/Women of Color, 1983. 356–368.

Reddy, Maureen T. *Crossing the Color Line: Race, Parenting, and Culture*. New Brunswick, N.J.: Rutgers UP, 1994.

Reiter, Rayna R., ed. *Toward an Anthropology of Women*. New York: Monthly Review P, 1975.

Rhea, Joseph Tilden. *Race Pride and American Identity*. Cambridge, Mass.: Harvard UP, 1997.

Riis, Jacob A. *How the Other Half Lives: Studies Among the Tenements of New York.* 1890. New York: Penguin, 1997.

Ritter, Gretchen. "Silver Slippers and a Golden Cap: L. Frank Baum's *The Wonderful Wizard of Oz* and Historical Memory in American Politics." *Journal of American Studies* 31.2 (1997): 171–202.

Robbins, Bruce. *Feeling Global: Internationalism in Distress.* New York: New York UP, 1999.

Robnett, Belinda. *How Long? How Long?: African-American Women and the Struggle for Civil Rights.* New York: Oxford UP, 1997.

Rofel, Lisa. *Other Modernities: Gendered Yearnings in China After Socialism.* Berkeley: U of California P, 1999.

Rosaldo, Michelle Z. "Toward an Anthropology of Self and Feeling." *Culture Theory: Essays on Mind, Self, and Emotion.* Ed. Richard A. Shweder and Robert A. LeVine. Cambridge, Mass.: Cambridge UP, 1984. 137–157.

Rosaldo, Michelle and Louise Lamphere, eds. *Woman, Culture, and Society.* Stanford, Calif.: Stanford UP, 1974.

Rosaldo, Renato. *Culture and Truth: The Remaking of Social Analysis.* Boston: Beacon, 1989.

Roscoe, Will. *The Zuni Man-Woman.* Albuquerque: U of New Mexico P, 1991.

Rose, Gillian. *Feminism and Geography: The Limits of Geographical Knowledge.* Minneapolis: U of Minnesota P, 1993.

Roseberry, William. *Anthropologies and Histories: Essays in Culture, History, and Political Economy.* New Brunswick, N.J.: Rutgers UP, 1989.

Rotman, Brian. *Signifying Nothing: The Semiotics of Zero.* Stanford, Calif.: Stanford UP, 1987.

———. *Ad Infinitum: The Ghost in Turing's Machine: Taking God Out of Mathematics and Putting the Body Back In.* Stanford, Calif.: Stanford UP, 1993.

———. *Mathematics as Sign: Writing, Imagining, Counting.* Stanford, Calif.: Stanford UP, 2000.

Rowe, Jonathan. "The Growth Consensus Unravels." *Dollars and Sense* (July–Aug. 2000): 15–18, 33.

Rubin, Gayle. "The Traffic in Women." *Toward an Anthropology of Women.* Ed. Rayna R. Reiter. New York: Monthly Review P, 1975. 157–210.

———. "Thinking Sex: Notes for a Radical Theory of the Politics of Sexuality." *Pleasure and Danger: Exploring Female Sexuality.* Ed. Carole S. Vance. New York: Routledge, 1984. 267–319.

Ruiz, Vicki L. *From Out of the Shadows: Mexican Women in Twentieth-Century America.* New York: Oxford UP, 1998.

Russell, Kathy, Midge Wilson, and Ronald Hall. *The Color Complex: The Politics of Skin Color Among African Americans.* New York: Anchor, 1992.

Russo, Mary. "Female Grotesques: Carnival and Theory." *Feminist Studies/Critical Studies.* Ed. Teresa de Lauretis. Bloomington: Indiana UP, 1986. 213–229.

Rydell, Robert. *All the World's a Fair: Visions of Empire at American International Expositions, 1876–1916.* Chicago: U of Chicago P, 1984.

Said, Edward W. "Invention, Memory, and Place." *Critical Inquiry* 26.2 (2000): 175–192.

Samois. *Coming to Power: Writings and Graphics on Lesbian S/M.* Boston: Alyson, 1982.

Sandoval, Chela. "U.S. Third World Feminism: The Theory and Method of Oppositional Consciousness in the Postmodern World." *Genders* 10 (1991): 1–24.

Sangari, Kumkum, and Sudesh Vaid, eds. *Recasting Women: Essays in Colonial History.* New Delhi: Kali for Women P, 1989.

Santos-Granero, Fernando. "Writing History into the Landscape: Space, Myth, and Ritual in Contemporary Amazonia." *American Ethnologist* 25.2 (1998): 128–148.

Sassen, Saskia. *Globalization and Its Discontents.* New York: New Press, 1998.

Scales-Trent, Judy. *Notes of a White Black Woman: Race, Color, Community.* University Park: Pennsylvania State UP, 1995.

Schama, Simon. *Landscape and Memory.* New York: Knopf, 1995.

Scheper-Hughes, Nancy. "Joining the Witch-Hunt." *New Internationalist* (April 1999): 14–17.

Schimmel, Annemarie. *The Mystery of Numbers.* New York: Oxford UP, 1993.

Schwartz, Barry. "Social Change and Collective Memory: The Democratization of George Washington." *American Sociological Review* 56 (1991): 221–236.

Scott, David. "That Event, This Memory: Notes on the Anthropology of African Diasporas in the New World." *Diaspora* 1.3 (1991): 261–284.

———. *Refashioning Futures: Criticism After Postcoloniality.* Princeton, N.J.: Princeton UP, 1999.

Scott, James C. *Seeing Like a State: How Certain Schemes to Improve the Human Condition Have Failed.* New Haven, Conn: Yale UP, 1998.

Scott, Joan Wallach. *Gender and the Politics of History.* New York: Columbia UP, 1988.

Searle, John. *Speech Acts.* Cambridge, Mass.: Cambridge UP, 1969.

Sedgwick, Eve Kosofsky. *Epistemology of the Closet.* Berkeley: U of California P, 1990.

Seidenberg, A. "The Zero in the Mayan Numerical Notation." *Native American Mathematics.* Ed. Michael P. Closs. Austin: U of Texas P, 1986. 371–386.

Seidman, Steven. *Romantic Longings: Love in America, 1830–1980.* New York: Routledge, 1991.

Seife, Charles. *Zero: The Biography of a Dangerous Idea.* New York: Viking, 2000.

Sen, Satadru. *Disciplining Punishment: Colonialism and Convict Society in the Andaman Islands.* New Delhi: Oxford U, 2000.

Sherman, Daniel J. *The Construction of Memory in Interwar France.* Chicago: U of Chicago P, 1999.

Shulevitz, Judith. "Keepers of the Tenure Track." *New York Times* 29 Oct. 1995.

Silverman, Kaja. *Male Subjectivity at the Margins.* New York: Routledge, 1992.

Slyomovics, Susan. *The Object of Memory: Arab and Jew Narrate the Palestinian Village.* Philadelphia: U of Pennsylvania P, 1998.

Smith-Rosenberg, Carroll. "Discourses of Sexuality and Subjectivity: The New Woman, 1870–1936." *Hidden From History: Reclaiming the Gay and Lesbian Past.* Ed. Martin Duberman, Martha Vicinus, and George Chauncey, Jr. New York: Penguin, 1989. 264–280.

Social Justice Group. *Is Academic Feminism Dead? Theory in Practice*. New York: New York UP, 2000.

Soley, Lawrence C. *Leasing the Ivory Tower: The Corporate Takeover of Academia*. Boston: South End P, 1995.

Solomon, Alisa. "Identity Crisis: Queer Politics in the Age of Possibilities." *Village Voice* 37.26 (1992): 27–33, 29.

Somerville, Siobhan. *Queering the Color Line: Race and the Invention of Homosexuality in American Culture*. Durham, N.C.: Duke UP, 2000.

Soyinka, Wole. *The Burden of Memory, the Muse of Forgiveness*. New York: Oxford UP, 1999.

Spence, Jonathan D. *The Memory Palace of Matteo Ricci*. New York: Penguin, 1984.

Spivak, Gayatri. *In Other Worlds: Essays in Cultural Politics*. New York: Methuen, 1987.

———. "Can the Subaltern Speak?" In *Marxism and the Interpretation of Culture*. Ed. Cary Nelson and Lawrence Grossberg. Urbana: U of Illinois P, 1988. 271–313.

———. *A Critique of Postcolonial Reason: Toward a History of the Vanishing Present*. Cambridge, Mass.: Harvard UP, 1999.

Stacey, Judith. *In the Name of the Family: Rethinking Family Values in the Postmodern Age*. Boston: Beacon, 1996.

Stanley, Amy Dru. *From Bondage to Contract: Wage Labor, Marriage, and the Market in the Age of Slave Emancipation*. New York: Cambridge UP, 1998.

Stein, Arlene. "All Dressed Up, But No Place to Go? Style Wars and the New Lesbianism." *Out/Look* 1.4 (1989): 38.

Stein, Edward, ed. *Forms of Desire: Sexual Orientation and the Social Constructionist Controversy*. New York: Routledge, 1990.

Stewart, Ian. *Nature's Numbers: The Unreal Reality of Mathematics*. New York: Basic, 1995.

Stewart, Ian. *From Here to Infinity*. New York: Oxford UP, 1996.

Stockes, Brian. "Sand Creek Historic Landmark a Reality." *Indian Country Today* 8 Nov. 2000.

Stocking, George W., Jr. "The Turn-of-the-Century Concept of Race." *Modernism\modernity* 1.1 (1993): 4–16.

Stone, Alluquère Rosanne. *The War of Desire and Technology at the Close of the Mechanical Age*. Cambridge, Mass.: MIT P, 1995.

Strathern, Marilyn. "Making Incomplete." *Carved Flesh/Cast Selves: Gendered Symbols and Social Practices*. Ed. Vigdis Broch-Due, Ingrid Rudie, and Tone Bleie. Oxford: Berg, 1993. 41–51.

Streng, Frederick J. *Emptiness: A Study in Religious Meaning*. Nashville, Tenn.: Abingdon, 1967.

Sturken, Marita. *Tangled Memories: The Vietnam War, the AIDS Epidemic, and the Politics of Remembering*. Berkeley: U of California P, 1997(a).

———. "Absent Images of Memory: Remembering and Reenacting the Japanese Internment." *positions* 5.3 (1997): 687–707. (b)

Susser, Ida. "The Construction of Poverty and Homelessness in US Cities." *Annual Review of Anthropology* 25 (1996): 411–435.

Swedenburg, Ted. *Memories of Revolt: The 1936–1939 Rebellion and the Palestinian National Past*. Minneapolis: U of Minnesota P, 1995.

Swetz, Frank J., and T. I. Kao. *Was Pythagoras Chinese?* University Park: Pennsylvania State UP, 1977.

Szamosi, Géza. *The Twin Dimensions: Inventing Time and Space*. New York: McGraw-Hill, 1986.

Takaki, Ronald. *A Different Mirror: A History of Multicultural America*. Boston: Little, Brown, 1993.

Terry, Jennifer. "Anxious Slippages between 'Us' and 'Them': A Brief History of the Scientific Search for Homosexual Bodies." *Deviant Bodies: Critical Perspectives on Difference in Science and Popular Culture*. Ed. Jennifer Terry and Jacqueline Urla. Bloomington: Indiana UP, 1995. 129–169.

———. *American Obsession: Science, Medicine, and Homosexuality in Modern Society*. Chicago: U of Chicago P, 1999.

Terry, Jennifer, and Jacqueline Urla. *Deviant Bodies: Critical Perspectives on Difference in Science and Popular Culture*. Bloomington: Indiana UP, 1995.

Thelan, David, ed. *Memory and American History*. Bloomington: Indiana UP, 1989.

Third World Institute, ed. *The World Guide*. London: New Internationalist, 2000.

Thomas, Nicholas. *Out of Time: History and Evolution in Anthropological Discourse*. 2nd ed. Ann Arbor: U of Michigan P, 1996.

Thompson, E. P. *Customs in Common: Studies in Traditional Popular Culture*. New York: New P, 1993.

Tolstaya, Tatyana. "Out of This World?" *New York Review of Books* 13 Apr. 2000: 50–51.

Torgovnick, Marianna. *Gone Primitive: Savage Intellects, Modern Lives*. Chicago: U of Chicago P, 1990.

Tuan, Mia. *Forever Foreigners or Honorary Whites?: The Asian Ethnic Experience Today*. New Brunswick, N.J.: Rutgers UP, 1998.

Turner, Howard R. *Science in Medieval Islam*. Austin: U of Texas P, 1995.

Turner, Patricia A. *Ceramic Uncles and Celluloid Mammies: Black Images and Their Influence on Culture*. New York: Anchor, 1994.

Urrea, Luis Alberto. *Across the Wire: Life and Hard Times on the Mexican Border*. New York: Anchor, 1993.

U.S. Census Bureau. "Household Income at Record High; Poverty Declines in 1998, Census Bureau Reports." Press release archived at *http://www.census.gov/Press-Release/www/1999/cb99–188.html* 25 June 2000.

Valdez, Luis. *Zoot Suit and Other Plays*. Houston: Arte Publico P, 1992.

Van Egmond, Warren. "How Algebra Came to France." *Mathematics from Manuscript to Print, 1300–1600*. Ed. Cynthia Hay. Oxford: Clarendon P, 1988. 127–144.

Vance, Carole S., ed. *Pleasure and Danger: Exploring Female Sexuality*. Boston: Routledge, 1984.

———. "Social Construction Theory: Problems in the History of Sexuality." *Homosexuality, Which Homosexuality?* Ed. Anja van Kooten Niekerk and Theo van der Meer. Amsterdam: An Dekker/Schorer, 1989. 13–34.

Vásquez, Ian. "Introduction: The Return to a Global Economy." *Global Fortune: The Stumble and Rise of World Capitalism.* Ed. Ian Vásquez. Washington, D.C.: Cato Institute, 2000. 1–11.

Vázquez, Carmen. "Appearances." *Homophobia: How We All Pay the Price.* Ed. Warren Blumfeld. Boston: Beacon, 1992. 157–166.

Verlichak, Carmen. "The Crime of Cultural Cleansing." *World Press Review* (Sept. 2000): 38–39.

Vigil, James Diego. *From Indians to Chicanos: The Dynamics of Mexican-American Culture.* 2nd ed. Prospect Heights, N.J.: Waveland, 1998.

Virilio, Paul. *Speed and Politics (Vitesse et politique).* Trans. Mark Polizzotti. New York: Columbia UP, 1986.

Vizenor, Gerald. *Crossbloods: Bone Courts, Bingo, and Other Reports.* Minneapolis: U of Minnesota P, 1990.

Volcano, Del LaGrace, and Judith "Jack" Halberstam. *The Drag King Book.* London: Serpent's Tail, 1999.

Walker, Lisa M. "How to Recognize a Lesbian: The Cultural Politics of Looking Like What You Are." *Signs* 18.4 (1993): 866–890.

Ward, Peter D. *Time Machines: Scientific Explorations in Deep Time.* New York: Copernicus, 1998.

Warner, Sam B., Jr. *Streetcar Suburbs: The Process of Growth in Boston, 1870–1900.* New York: Atheneum, 1974.

West, Candace and Don H. Zimmerman. "Doing Gender." *Gender & Society* 1.2 (1987): 125–151.

Weston, Kath. *The Apprenticeship and Blue Collar System: Putting Women on the Right Track.* Sacramento: California State Department of Education, 1982.

———. "Production as Means, Production as Metaphor: Women's Struggle to Enter the Trades." *Uncertain Terms: The Negotiation of Gender in American Culture.* Ed. Faye Ginsburg and Anna Lowenhaupt Tsing. Boston: Beacon, 1990. 137–151.

———. *Render Me, Gender Me: Lesbians Talk Sex, Class, Color, Nation, Studmuffins . . .* New York: Columbia UP, 1996.

———. *Families We Choose: Lesbians, Gays, Kinship.* 2nd ed. New York: Columbia UP, 1997.

———. *Long Slow Burn: Sexuality and Social Science.* New York: Routledge, 1998.

———. "Kinship, Controversy, and the Sharing of Substance: The Race/Class Politics of Blood Transfusion." *Relative Values.* Ed. Sarah Franklin and Susan McKinnon. Durham, N.C.: Duke UP, 2002. 147–174.

Wikan, Unni. *Behind the Veil in Arabia: Women in Oman.* Baltimore: Johns Hopkins UP, 1982.

Williams, Gregory. *Life on the Color Line: The True Story of a White Boy Who Discovered He Was Black.* New York: Dutton, 1995.

Willis, Susan. *A Primer for Everyday Life.* New York: Routledge, 1991.

Wills, Garry. "Message in the Deodorant Bottle: Inventing Time." *Critical Inquiry* 15 (1989): 497–509.

Wilson, Elizabeth. "Deviant Dress." *Feminist Review* 35 (1990): 67–74.

Winter, Jay. *Sites of Memory, Sites of Mourning: The Great War in European History.* Cambridge: Cambridge UP, 1995.

Wittig, Monique. *The Straight Mind and Other Essays.* Boston: Beacon, 1992.

Woodard, Stephanie. "Young Yankton Women Come of Age: Gain Appreciation of Culture, Womanhood." *Indian Country Today* 25 July 2001: C1–C2.

Yan, Li and Dù Shírán. *Chinese Mathematics: A Concise History.* Trans. John N. Crossley and Anthony W. C. Lun. Oxford: Clarendon P, 1987.

Yanagisako, Sylvia, and Carol Delaney. *Naturalizing Power: Essays in Feminist Cultural Analysis.* New York: Routledge, 1995.

Yates, Frances. *The Art of Memory.* New York: Routledge, 1999.

Yoder, Joella G. *Unrolling Time: Christiaan Huygens and the Mathematization of Nature.* Cambridge: Cambridge UP, 1988.

Yoneyama, Lisa. *Hiroshima Traces: Time, Space, and the Dialectics of Memory.* Berkeley: U of California P, 1999.

Young, Robert J. C. *Colonial Desire: Hybridity in Theory, Culture and Race.* New York: Routledge, 1995.

Zeig, Sande. "The Actor as Activator: Deconstructing Gender Through Gesture." *Women and Performance* 2.2 (1985): 12–17.

Zerubavel, Yael. *Recovered Roots: Collective Memory and the Making of Israeli National Tradition.* Chicago: U of Chicago P, 1995.

Zinn, Maxine Baca, Pierrette Hondagneu-Sotelo, and Michael A. Messner, eds. *Through the Prism of Difference: Readings on Sex and Gender.* Boston: Allyn and Bacon, 1997.

# INDEX